THE ECUMENICAL WITNESS
OF
THE UNITED PRESBYTERIAN CHURCH
IN THE U.S.A.

THE ECUMENICAL WITNESS *of* THE UNITED PRESBYTERIAN CHURCH IN THE U.S.A.

BY W. STANLEY RYCROFT

Published for

Commission on Ecumenical Mission and Relations of

The United Presbyterian Church in the U.S.A.

by the

Board of Christian Education of

The United Presbyterian Church in the U.S.A.

Dedicated to
Charles Tudor Leber

CONTENTS

FOREWORD

This book is a history, but it is more than history.

As history it brings up to date the record of the United Presbyterian Church as it expressed itself in the missionary movement of the nineteenth and twentieth centuries. It continues the histories of the Boards of Foreign Missions of the Presbyterian Church in the U.S.A. and of the United Presbyterian Church of North America dealt with in earlier volumes. Dr. Rycroft adds to this account the records of the Permanent Commission on Interchurch Relations of the Presbyterian Church in the U.S.A., the Committee on Ecumenical Affairs and the Permanent Committee on Inter-Church Relations of the United Presbyterian Church of North America, with particular emphasis upon their union in the Commission on Ecumenical Mission and Relations as The United Presbyterian Church in the U.S.A. was formed in 1958.

This book is also more than a record of past events. It is an interpretation of radical contemporary changes in the world and in the church, revealing an ecumenical character deep within the United Presbyterian Church which leads it irresistibly to be an ecumenical witness. This ecumenical development is traced in the Presbyterian concept of the church and the "coercions of history" as well as in the many organizations established by the church as instruments of mission. With remarkable skill it reveals how the two streams of "mission" and "unity" emerged in history and finally joined together in the Commission.

Although this book focuses upon the experience of the United Presbyterian Church, that experience is always in relationship to other denominations and to many ecumenical agencies in which a

11

great variety of churches all over the world also participated. As such, it will be of interest to the entire world Christian community.

Those who planned for this book three years ago believed that it would be important. Each year that has passed has increased that belief. The ecumenical movement has touched every community of believers and its implications for the future are only beginning to be understood.

Studies such as this will contribute to that understanding.

We are indebted to Stanley Rycroft for this book. Born in England and recruited by Dr. John A. Mackay for Christian service in Peru in 1922, Dr. Rycroft has been part of the history. His subsequent service has been in the National Council of Churches and with the Commission. Although primarily concerned with affairs in Latin America he was soon involved in the ecumenical movement. Beginning with the Tambaram Conference in 1938 he has participated in much of that about which he writes. His previous books are valuable contributions to the Christian movement, and the results of his research are used by many churches and educational institutions. His scholarship and skill in writing make this a dependable and readable record of an exciting and important period in the history of the church.

INTRODUCTION

IN March, 1964, the Commission on Ecumenical Mission and Relations took action requesting "the preparation of a history of the Commission on Ecumenical Mission and Relations by the Office for Research." The action stated that the purpose of such a study would be "to inform the churches in the United States, and churches overseas, concerning the nature of the Commission and its task." The intention of the Commission was to have a book that would provide comprehensive interpretation as well as pertinent historical data and background.

An Advisory Committee, appointed by the Commission to work with the author on the structure of the book, felt that a history of the Commission should not be a mere chronicle of events but rather an interpretation of both the missionary movement and the unitive movement in their historical contexts, as far as the United Presbyterian Church is concerned.

The changes that have taken place in the world and in the Christian church in recent times are reflected in the title of this book, THE ECUMENICAL WITNESS OF THE UNITED PRESBYTERIAN CHURCH IN THE U.S.A. From histories of the work of boards of foreign missions we have moved to a contemplation in dimension and depth of an ecumenical witness of the church as a whole, and this represents a profound and dramatic change in the mission of the church.

In 1936, Arthur Judson Brown published his monumental work entitled *One Hundred Years*. This was a centennial volume, celebrating the completion of a century of work by the Board of Foreign Missions of the Presbyterian Church in the U.S.A. No similar book has been written in such depth and with so much insight, either before or since. The subtitle of the book describes it as "A History of the Foreign Missionary Work of the Presbyterian Church in the U.S.A.

with Some Account of Countries, Peoples and the Policies and Problems of Modern Missions."

Dr. Brown's book was followed by W. Reginald Wheeler's *The Crisis Decade*, which was published in the nature of a supplement to *One Hundred Years*. The book was a symposium, and covered the period 1937 to 1947, the authors describing conditions in many countries where the Presbyterian Church in the U.S.A. had missionary work during the crucial period, before, during, and after World War II.

In 1958, Wallace N. Jamison published *The United Presbyterian Story*, covering a century (1858–1958) of the life and work of the United Presbyterian Church of North America, with some chapters on the development of the missionary work of that church.

In a sense, it can be said that the present volume is a sequel to these three books, and yet it is quite different from them in treatment and content. The world with which they dealt had not yet begun to feel the impact of the ecumenical era, or the "one world" concept with which we are now familiar. In the past twenty-five years there has developed a sense of a world neighborhood, with all its agonizing conflicts and confrontations. New nations try desperately to overcome age-old handicaps of poverty, disease, ignorance, and backwardness. The social changes that have been generated have produced a revolutionary situation that has profoundly affected the nature and the scope of the mission of the church.

The three books mentioned depicted the history of the work carried on by boards of foreign missions and the women's organizations of the two former churches, the Presbyterian Church in the U.S.A. and the United Presbyterian Church of North America. The present volume deals interpretatively, as well as historically, with the Commission on Ecumenical Mission and Relations, the body that was created in 1958 by The United Presbyterian Church in the U.S.A., which had just come into being. The Commission's story goes much farther back than 1958. Therefore, an attempt has been made to show how the two uniting churches were first established, the manner in which they developed a sense of missionary obligation, and the unitive movement that unfolded in the nineteenth century, a movement in which the two churches were greatly involved.

It is hoped that the reader will discern in this book how the philosophy of missions has changed in recent decades. Foreign missions were promoted, organized, and run by mission boards from the West.

The *mission* of the church now supersedes the role of *foreign missions*. In that mission, Christians from countries formerly called "mission lands" now participate along with those from the West. Moreover, foreign missions, which in former years were largely denominational in character, have given way to a new concept, described as partnership in mission, across denominational lines, as Christians of different persuasions are drawn together by their loyalty to a common Lord.

The missionary movement and the unitive movement find their symbolic representation in the inclusion of "ecumenical mission" and "ecumenical relations" in the task of the Commission. All this is caught up in the ecumenical witness, not merely of the Commission, but of the United Presbyterian Church as a whole. The sense of wholeness is very pronounced in Presbyterian tradition and in its concept of the church, and that is why it became apparent as the form and structure of this book evolved that the story of the Commission on Ecumenical Mission and Relations must be closely related not only historically with missions, in the traditional sense, but also with the development of the ecumenical movement. Unity in mission is the goal toward which the United Presbyterian Church strives in its ecumenical witness, but in the nature of the case, it must do so with other branches of the Christian church.

When the author was asked by the Commission to write this book, he soon became aware of the dimensions and the difficulties of the undertaking. Fortunately, he has had at his disposal the advice and wise suggestions of his colleagues on the Commission staff, and also of some competent authorities, with knowledge and experience in both the missionary enterprise and the ecumenical movement.

The author wishes to express his gratitude to the members of the Advisory Committee appointed by the Commission to help with their counsel: Archie R. Crouch (chairman), Donald Black, Myrtle M. Clemmer, Theodore F. Romig, Margaret Shannon, John Coventry Smith, William R. Stackhouse, and Mary E. Turrentine.

Other colleagues on the Commission staff were helpful in providing data and material for various portions of the book: William K. DuVal, Ernest L. Fogg, Margaret Flory, Abby Jacobs, Alcwyn L. Roberts, Albert J. Sanders, John H. Sinclair, Donald P. Smith, Rodney A. Sundberg, L. Newton Thurber, and Frederick R. Wilson.

The author is particularly indebted to the following who were willing to spend the necessary time reading, evaluating, and commenting on the manuscript: R. Pierce Beaver, Evlyn W. Fulton, Ray-

mond V. Kearns, Edith L. McBane, James I. McCord, and David M.
Stowe. In addition to reading the manuscript, the following spent
time discussing it with the author and offering valuable suggestions:
Roswell P. Barnes, Donald Black, John A. Mackay, Hermann N. Morse,
John Coventry Smith, and Theophilus M. Taylor.

Gratitude is also expressed to Miss Myrtle M. Clemmer, research
assistant in the Office for Research, for her extraordinary service in
the seemingly interminable search for pertinent facts and relevant
material and for her collaboration with the author in the editing of
the manuscript.

The author also expresses his appreciation to his secretary, Mrs.
Margaret Breukel, and to Mrs. Gertrude Lipson, for their part in
typing various drafts of the manuscript.

The United Presbyterian Library was founded in 1840, that is, three
years after the Board of Foreign Missions of the Presbyterian Church
in the U.S.A. was created, and the author used its excellent resources
accumulated over many years. His thanks go to Miss Madeline
Brown, librarian of the United Presbyterian Mission Library, and to
her assistant, Miss Nancy Jennings, for their unfailing courtesy and
their willingness at all times to discover the necessary sources of information. In addition, the author availed himself of the books and
magazines of the Missionary Research Library, and the library of
Union Theological Seminary in New York City.

                                                                    W. S. R.

New York City, New York

Chapter I

THE ECUMENICAL WITNESS OF THE UNITED PRESBYTERIAN CHURCH

A Union of Two Churches and the Emergence of Ecumenical Mission

May 28, 1958, was a day to be remembered by Presbyterians in the United States. The historic occasion was the merger of two denominations, the United Presbyterian Church of North America and the Presbyterian Church in the United States of America, to form a single church, The United Presbyterian Church in the United States of America. This was the third time in just over one hundred years that Presbyterian churches had met in Pittsburgh for the purpose of effecting church union. In 1858, the Associate Presbyterian Church and the Associate Reformed Presbyterian Church met to form the United Presbyterian Church of North America. In 1870, also in Pittsburgh, the Old School and the New School Presbyterian Churches, which had constituted two separate denominations for thirty-two years, reunited into a single church, the Presbyterian Church in the U.S.A.

Before 1958, years of preparation, in the form of study, discussion, organization, and prayer, went into the decision that the time had come for the two denominations, the United Presbyterian Church of North America and the Presbyterian Church in the United States of America, to become one.

Early in the morning of May 28, 1958, the historic day in Pittsburgh, the sky was gray and overcast. It had been agreed that in case of rain the procession of 1,200 ministers and elders would assemble in the Syria Mosque auditorium, where the Assembly was to be held. At

17

9:50 A.M. two great columns were to leave the Oakfield and Bellefield churches of their respective denominations and join in one united procession. However, it was raining hard at the appointed hour and the streets were almost deserted, except for some policemen, honking cars, and a few hundred spectators. It was expected that the procession would be called off. "But this was not for the twentieth century descendants of the intrepid Scotch-Irish pioneers who helped to settle Pittsburgh two hundred years ago. The 1,200 commissioners of the first General Assembly of The United Presbyterian Church in the United States of America strode bravely off into the downpour."[1] At 9:58 A.M. the Moderators of the two churches, both bareheaded and dripping wet, shook hands at the intersection of Fifth Avenue and Bigelow Boulevard, while the Stated Clerks and other leaders exchanged greetings.

The commissioners heard Robert Montgomery, Moderator of the United Presbyterian Church of North America, say in his sermon that "this is the hour in history . . . for Christians to so live in harmony that the peoples of the world might have a foretaste of the possibility of the world becoming one spiritually. . . . The quest for unity . . . has led us to become one. . . . We must be open to what the Spirit may have to say to us through those other members of the Body of Christ whose tradition differs from our own."[2]

Later in the day, as the business session of the General Assembly was beginning, the sun broke through the skies of Pittsburgh, bringing warmth and light as a symbolic token of God's approval of the historic events that were taking place.

By a unanimous vote the uniting Assembly elected the Rev. Theophilus M. Taylor as its Moderator. It was meaningful that the Moderator of the first General Assembly of The United Presbyterian Church in the U.S.A. should be chosen from the ministerial ranks of the smaller of the two uniting churches. At the time of this election, Dr. Taylor was a distinguished professor of New Testament literature and exegesis at Pittsburgh-Xenia Seminary of the United Presbyterian Church of North America.

In addition to the merger of the two churches on May 28, 1958, another event of significance took place at the first General Assembly of the united church, one that began a new era in the life of the church as a missionary community and constitutes the basis and *raison d'être* of this book.

After extended study by the two churches, a recommendation was brought to the united General Assembly by the Special Commission on Consolidations to create the Commission on Ecumenical Mission and Relations. Commenting on this far-reaching action of the new church body, and referring particularly to the Presbyterian Church in the U.S.A., *Presbyterian Life* said, "For the first time in Protestant history, a major denomination has chosen to eliminate its board of foreign missions, in favor of an agency which would handle the church's diplomatic and mission relations together."[3]

The newly created agency combined the operations of the boards of foreign missions of the two former churches, the Permanent Commission on Interchurch Relations of the Presbyterian Church in the U.S.A., the Committee on Ecumenical Affairs and the Permanent Committee on Inter-Church Relations of the United Presbyterian Church of North America.

Thus, on May 28, 1958, The United Presbyterian Church in the United States of America came into being, and among its first actions was the creation of the Commission on Ecumenical Mission and Relations. Without a doubt, these two events, the merger of the historic communions and the formation of the Commission, combined to make this day a very important one in the entire history of Presbyterianism in the United States, and behind the events lay the deep conviction that God was calling the churches to something new in a time of unprecedented revolutionary change in the life of the world.

It will become apparent in later chapters of this book that The United Presbyterian Church in the U.S.A. and its predecessors which merged in 1958 have been historically very much involved in the rise and development of the ecumenical movement. Therefore, as we analyze what might be called the dynamics of the ecumenical movement, we are seeking to understand the developments and concerns that brought about the creation of the Commission on Ecumenical Mission and Relations. Behind the creation of the Commission lay the coinciding of a basic theological concept concerning the nature of the church with the imperatives of a historical process, or what we might call "the coercions of history."

The Presbyterian Concept of the Church

In the Presbyterian Confession of Faith are found the common heritage and tradition of the two churches. The Plan of Union stated: "The Constitution holds The United Presbyterian Church in the United States of America firmly in the great heritage and tradition of the Confessional Churches, of historic Presbyterianism, and of the Westminster Standards. . . . The Westminster Confession of Faith and Catechisms continue to have the same basic significance in the Constitution of the united Church as they had in the Constitution of each of the two separate Churches before union."[4]

For our purpose here we shall refer to two sections of the Confession of Faith dealing with the church. In Chapter XXV, called "Of the Church," it is stated: (1) "The catholic or universal Church, which is invisible, consists of the whole number of the elect, that have been, are, or shall be gathered into one, under Christ the head thereof; and is the spouse, the body, the fullness of Him that filleth all in all"; (2) "The visible Church, which is also catholic or universal under the gospel . . . , consists of all those throughout the world that profess the true religion, . . . and is the Kingdom of the Lord Jesus Christ, the house and family of God."[5]

In the same Constitution, under the section titled "Form of Government," there is also reference to "the universal Church [which] consists of all those persons, in every nation, . . . who make profession of the holy religion of Christ. . . . Communions and particular churches ought to co-operate in so far as possible in giving expression to their oneness in Jesus Christ within his body, the *ecumenical, catholic Church*."[6] (Italics added.)

In these paragraphs we see an underlying principle of the ecumenical movement itself, the idea of the wholeness of the church as the body of Christ, the oneness of the church in Christ. This wholeness is part of the "givenness" of the Christian gospel, something that *is*, and not something that the church itself creates. The church accepts this spiritual unity in Christ, and strives to give expression to it in many ways. The same section of the Constitution describes these forms of expression as follows: "The great ends of the Church are the proclamation of the gospel for the salvation of men; the shelter, nurture, and spiritual fellowship of the children of God; the maintenance of divine worship; the preservation of the truth; the promotion of social righteousness; and the exhibition of the Kingdom of Heaven to the world."[7]

The United Presbyterian Church in the United States of America has pledged, as did its predecessors, to seek to give expression to the wholeness of the body of Christ, and it does so by pursuing the ends of the church to which we have just referred. From this it is apparent that The United Presbyterian Church in the U.S.A. is ecumenical in purpose, both by heritage and by commitment.

God's purpose for his church is that it should be a worldwide community transcending all barriers of race, culture, nationality, and ecclesiastical affiliation. However, although the church believes this is in the purpose of God, achieving wholeness or oneness is not an end in itself, but is in order to fulfill its mission in the world, and so that all barriers of separation in the family of mankind shall be broken down.

The historical events, and the convulsions of our time, have raised some agonizing questions concerning the nature of the church, and especially its relation to the world. These events have compelled the church to make a reappraisal of its very being as well as of the nature of its calling. From the Life and Work Conference of 1937 came the dictum, "Let the church be the church," and this dynamic phrase is at the heart of the reappraisal.

Contemporary literature gives us a vivid portrayal of a modern concept of hell as it describes the end result of man's alienation from God and from man, his corruption, greed, and hate. The seemingly impending doom has dispelled the hope of a brave, new world's arising. Arnold Come refers to the false hopes in these words: "The hope and vision, during World War II, that man would at least return to 'normal' or possibly even actualize 'one world' has not risen concretely for a single instant out of the ashes of the recent holocaust of human fear and hate."[8]

There is little doubt that the crisis of our time springs largely from the separation of man from man, man from community, nation from nation, and mankind from God. "Nations face each other in hostility; and prejudices, injustices, and hatreds divide the races of mankind. Man sees himself enslaved by the forces of history, . . . separated from God and from his fellow man by barriers of violence, self-interest, and meaninglessness. He is tyrannized by nature, totalitarian governments, national ambitions, mass society, religion, rules of conformity, secular messianisms, technology and automation."[9]

This desperate plight in which mankind finds itself has raised afresh the role of the church. Along with sister denominations, the United Presbyterian Church is becoming aware of two basic realities. The first is that the church exists not for itself but for the world, the world that "God so loved . . . , that he gave his only begotten Son."

The second reality is that a church, divided and fragmented, cannot properly fulfill its task of healing, reconciliation, and proclaiming a gospel of redemption through Christ to a suffering and sundered world.

The church of Jesus Christ has become worldwide in extent during the past few decades, although its total membership constitutes a minority of the world population. The church is called upon to witness unto all nations, and this witness, no longer confined to churches of the West, within the purpose of God is the witness of a worldwide Christian community. Dr. John A. Mackay, speaking at the 1957 General Assembly of the former Presbyterian Church in the U.S.A. concerning the proposal for a new name to replace that of the Board of Foreign Missions, said, "World-wide Christianity has reached a crucial moment . . . not because of failure, but because of success."[10] Within the purpose of God the churches of Asia, Africa, the Middle East, and Latin America have grown numerically and in stature. Their development has "transformed the Protestant Christian mission from a unilateral Western sending operation into a missionary enterprise with a world-wide base and a world-wide field of operation."[11]

The Coercions of History

The Christian church has always carried on its mission within the context of history, adjusting to the realities of the period. During the first century of the Christian era, conditions arising out of the existence of Roman roads, the extension of Roman law, and the prevalence of a Pax Romana provided some of the context within which Paul, the first great missionary, was able to carry the gospel to many parts of the then known world. During the nineteenth century, the century of Christian missions, the missionary enterprise flourished within the context of a Western colonial system in an expansionist period.

The first factor we must consider is the decline of colonialism. Whether we like it or not, the greatest development of the Christian church across the world coincided with the colonial expansion of Christian nations of the West. Following the industrial revolution, these nations needed raw materials for their industrial growth. When these nations conquered or occupied and controlled underdeveloped areas abroad, particularly in Africa and Asia, vast sources of raw materials were made accessible at a minimum cost, because of cheap labor, while at the same time new markets for manufactured goods were opened up, and countless jobs for colonial administrators, businessmen, and traders were made available for thousands of Europeans. All this meant prestige and power for the Western nations concerned, but also certain resentments and critical attitudes. Christianity moved forward within this context. During the twentieth century the United States joined Europe in the extension of its markets and contacts overseas, and also became a large importer of raw materials from the underdeveloped countries.

The leadership of the world was clearly in the hands of the white race, with all its prestige, power, and wealth. During the recent decades, however, and particularly since World War II, the situation has changed radically and dramatically. There has been a revolt against the West, and the great new fact of our time is the end of colonialism. Between 1943 and 1965, fifty-six nations became independent, including large countries such as India, Indonesia, and the Philippine Islands, but principally on the continent of Africa. In some of these new nations—culturally old but politically new—many of the leaders are either Christians or have been brought in some way under the influence of Christianity, particularly in Africa, where for a long time education was largely carried on by Christian missionaries. At the same time, it must be recognized that some leaders of new nations, reared in Christian culture, have repudiated their Christian rootage. "In more than one non-Western government there have been and are high officials who gave up Christianity and later espoused the national religion. Religious resurgence—or nationalism?"[12]

The second factor is the extension of nationalism. The results and effects of Western expansion were far-reaching. Colonialism provided vast areas of the world with a glimpse of world civilization and the totality of human life, bringing word about a certain kind of unification, and undoubtedly preparing the way for the global unity of the twentieth century. However, colonialism was exploitative as well as self-serving, and was bound to produce a profound reaction among the oppressed peoples of the world. The feeling against the West gathered momentum after World War II, and this partly explains the strong independence movements. It also accounts for the awakening of nationalist passion. Nationalism has both its positive and its negative aspects. It has often called forth noble sentiments of self-sacrifice and devotion in the interests of nation-building, but it has also led to unreasonable attitudes and, in some cases, to extreme forms of violence. With a heightened sense of nationality has come also a resurgence of ancient religions such as Buddhism, Hinduism, and Islam.

Later on in this book we shall refer more in detail to the ecumenical era, but let it be said at this point that the dawn of this ecumenical era represents one of the coercions of history. There has emerged in our time the concept of one world, discernible in terms of a kind of global unity with aspects of world culture. The extraordinary advance of science and technology in recent times, especially in their application in the fields of transportation and of mass communication, has tended to bring the peoples of the world together into a neighborhood, and the process involves a sort of frightening propinquity. "Human history has, in a very real sense, been a record of global unification through the process of simultaneous expansion and contraction."[13] The world has become larger and smaller at the same time. Even two world wars, with all their destructiveness and bitter strife, served ultimately to enmesh the affairs and destinies of many nations and groups of people hitherto isolated from one another.

The rival processes of political independence and interdependence can be seen by the fact that although fifty-six nations have achieved their national identity, these same nations, immediately upon securing their independence, have sought membership in the United Nations, thus recognizing their achievement of nationhood in today's world.

An important feature of the one world culture that is emerging is its secular character. "We move amidst a technological revolution, the full significance of which can only be grasped in the context of the overall development which goes by the name of 'secularization.' "[14] Van Leeuwen has pointed out that this process of secularization which now reaches out into practically every part of the globe is a product of the Christian West, and he observes that for Christian churches in East and West alike, "what has first priority here and now is this business of secularization and of our encounter with it."[15]

Related to the concept of one world, we can discern also the development of a single world history. "What we see happening," says Bishop Newbigin, "is that the people of East Asia are being drawn out of their separate pools of existence into the current of a single history."[16] He points out that countries dominated by Hindu or Buddhist cultures have no real sense of history. Changes in human experience are viewed as recurrent cycles, rather than forms of development. In the Indian village, for example, "the only records are those of the purchase and sale of land. Life is interpreted in terms of the natural rhythms of day and night, summer and winter, birth, age and death."[17] Similar examples from African culture could also be cited.

The pattern of life among the peoples of Asia and Africa has begun to change, and national experiences and developments are fast becoming part of a single world history and culture, where all share the benefits and hazards of a technological civilization. This concept of a single history originated in the Christian West. "It is a secularized form of the Christian eschatology,"[18] and moreover, "the secular order is precisely this created order in which God has set us to do His will."[19]

The Guidance of the Holy Spirit

The ecumenical movement has developed under the guidance and inspiration of the Holy Spirit. Faced with the coercions of history and the dynamics of a fast-changing world, the churches have been led by the Holy Spirit into a new and more direct confrontation with one another, with a deeper desire for mutual understanding and appreciation. In so doing, the leaders of many denominations have discovered a renewed sense of mission together in the world. "The ecumenical movement is the arena where the churches expose their own responses to the operation of the Holy Spirit [that is, their traditions] to judgment by the Holy Spirit, in the presence of other churches and in the light of their different responses, in the hope that by reassessing them the incongruity between the unity that *is* and the disunity that *is* may be overcome."[20] As in its Confession of Faith the United Presbyterian Church gives expression to its belief in the wholeness or oneness of the Christian church, so it also confesses its faith that "by the indwelling of the Holy Spirit all believers being vitally united to Christ, who is the head, are thus united one to another in the Church, which is his body."[21]

Not only has the work of the Holy Spirit brought leaders and members of Protestant denominations together in a spirit of Christian unity and renewal of life, it has also brought into closer relationship Protestants, Roman Catholics, Orthodox Christians, and Conservative Evangelical Protestant groups, all of whom have been separated from one another by historical developments.

In some instances, the Commission on Ecumenical Mission and Relations has taken the initiative. For example, the Commission presented a statement to the 1965 General Assembly of the United Presbyterian Church which began with these words: "In the providence of God and by the power of his Spirit, changes are coming in attitudes and circumstances which have been frustrating for all of us who are members of his holy catholic Church. Now doors have been opened for conversation and cooperation between Protestant and Roman Catholic, and for ventures in ecumenical trust and faith."[22] In a similar fashion, the Commission, acting for the United Presbyterian Church, has sought dialogue and conversation with Christians in the other groups we have mentioned.

The United Presbyterian Church moves to fulfill its share of the mission of the church in the world, convinced that the contemporary sweeping changes that affect all mankind are evidence of the hand of

God in history. According to John Macmurray, the English writer: "History is the continued act of God, and it is in his working in history that God is known. God is known as a worker, in the work; and his work is history. The knowledge of God and the knowledge of history are inseparably bound up."[23]

As the first half of the twentieth century saw the rapid decline of colonialism, so the second half witnessed the rise of many new independent nations across the world, particularly in Asia and Africa. The consequent growth of nationalism has had a corresponding effect on the missionary enterprise. Until relatively recent years, this enterprise had been largely a one-way process, that is, personnel and funds went from the sending countries of the West to the receiving countries in Asia, Africa, and Latin America. In the meantime the so-called younger churches had achieved a degree of maturity as well as a status of independence and selfhood. These churches began to move out of their isolationism and to reach out for relationships with other churches across the world.

If the secular world was fast becoming one world, due to the technological revolution, so was the world of the Christian churches. These could now be found in practically every part of the world, and through the ecumenical movement were being drawn together. Christ was no longer "foreign" in these lands where his gospel had been preached, and had become part of the culture of sizable segments of the people. In this situation, the names of the two boards of foreign missions of the churches that were united in Pittsburgh were seen to be anachronistic.

Churches in Asia, Africa, and Latin America, as they sent their fraternal delegates to the General Assemblies of the Presbyterian Church in the U.S.A. and the United Presbyterian Church of North America, did so in a direct kind of church-to-church relationship rather than through the boards of foreign missions. The time had come for the boards to be transformed from the status of a kind of colonial office of the church into a body or organization which could represent, and in fact involve, and speak for the whole church in carrying out its mission. The Commission on Ecumenical Mission and Relations, as a newly formed body, was in a position to act for The United Presbyterian Church in the U.S.A. in a fraternal way in relation to other Presbyterian churches which had originated in Europe and Australia, as well as to churches of other denominations across the world, and to the emerging ecumenical bodies of the world Christian community.

In this way, The United Presbyterian Church in the U.S.A., through the Commission on Ecumenical Mission and Relations, was better able to play its part in the great task to which God was calling his church as a whole church in the contemporary world, namely, to carry the gospel to the whole world. Faced with the challenge of a dynamic world revolution, and given the new dimensions of the total missionary task in the world, the United Presbyterian Church felt that God was summoning it to witness and to serve on the frontiers of an ecumenical era with all its complexity and challenge.

Chapter II

COLONIAL PRESBYTERIANISM
AND EARLY MISSIONARY EFFORTS

As one of its major themes, this book attempts to trace the history and development of The United Presbyterian Church in the U.S.A. and its predecessors, the Presbyterian Church in the U.S.A. and the United Presbyterian Church of North America, with particular emphasis on the missionary aspect of their calling. Before a church engages in missionary work, it usually goes through an initial phase of establishment, and achieving identity as a church. While it is true that what is known as Presbyterianism, or the family of Reformed Churches, was brought to these shores by the settlers from the British Isles and the continent of Europe, it must be remembered that these churches were not the mere continuation of any one Presbyterian tradition on American soil. They were brought here by Dutch, English, Scottish, Welsh, French, and German settlers.

The early Presbyterians had in common a loyalty to the Calvinistic tradition, and in the formation of the Presbyterian system in the American colonies, people with strong ideas concerning freedom and independence participated. "These searchers for freedom together formed a native Presbyterian Church, an independent, self-sustaining, and self-directing body of American Presbyterians,"[1] but the process of development was slow, and it was not until the eighteenth century that the Presbyterian Church became independent and "American."

In outlining the establishment of Presbyterian congregations in the American colonies, we shall also point out some of the characteristics of the Reformed family of churches and the contribution it made to the nascent American nation. "The influence of religious forces upon human affairs is too often overlooked by secular historians."[2]

29

The Formation and Establishment of Presbyterianism in America

As far as is known, the first Presbyterians or Calvinists to reach the New World were a group of French Huguenots who went to Brazil in 1557. The idea of establishing a Calvinistic Huguenot colony there was conceived by a group of leading French Protestants, and the scheme had the blessing of John Calvin. The expedition ended in failure, chiefly through the treachery of the leader, Villegagnon; some members of the group forfeited their lives, while the rest were dispersed.

In 1562 some French Huguenots also reached what is now Florida, and others arrived in what are now the Carolinas. However, no record of their activities is available.

Among the settlers at Jamestown, Virginia, beginning in 1611, and in New England from 1620, were Puritans with Presbyterian tendencies and convictions. This was accounted for by the fact that in England, Presbyterianism was a strong element among the Puritans. The first church officer to reach Plymouth Rock in 1620 was William Brewster, who was a ruling elder. According to Cotton Mather, "at least 4,000 Presbyterians were included among the 21,000 Puritans who landed in New England between 1620 and 1640."[3] This would mean that in the first two decades of colonial history about 20 percent of the Puritan settlers in New England were Presbyterians, either by choice or by heritage. However, many of these worshiped in Congregational churches in that area. In 1630 the Rev. Richard Denton, a Presbyterian minister from Yorkshire, England, settled in Massachusetts with part of the congregation he had served in Halifax, England, and in 1637 the Rev. Francis Doughty settled in Taunton, Massachusetts, but was driven out by the civil authorities because of his views on infant baptism. "Early Congregationalism was nearly as intolerant of opposing opinions as was Episcopacy."[4] Later Mr. Denton established a congregation in Hempstead, Long Island, in 1644, where the Dutch government granted land "to build a town or towns . . . with a temple or temples to exercise the Reformed religion."[5] Mr. Doughty and his followers fled from Maspeth, Long Island, when their church was burned down by the Indians, and established the first Presbyterian church in Manhattan in 1643.

Among the early Puritans in New England, some favored the presbyterian form of church government; others preferred episcopalian practices, but the majority wished to have an independent congregational church. One concession to those who had presbyterian views was to allow the election of elders in the church. In the congregational system, the local congregation was the church, and church government was the function of that congregation. For the Presbyterians, the church signified the whole company of Christians, the one body of Christ, manifested locally. Church government belonged to the whole body of Presbyterians of a particular denomination, and authority was exercised by judicatories called presbyteries and synods.

As early as 1640, there was a movement of Presbyterians from New England to New York, Connecticut, and New Jersey. The Rev. John Young, a Presbyterian Puritan minister, organized a congregation in Southold, Long Island, in 1640, and a year later the Rev. Abraham Pierson settled in Southampton, Long Island, with his entire congregation from Lynn, Massachusetts. These two churches are often referred to by church historians as the oldest Presbyterian churches in the Middle Colonies, although it has not been established whether they were Congregational or Presbyterian in the early years. We do know, however, that both churches were included in the Long Island Presbytery, which was formed in 1717.

Similarly, churches were established by Presbyterians in Elizabeth, New Jersey, in 1665, Newark in 1666, and Woodbridge in 1680. "By the beginning of the seventeenth century Presbyterian immigrants had pushed their way into all the colonies. Some of these appear to have entered North Carolina as early as 1650, driven there by persecution in Virginia."[6]

In Connecticut we find Presbyterian tendencies being asserted by church people in the latter part of the seventeenth century, "after the ejection of many Presbyterian Anglicans from English parishes in 1662."[7] In 1706 the Saybrook Platform was adopted in London by Presbyterians and Congregationalists, whereby "Consociations" of churches were set up. These were similar in form to presbyteries, as the Connecticut churches called themselves Presbyterian thereafter.

This southward movement of Puritans from New England to the Middle Colonies was due partly to economic reasons, for some people were in search of better opportunities. However, others went south because in their communities "their distinctive presbyterian practices had made them an unwelcome and disturbing minority."[8]

As we have seen, the beginnings of Presbyterianism in America are not easy to trace. Whereas the Quakers had their Pennsylvania, the Baptists Rhode Island, the Episcopalians Virginia, and the Congregationalists Massachusetts and Connecticut, the Presbyterians cannot point with pride to any predominantly Presbyterian colony. There were only scattered groups of Presbyterians. Puritan churches, which were Presbyterian in theology but not in church government, were formed. Only the Dutch Reformed and the German Reformed Churches were Presbyterian in both theology and government.

The real foundations of Presbyterianism were laid when the Scotch-Irish immigration reached these shores, beginning about 1680. Persecuted in Scotland, large numbers of Presbyterians had fled to Northern Ireland, where they found that the King of England continued to harass them. As a result of this persecution, large numbers emigrated to the American colonies. By the middle of the eighteenth century, "a quarter of a million of Ulster County Presbyterians had landed upon our shores."[9] The term "Ulster County Presbyterians" (or Ulstermen) is more accurate than "Scotch-Irish" because the Scots who fled to Northern Ireland never intermarried with the Irish. It was these Scots, rather than the early Presbyterian settlers in New England, who played such an important part in shaping not only the spiritual but also the political destinies of the American people. It must be clearly stated that not all the Scotch-Irish who migrated were good churchgoers. However, as a whole the group seems to have been composed of sturdy, rugged, freedom-loving people. William Thomson Hanzsche maintains that "with the coming of large numbers of these tenacious Scotch-Irish, Presbyterianism was in America to stay."[10]

Among the Scotch-Irish immigrants was an energetic, forceful young minister named Francis Makemie, who reached Maryland in 1683. Makemie is referred to by church historians as "the Father of American Presbyterianism." In addition to exercising a Christian ministry, Makemie was a businessman, following in the Pauline tradition by earning his living outside the ministry. His private income was augmented by marrying the daughter of a wealthy Viriginia landowner.

him to pay the cost not only of the defense but also of the prosecution, amounting to eighty-three pounds. The trial and acquittal of Makemie were widely publicized in Boston and New York, and this led to the recall of the governor. The trial was a victory for freedom of speech in the colonies, and it also brought into prominence the newly formed Presbytery of which Makemie was Moderator. The establishment of an independent American church was an important event in the history of the colonies, for seventy years later the struggle for independence was not only political but ecclesiastical as well, and religious freedom was of major importance in the founding of the republic.

The Covenanters and the Seceders

The United Presbyterian Church of North America, which came into being in 1858, had a rich heritage of individual courage and fortitude in the face of persecution, and a strong tradition of resistance to royal encroachments on freedom and independence, and most of all, of dissent.

These early settlers were fiercely independent and suspicious of any external discipline or governmental authority. They were " 'bold, stout and industrious men, sharp at religious controversy and not strongly attached to government, whether of the royal or proprietary kind. In nearly every cabin three articles were to be found: a Bible, a rifle, and a whisky jug.' Such were the forebears of the United Presbyterian Church of North America."[14]

In Scotland, both Covenanters and Seceders had been opposed to tyranny for similar reasons. The former originally were those who signed the Solemn League and Covenant in 1638, which was a revised and an enlarged version of the Covenant of 1561. The Covenant of 1638 is described as "one of the most significant documents in the history of religious liberty."[15] During the reigns of King Charles I and King Charles II, the Covenant became a rallying point for those who opposed the institution of the episcopate, the Book of Ordination, and the Book of Canons. Historians estimate that about 2,000 Covenanters died in the struggle that ensued, while 16,000 fled into exile.[16]

From 1680 onward, the Covenanters who had been routed at the

As well as being a gifted man, Makemie was an invet(
and itinerant missionary. He founded five Presbyterian
Maryland, and in 1704 went to London to recruit more
ministers and resources. In 1706 he was largely respon
organization of a Presbytery in Philadelphia, the first I
America. Makemie was elected Moderator.

In view of the power of colonial administration and
England, the establishment of the Presbyterian Churc
clesiastical body was not only an important step, but a b
"It was an epoch-making achievement, a masterful stro
which was to give the weak, scattered Presbyterian chu
ganizational unity."[11] Moreover, it gave the Presbyteriar
advantage over other ecclesiastical colonial bodies, bec
organized four decades before any of these. The Presb)
was formed in Philadelphia in 1706, was the origin in a
way, of what came to be known as the Presbyterian Ch
United States of America, when the General Assembly
lished in 1789.[12]

In 1787 and 1788, during the discussions in the Synod o
and Philadelphia which led to the organization of the (
sembly, the following names were used: The Presbyteriar
America, The Presbyterian Church in the United State
Presbyterian Church in the United States of America. A
formal action seems to have been taken on the name, th
record was made: "The Synod having also 'revised and co
Directory for Worship, did approve and ratify the san
hereby appoint the said Directory, as now amended, to be
tory for the public worship of God in the *Presbyterian Ch*
United States of America.'"[13] (Italics added.)

Following the establishment of the Presbytery of Pl
Makemie visited New York, and was invited to preach in
Puritan churches. He was arrested and imprisoned by the
Lord Cornbury, for preaching without a license. With t
three able lawyers, Makemie won his case in the courts on
that he had been given a license to preach while in B
license that was valid throughout the Queen's dominions.
brilliant defense resulted in his acquittal. The angry goverr

Battle of Bothwell Bridge the previous year were forced to organize into neighborhood societies that met secretly. In December, 1681, the first general meeting of commissioners from the various local societies was held. Policy and action on the part of the Covenanters were determined at such general meetings. This system of local societies with general meetings three or four times a year provided the only means of organization until August, 1743, when the Rev. John Mc-Millan and the Rev. Thomas Nairne, with some ruling elders, constituted themselves as "The Reformed Presbytery." The same loose system of neighborhood societies related to one another in general meetings was employed in Northern Ireland, and it served in North America until March, 1774, when "The Reformed Presbyterian Presbytery of America" was established in Paxtang, Pennsylvania.

The Secession movement was a later development. It was precipitated in 1733 by a sermon preached by the Rev. Ebenezer Erskine, moderator of the Synod of Sterling and Perth. In his sermon, Erskine attacked the evils of patronage whereby the King controlled ecclesiastical appointments. In 1733, when the General Assembly of the Church of Scotland censured Erskine and three other ministers who supported him, they shortly thereafter constituted themselves as "The Associate Presbytery." These men and their followers were called Seceders. They grew so rapidly that the General Assembly of the Church of Scotland, taking second thought, invited Erskine to return, and even elected him moderator, but he refused the honor. By 1744 the Associate Presbytery numbered twenty-six settled charges, and, being so widely scattered, they reconstituted themselves into three presbyteries under an "Associate Synod." About this time many Scots were emigrating to the New World, Covenanters and Seceders among them.

The Scottish immigrants who came to America in the seventeenth century came singly or in small groups, and settled largely in Pennsylvania, New York, New Jersey, and Virginia. It was not until 1743 that a minister was available to the Covenanter groups. The Rev. Alexander Craighead left the Presbyterian Church, which had been established in 1706, and he became the first Reformed Presbyterian minister in this country. Mr. Craighead served the Reformed Presbyterian congregation at Middle Octorara, Pennsylvania.

The first minister to leave Scotland to minister to the Covenanters was the Rev. John Cuthbertson, and for forty years thereafter he traveled widely among the early Covenanter families, sharing with them the rugged pioneer life of those times. "It was a rough life, most of it in the saddle with often less than a week in any one place. Bible study and the preparation of the customary two- and three-hour sermons had to be done on the way from one settlement to another, over roads that were often little more than dirt tracks, and in all kinds of weather."[17] Few church buildings existed and congregations often worshiped outdoors, with the minister standing on a raised wooden platform, covered by a sloping roof in case of rain. As the work developed, churches were built of logs, but they were unheated, and in cold weather the people used to leave the church during an intermission in the long service and gather round a big bonfire for a while. In warm weather the minister still wore a long frock coat, but usually took it off after he had announced the text of his sermon!

The Seceders also faced many of the same difficulties as the Covenanters did. Repeated attempts were made to secure a minister from Scotland, but it was not until 1753 that a young man, the Rev. Alexander Gellatly, and an older man, the Rev. Andrew Arnot, offered to leave for America. Soon after arrival in November, 1753, these two ministers constituted "The Associate Presbytery of Pennsylvania, subordinate to the Associate (Anti-Burgher) Synod of Scotland."

In 1777 the possibility of union was first discussed when a group of Associate Presbyterians (Seceders) and Reformed Presbyterians (Covenanters) met in Lancaster County, Pennsylvania. The Associate Presbytery of New York in 1780 drafted and unanimously adopted a Basis of Union consisting of ten brief statements, and submitted the Basis to the Reformed Presbyterian Presbytery and the Associate Presbytery of Pennsylvania. The former, with a few minor modifications, unanimously adopted the Basis in December, 1781, and the latter adopted the Basis by a majority vote in June, 1782, with two ministers and three elders dissenting. On October 30, 1782, the three presbyteries met in convention in Philadelphia and drew up eight articles for the guidance of the proposed new American synod. On November 1 the Associate Reformed Synod was constituted on the Basis of Union and the eight articles. These eight articles were subsequently published under the erroneous title, *The Constitution of the Associate Reformed Church.*

The two ministers of the Associate Presbytery of Pennsylvania who dissented from the Basis of Union continued the Associate body, placing themselves under the General Associate Synod in Scotland. Although all three ministers of the Reformed Presbytery and all its organized congregations went into the Associate Reformed Synod, a few individual members withdrew, and upon appeal to the Reformed Synod in Scotland eventually secured new ministers, thus continuing a separate existence.

By comparison, the newly formed Associate Reformed Synod was, from its inception, an independent body, free from foreign control. Statement 10 in the Basis of Union said, "They shall claim the full exercise of church discipline, without dependence upon foreign judicatories." Moreover, this group held firmly to the principle of separation of church and state, a principle that was soon to achieve importance as part of the First Amendment to the Constitution of the United States. The Associate Reformed Synod of North America grew in numbers, particularly in New York, Pennsylvania, and New Jersey, and in 1802 four synods were created.

The Contribution of Presbyterianism in Colonial America

The contribution of Protestant churches during the formative period of American life was considerable. Congregationalists, Baptists, Episcopalians, Methodists, Quakers, and Presbyterians all exercised their particular influence on the developing society. This is attested to by historians, in spite of the fact that during the eighteenth century the large majority of the white population had no church connection. According to Kenneth Latourette, in 1800 only 6.9 percent of the colonial population had any church affiliation.[18] Other historians put the figure even lower than that. And yet, the verdict of history in general, and in America in particular, is that "the spirit of democracy has been cradled in religion—and with confidence we can say that the spirit of American democracy has been nourished at all times by the spiritual zeal of devout members of the Church of Christ."[19]

At the heart of democracy is the question of authority. Does it rest in the people who are governed, or is it in the hands of one man or a small group of men with dictatorial powers? To John Calvin is mainly attributed the important principle that power rests with the people.

The church in Geneva was governed on the principle that authority begins at the bottom, that is, among the people, and by representation moves upward to the highest body. The movement is from the session of the local congregation to the presbytery, to the synod, and up to the General Assembly. Moreover, the highest judicatory, the General Assembly, as well as the delegate synods, must be composed of elders and clergy in equal proportions.

The principle of government by consent, or through representation of the governed, is enshrined in the United States Constitution in the phrase "We, the people." Interestingly enough, this principle, in various forms of language, has been incorporated into all the Latin American constitutions, as the people sought to emerge from colonialism and authoritarianism into a democratic life. Prof. Alfonso López, son of a former president of Colombia, describes the origin of this principle in his book *La Estirpe Calvinista de Nuestras Instituciones* (The Calvinistic Origin of Our Institutions), originally given as lectures at the National University of Colombia. "Before there were any democratic states, in the modern sense of the word, there existed already a democratic church, that of Calvin."[20]

The Presbyterians brought to the American scene an attachment for system and order. "Liberty in law is the watchword of Presbyterianism."[21] The *Encyclopedia of the Presbyterian Church*, from which this sentence is taken, goes on to affirm that "the Presbyterianism of these colonists was the very form and mold of a free government. . . . In this Church [the Presbyterian] all power proceeds from the people; but presbytery is not democracy, it is not a weak confederation. It is a compact representative government, with a written constitution."[22]

Congregationalism was also founded on the democratic principle that power proceeds from the people, and indeed the Congregationalists carried this principle farther than the Presbyterians did. However, the formulation of principles of church government in a constitution came much later.

In his book *Piety and Politics*, Alan F. Geyer shows how political and religious ideas were intermingled, and that the United States is the one nation where the social contract of the seventeenth- and eighteenth-century philosophers was translated into practical reality, "like a covenant between a chosen people and its Sovereign Lord."[23]

The early Puritans, as well as the Jeffersonian rationalists, saw their country as a sort of "Promised Land." "The ancient community of the Covenant had become the American Commonwealth. . . . Calvinism, most conspicuously in New England, linked the doctrine of the Covenant with American constitutionalism and politics."[24]

A further idea of Calvinistic origin that was also incorporated into the American political system was the limitation of power through the three branches of government, a bicameral Congress, and the federal system. "Not only was the structure of constitutional government in America responsive to Calvinist influence: the very image which Americans formed of their own nation was largely shaped by that influence."[25] However, we must be careful not to give the impression that the Presbyterian form of government had any decided effect as such on the American form of government. Trinterud maintains that "of direct influence of American Presbyterian ecclesiastical polity upon the framers of the Constitution, none can be traced."[26] What he does affirm is that Calvin's ideas on the state greatly influenced Locke, and that "the framers of the Constitution leaned heavily upon those political theorists who had been influenced most by Calvin."[27]

Another Presbyterian contribution to the development of the American nation in its formative period was the fierce love of independence and freedom, and a hatred of hierarchical authority, which characterized the Scotch-Irish. "Revolt against the tyranny of the English rule was bred in their bones . . . [and] all the ardor of the English-Scotch border feuds came to the surface again in the colonies."[28] At the time of the War of Independence, the population in the colonies was about three million people, and of these, some nine hundred thousand were Scots or of Scottish descent, whereas another million were other Calvinist groups such as English, Dutch, and German. It is not surprising, therefore, that the majority of those who fought in Washington's army were either Scottish or Scotch-Irish, at least in origin, from New Jersey and Pennsylvania. According to Charles A. and Mary R. Beard, the first census taken in the United States was in 1790, and at that time there were 3,172,000 whites and 700,000 Negroes, of whom 75.2 percent were of English, Scotch, or Scotch-Irish origin, 3.7 percent South Irish, 8.7 percent Germans, and the remainder Dutch, Swedish, French, and so on.[29]

Worthy of note also are the Mecklenburg Resolves, which ante-
dated the Declaration of Independence by a year. This document consisted of twenty resolves, one of which declared that "all laws and
commissions confirmed or derived from the authority of the King or
Parliament are annulled and vacated, and the former civil constitution
of these colonies for the present wholly suspended."[30] The Mecklenburg Resolves were approved at a meeting of citizens, all of Scottish
or Scotch-Irish origin, in Charlotte, North Carolina, on May 31, 1775.
The document was sent by special messenger to the Continental Congress. Its direct influence on the Declaration of Independence has been
questioned by historians, but the similarity of interest and spirit cannot be denied. " 'The first public voice in America for the dissolving
of all connection with Great Britain, came not from the Puritans of
New England, the Dutch of New York, nor the planters of Virginia,
but from the Scotch-Irish Presbyterians.' "[31] A footnote to the history
of the independence movement is the fact that the Rev. John Witherspoon, who later presided at the opening session of the first General
Assembly of the Presbyterian Church in the U.S.A. in 1789, not only
was tireless in his advocacy of principles of political and religious
freedom but also was the only clergyman who signed the Declaration
of Independence.

The emphasis on education was a further contribution made by
Presbyterians in the New World. Scotland promoted popular education more than any other country at the time of the Reformation. The
Reformed Churches felt the need to place a school alongside every
local church in order to produce a population that could read the
Bible, which had recently been translated into the English language.
The Scotch-Irish brought this traditional love of education to America
and helped build its educational system from the common school to
the university. Of the forty colleges established between 1780 and
1829, thirteen were founded by Presbyterians.[32] It should be added
that the Episcopalians, the Baptists, and the Congregationalists also
founded what are today well-known institutions of higher learning,
and thus made their contribution to education.

The Presbyterian emphasis on an educated ministry and the requirement that all ministerial candidates should have at least a degree
of Bachelor of Arts was indeed commendable, but it meant that the

Presbyterian Church was not as flexible in its operations on the expanding frontiers as were the Baptists and Methodists. "These [the Baptists and Methodists] were not concerned at that time about educational standards for their missionary evangelists and circuit riders."[33] However, Loetscher maintains that when the trek westward began with the opening of the Erie Canal in 1825, Presbyterians were well prepared to serve the people on the new frontiers.[34]

The Development of a Missionary Church

We have outlined the establishment of Presbyterianism in the New World, and have referred to the distinct contribution that it made together with other religious groups in the building up of a new nation. How did the Presbyterian churches become missionary churches? The missionary impulse was first manifested in the desire to reach the unchurched with the gospel. Early in the eighteenth century dedicated ministers traveled on foot or on horseback to evangelize the settlers. This same impulse led Christians to undertake missionary work among the Indian tribes.

Between 1776 and 1830 the population of the new nation multiplied five times, but although gains were made in church membership and the number of churches, churchmen were still a small minority. It is remarkable that missionary zeal should have developed, and indeed that a missionary movement itself in the Presbyterian Church could have been initiated during that period. Church life had not yet become ecclesiasticized, and so it can be said that missionary interest grew largely out of personal piety. " 'The Spirit of missions . . . is the spirit of piety,' and increasingly the mission movement became the vehicle for the development of personalistic piety."[35] However, more than this was involved. In those early days of the Presbyterian Church a tradition was established, namely, that the church exists not as an end in itself, but for mission, to serve Christ in the world.

A widespread interest in missions did not arise easily in the Presbyterian Church. The closing years of the eighteenth century were a time of great turmoil. Fresh in the minds of people was the Reign of Terror in France; there were wars and rumors of wars, and atheistic philosophy made inroads into Christianity. All these factors spurred

preachers of the day to search the Scriptures for some basis of interpretation. They found it in the book of Revelation. Timothy Dwight,
an outstanding figure in the Calvinistic Federation in Connecticut,
and president of Yale, was convinced that the apocalyptic writers of
the Bible had the closing years of the eighteenth century in mind. His
analysis of the international turmoil was made in the light of the
sixteenth chapter of Revelation.[36]

Many preachers were convinced that the events of the time were
sufficient indication that the end of the age was approaching. It was
believed that the Jews were about to accept Christianity. "The conversion of the Jews would constitute a very important part of the
approaching prosperity of the Church. It would, without doubt, be a
prelude to the general acceptance of Christianity by the heathen
peoples of the earth."[37]

The spirit of Old Calvinism, however, was still prevalent, and it was
believed by many that God would convert the Jew and the pagan
when and how he pleased, and there was not much that mortals could
do about it. The teachings and preachings of men like Edwards,
Hopkins, Witherspoon, and Tennent began to influence a new generation, and to change the ideas and attitudes of church people, especially
the Presbyterians. The Second Great Awakening, which began in
1797, had considerable effect upon the life of the churches, starting
revivals not only in New England but also in the West and the South.

It can be said that to a great extent the missionary motivation in the
early part of the nineteenth century was derived from the conviction
that Bible prophecies were clearly related to the events of those years.
"To save countless millions of heathen from everlasting punishment,
to emulate their British brethren in their heroic efforts to evangelize
the world, to obey the Great Commission which had enjoined missions on a universal scale, and to put into practice the principle of
disinterested benevolence out of pure love to God and to all 'beings
capable of good,' were the most conspicuously stressed motives for
Christians to engage in Foreign Missions."[38]

The Missionary Societies

Beginning with the last decade of the eighteenth century, a number
of missionary societies were formed, representing what might be

termed the pioneer organizational phase of missionary work. The interesting feature about these early societies is that some of them crossed denominational lines. According to an article with the title "Some 'Very Respectable Missionary Societies,'" some of the earliest of these societies were The New York Missionary Society (1796), The Northern Missionary Society (1797), The Berkshire and Columbia Missionary Society (1797), The Missionary Society of Connecticut (1798), The Massachusetts Missionary Society (1799), and The Boston Female Society for Missionary Purposes (1800).[39]

Not all of these were Presbyterian societies, but Presbyterians were prominent in them, especially in the New York and Northern Societies. "While they were primarily for what would now be deemed home missions, their constitutions and announcements showed that they contemplated work among the Indians, which was then considered foreign missions."[40]

The New York Missionary Society was the first voluntary interdenominational organization of a missionary character in the United States.[41] It drew upon the experience of British missionary societies, and, in particular, from the famous London Missionary Society, which had been formed in 1795.[42] From the beginning the work of the Society was undergirded by prayer. "The Concert of Prayer was a very prominent aspect of the missionary movement on both sides of the Atlantic."[43] The practice began in Scotland in 1744, when time was set aside on Saturday evening, Sunday morning, and the first Tuesday in February, May, August, and November for public and private prayer for the extension of the Kingdom of God. The plan was first used in America in 1794.

The minutes of December 11, 1797, of the New York Missionary Society record that the Directors of the Society sent to the judicatories of the several churches connected with the Society a proposition that "the second Wednesday of every month, beginning at candlelight, be observed by meetings for prayer in behalf of missions, these meetings to be held in succession at the Old Presbyterian Church, the Scots' Presbyterian Church, the new Dutch Church, the First Baptist Church, the Brick Presbyterian Church, the North Dutch Church, and then to revert to the place of beginning."[44]

In 1816 the General Assembly of the Presbyterian Church entered into correspondence with the Dutch Reformed Church and the Associate Reformed Church, and out of the proposals made came the formation in 1818 of the United Foreign Missionary Society. The object of the Society was stated in the Constitution as being "to spread the Gospel among the Indians of North America, the inhabitants of Mexico, and South America, and other portions of the heathen and anti-Christian world."[45] For many years this Society was regarded as under the peculiar protection of the General Assembly. In 1818 The Northern Missionary Society merged with The United Foreign Missionary Society, and The New York Missionary Society did likewise in 1820.

An outstanding event in the annals of missions is the famous Haystack Prayer Meeting of four students from Williams College of Williamstown, Massachusetts, in 1806. Samuel J. Mills, who was the central figure in the Society of the Brethren which was formed two years later, was joined by Adoniram Judson and other students at Andover Theological Seminary in the sending of a petition to the clergy of New England that a missionary society be formed. As a result of this petition, the American Board of Commissioners for Foreign Missions was established in 1810, and this was the first overseas missionary organization in the United States. In this organization Presbyterians, Reformed Church leaders, as well as Congregationalists, cooperated. The records of the period from the middle of the eighteenth century to 1810 indicate that many sermons revealed a remarkable vision of world mission. Evidently it was the demands of the American frontier, and especially the need to spread the gospel among the Indians, which postponed the extension of missions to distant lands before the end of the first decade of the nineteenth century.

In 1812 the American Board of Commissioners for Foreign Missions suggested to the General Assembly of the Presbyterian Church in the U.S.A. that it form "an institution similar to theirs, between which and them may be such co-operation as shall promote the great object of missions."[46] The Presbyterian General Assembly, however, did not consider it convenient to form such a society at that time and commended the American Board to its churches. "The American Board thus became the recognized foreign missionary agency for both Congregational and Presbyterian churches."[47] Presbyterian personnel and funds were contributed to the American Board, and the foundation for the Presbyterian mission work in the Middle East was laid by missionaries who went out under the American Board.

The Western Foreign Missionary Society

As we have seen, a number of foreign missionary societies were established in the last decade of the eighteenth century as well as in the early nineteenth, and they provided a great stimulus to interest in missions among the churches. However, it was the creation of The Western Foreign Missionary Society which in more ways than one laid the foundations of what was later to become the work of the Board of Foreign Missions of the Presbyterian Church in the U.S.A. In a sense this Society was the forerunner of the Board of Foreign Missions.

The Synod of Pittsburgh, from the time it was formed, took an active interest in missionary work, and at its first meeting in 1802 organized itself as The Western Missionary Society. This interest continued over the years and was later extended to cover foreign missions.

In 1831, the Synod of Pittsburgh constituted The Western Foreign Missionary Society. Details of the manner in which this was done will be given in the next chapter. Our purpose here is to draw attention to the formation of this Society as a foreign missions agency, one which in 1837 became the Board of Foreign Missions of the Presbyterian Church in the U.S.A.

The organ for promotion and publicity was *The Christian Advocate*, of which Ashbel Green was the editor for twelve years. In its April, 1833 edition, the magazine said in its section called "Religious Intelligence," "The Western Foreign Missionary Society has seen fit to provide this little Monthly Journal as a convenient organ of communication with its friends and patrons."[48]

The guiding spirit of the organization, and an eloquent and zealous advocate of foreign missions, was the Rev. Elisha P. Swift, D.D., who became the first Corresponding Secretary of the Society. In the Presbyterian Centenary Memorial Volume published in 1876, the Rev. Dr. Charles C. Beatty is quoted as having said, "I consider the

Rev. Elisha P. Swift, D.D., to have been really the father and founder of our Presbyterian Foreign Mission work."[49] Ashbel Green stated that "it is due to the Rev. Elisha P. Swift, the first Corresponding Secretary of this Society, to state, that its origin is to be traced, principally, to his ardent zeal in the missionary cause, and to his views of the importance of an institution organized in the manner exhibited in the foregoing documents [the Constitution]."[50]

Why should The Western Foreign Missionary Society be considered the forerunner of the Board of Foreign Missions, which came into being in 1837? In his address delivered at a missionary convention in Pittsburgh in January, 1872, the Rev. Dr. William D. Howard said: "The founders of The Western Foreign Missionary Society seem to have grasped all the essential features of the missionary work. The breadth and comprehensiveness of their views fill me with surprise. . . . And they not only selected Africa and India, but their eye was upon China, Japan, Persia, Asia Minor, South America, and other localities."[51]

The Synod of Pittsburgh, which from the time of its formation in 1802 had been called by its own action "The Western Missionary Society," had cooperated fully with the American Board in the interest of missions, and in 1831 there were some members who argued that it would be dishonorable toward that Board to set up an independent society.[52] Elisha P. Swift, who was in close touch with men like Ashbel Green, Archibald Alexander, and Samuel Miller,[53] drafted the constitution of the new society and was its foremost advocate. He was convinced that the Presbyterian Church should not leave foreign missions to a voluntary agency. The principle, therefore, that foreign missions should be part of the mainstream of the life of the church, rather than be promoted by an independent missionary society, is one that was early established in the Presbyterian Church. This differentiates it from many Protestant churches in Great Britain and Europe, where there are missionary societies still operating as separate entities. The principle became an important part of the controversy between the Old School and the New School which split the Presbyterian Church in the U.S.A. for over thirty years.

In 1835 the General Assembly of the Presbyterian Church became convinced that the time had come for it to have its own missionary society and resolved: "That a Committee be appointed to confer with the Synod of Pittsburgh, on the subject of a transfer of the supervision of The Western Foreign Missionary Society, now under the direction of that Synod; to ascertain the terms on which such a transfer can be made, to devise and digest a plan of conducting Foreign Missions under the direction of the General Assembly of the Presbyterian Church [in the U.S.A.] and to report the whole to the next General Assembly."[54]

To the chagrin of men like Ashbel Green and others who believed in the need to constitute a church mission board, the General Assembly of 1836 rejected by four votes (110 to 106) the proposal put forward by the committee. In other words, it voted in favor of the minority report presented by one dissenting member of the committee, who believed that there was no need for a missionary society under the General Assembly, since the Presbyterian Church had used the American Board as its agency from its inception, and a majority of its members were Presbyterian. Those who favored the majority report, and saw it defeated, called a conference at Philadelphia two weeks after the meeting of the General Assembly. In a 4,000-word statement to the conference, they said, "The constitution of the Presbyterian Church manifestly contains the presumption that operations of this kind [Foreign Missions] are to be carried on church-wise (Form of Government, Chapter 18)."[55]

Under The Western Foreign Missionary Society, the Rev. and Mrs. John C. Lowrie and the Rev. and Mrs. William Reed sailed for India in 1833. Mrs. Lowrie died a year later, but her husband remained and founded the Ludhiana Mission. However, due to ill health, Dr. Lowrie was forced to return to the United States in 1836. In 1838, he became executive of the newly formed Board of Foreign Missions and remained in its service until 1891.

The Society appointed the Rev. Joseph Barr and the Rev. John B. Pinney as missionaries to West Africa in 1832. Five days before he was to embark, Mr. Barr died of cholera; Mr. Pinney sailed for Monrovia, and shortly afterward was joined by other missionaries. In 1833 missionaries were sent to the Wea Indians in the territory that is now the State of Kansas.

In 1836 the Rev. Josiah Brewer and Mr. Thomas Brown, a printer, and his wife, sailed for Smyrna to open up work there, and later were joined by other missionaries. Within a short time Mr. Brown returned to the United States unexpectedly and without authorization from the Society. This caused the Society to study conditions of appointment more closely, for evidently Mr. Brown's support was supposed to come from some source other than the Society itself.

China was the fifth mission of the Society. The Rev. and Mrs. Robert W. Orr and the Rev. A. Mitchell sailed for that country in 1837, shortly before the Society was transferred to the Board of Foreign Missions.[56]

In later years the concerns of the Board of Foreign Missions were not confined to people in foreign countries. A particular responsibility was felt for those who were called Orientals, that is, Chinese and Japanese residing in this country. The shameful treatment to which they were subjected, and the conditions under which many of them lived, stirred the conscience of Christian people. To them it seemed intolerable that efforts should be made to carry the gospel to distant lands while there was indifference to the conditions under which Orientals lived in the United States.

With the discovery of gold in California, there was an immediate demand for cheap labor, and, to fill this, Chinese workers began to arrive in 1848. Before long, the influx of Chinese aroused much suspicion and opposition among people on the West Coast, who felt threatened. Newspaper articles whipped up resentment and hatred, and there were cases of mob violence and bloodshed. Immigration policies became more restrictive and unjust, and occasioned strong diplomatic protests from China. The worst feature of this whole unfortunate situation was the slave traffic. Girls were lured to this country under false pretenses. They were known as "picture brides." In order to evade the immigration laws, a girl was met on arrival at the pier by a Chinese young man who produced the girl's picture and swore that she was his wife. These girls were kept in wretched, dirty tenement houses and subjected to great abuse in dens of iniquity.

In 1873 a group of devoted Presbyterian women, shocked by the situation, organized the Women's Occidental Board of Missions and began a work of rescue and Christian ministry. The Board of Foreign Missions also began work among Japanese on the West Coast in the

1880's. Other groups from Asia, particularly Koreans, were also ministered to by the church. In 1922 this type of work was transferred by the Board of Foreign Missions to the Board of National Missions, and work administered by the Woman's Board of Foreign Missions was transferred to the Woman's Board of Home Missions of the Presbyterian Church in the U.S.A.

From 1831 to 1837 The Western Foreign Missionary Society succeeded in challenging the churches, not only in the Synod of Pittsburgh but in other sections of the country also, with the missionary message. The Society collected funds, and by 1837 had forty-five missionaries in five fields. It not only prepared the way for the formation of the Board of Foreign Missions, but in a very real sense The Western Foreign Missionary Society became the Board of Foreign Missions, which was to labor as the church's agency in foreign lands from 1837 to 1958, when the Commission on Ecumenical Mission and Relations was established.

In the development of the idea and the cause of missions in the Presbyterian Church in the U.S.A. in the 1830's, the influence of the Rev. Ashbel Green, D.D., was of paramount importance, and deserves some mention here. We have seen how he played a leading part in the controversy surrounding the establishment of a separate missionary organization, a Board of Foreign Missions, within the church's structure.

At its first meeting, held in Baltimore in 1837, the Board of Foreign Missions of the Presbyterian Church in the U.S.A. passed the following action: "RESOLVED, that the Rev. Dr. Ashbel Green be requested to draw up a history of the Foreign Missionary operations of the Presbyterian Church in the United States, to be published by the Executive Committee with the proceedings of this Board."[57] Some of the facts that we give, prior to 1837, are taken from this interesting book, which bears the title A Historical Sketch or Compendious View of Domestic and Foreign Missions in the Presbyterian Church of the United States of America. It was published in 1838 by William S. Martien, Philadelphia, and is an authentic source of information about Presbyterian missions prior to 1837. The outside cover bears the simple title of "Presbyterian Missions." In 1893 Dr. John C. Lowrie, who served the Board of Foreign Missions for a total of fifty-four years, first as Assistant Secretary (1838 to 1850) and then as Co-ordinate Secretary (1850 to 1891), reprinted Dr. Green's book under the same title, "Presbyterian Missions," with the addition of some supplemental notes and with a few minor changes in the text. The edition ran to only three hundred copies.

In a chapter bearing the title "Foreign or Heathen Missions," Dr. Green gives the following information about the first appointment of a missionary by the Presbyterian Church in the colonies in the New World:

> The Church of Scotland was their mother Church; and to her they looked, to enable them to send the Gospel to the pagans of the wilderness. "The Society in Scotland for propagating Christian knowledge" was instituted, in Edinburgh, in 1709. This Society, in 1741, established a Board of Correspondents in New York, who, on proper recommendation, appointed the Rev. Azariah Horton, a member of the Presbytery of New York, to labour as a missionary on Long Island, where a large number of Indians then resided. This was the first formal heathen mission instituted in the Presbyterian Church.[58]

Mention should also be made of a name well known in the early annals of Presbyterian missionary history, namely, that of David Brainerd, who was ordained as a missionary by the Presbytery of New York in 1744. Mr. Brainerd labored successfully among the Indians in Pennsylvania and New Jersey. "The wonders he saw wrought by the Spirit of God among the Indians at Crossweeksung have always been counted among the greatest achievements of missions."[59]

It should be noted that although Dr. Brown's book *One Hundred Years* was published on the completion of a century of missionary work by the Board of Foreign Missions which was established in 1837, there had been activities of a missionary nature for many years before that date, and, in the early part of the nineteenth century, at least eighty Presbyterian missionaries had been sent out under various missionary societies. Of these, twenty-seven labored among Indian tribes in the United States and the remainder went to Africa, China, and India.[60] Dr. Brown deals with these early missionary efforts as events leading to the formation of the Board of Foreign Missions of the Presbyterian Church in the U.S.A.

It is an interesting historical fact that what came to be known as "foreign missions" developed quite naturally out of missionary efforts by the Presbyterian Church in colonial times, and, after independence, in the newly formed States. In the early days, work among the Indian tribes, or nations, was considered "foreign missions." The supplemental notes in the 1893 edition of *Presbyterian Missions* by Ashbel Green, referring to the work carried on by the Synods of Virginia, the Carolinas, and Pittsburgh, record that "the Indian Missions of these Synods were regarded as *Foreign*. Such was the *usus loquendi*. Of course, they were also considered as missions to the Heathen. The Indians were foreigners in their language, way of life, religious usages, treatment by the Government in waging wars and forming treaties with them."[61]

In 1802 the General Assembly of the Presbyterian Church in the U.S.A. appointed a Standing Committee on Missions. This Committee was the first missionary organization with national responsibility in the church. *The Presbyterian Monthly Record* of 1879 said that this Committee was "the oldest sister, perhaps the mother, of the Assembly's Board of Education, Foreign Missions, Publication, Erection, Relief, etc." The first chairman of the Committee was Dr. Ashbel Green, and in one of its first meetings, four areas of concern were outlined: the frontiers, older settled communities without gospel privileges, Negroes, and Indians. In 1816 the Committee became the Board of Domestic Missions, and, later on, the Board of National Missions.

The same fundamental conviction that led the church in these early days to send missionaries to labor for the spreading of the gospel among the Indians of North America caused it to send them to distant countries as well. "Foreign Missions" and "Domestic Missions" were very closely related in the minds of Presbyterian church leaders—the purpose, motivation, and dedication being the same in both cases. This accounts for the words with which Ashbel Green begins his book on Presbyterian missions: "The propagation of the Gospel in North America possessed, essentially, the character of a Missionary enterprise."[62]

Thus, it can be said that after the Presbyterian Church was firmly established in America it began to achieve a distinct identity as a missionary church. Even in the late eighteenth century, it produced some outstanding missionary figures, and they were supported by the prayers, interest, and contributions of the local churches. As early as 1763 a collection for missions was ordered by the Synod of New York, and in 1766, the Synod of New York and Philadelphia voted that "an offering should be taken in all congregations to inaugurate church work in destitute places."[63] The members of the early missionary societies, founded at the end of the eighteenth century, "were spiritually-minded men and women, and they realized the essential place of prayer in any sound missionary programs."[64] Undoubtedly, the experience of the church in spreading the gospel among the Indians in North America was the basis, and in a sense provided the urge for extending the work beyond the shores of the American continent.

The Plan of Union of 1801

Reference has been made to the missionary tradition that developed early in the Presbyterian Church in the United States. Mention must also be made of a deep desire for unity in the church of Jesus Christ, and what we in our day would call ecumenicity, which developed at the beginning of the nineteenth century. This desire found expression in the Plan of Union of 1801, which "provided for combined work in villages where Congregational emigrants were settling side by side with Presbyterians."[65] A committee appointed to consider and digest a plan of government for the churches in the settlements of that time was approved by the General Assembly of the Presbyterian Church in the U.S.A. in 1802. The Plan stated: "It is strictly enjoined on all their missionaries to the new settlements, to endeavor, by all proper means, to promote mutual forbearance, and a spirit of accommodation between those inhabitants of the new settlements who hold the Presbyterian, and those who hold the Congregational form of church government."[66] There was to be a mutual exchange in matters of discipline, right of appeal, and the calling of a minister to a local church. A Presbyterian minister could serve as pastor of a Congregational church and vice versa.

In the minutes of the General Assembly of 1831, when the Plan was called into question, it was stated that it originally came before the General Assembly in 1790. The Plan was consummated in 1794 and further extended in 1801. It was then considered as a plan "in which Presbyterians and Congregationalists were harmoniously united in the same Church."[67]

Dr. Douglas Horton, former president of the International Congregational Council, called the Plan "the first ecumenical venture of national proportions in the history of the country, and though it came to an end with the first generation of its supporters, the high purpose which informed it gives it a distinction which does not die."[68] The writer of the article sees the Plan as a serious attempt to foster cooperation at the grass-roots and the national levels, and for the purpose of eliminating unchristian competition between the denominations in upper New York, where Congregational emigrants from Connecticut and Presbyterians from New Jersey and Pennsylvania were moving in large numbers.

The Plan was repudiated by the Presbyterians in 1831 and by the Congregationalists in 1852. Horton maintains that it failed because "it was an attempt to unite a fully-formed Presbyterianism with a half-formed Congregationalism. The latter was in process of losing its seventeenth century structure, and had not yet acquired its present one. The Congregationalism of early New England was not a type of church polity merely; it was a philosophy of civilization in that it involved both the Church and the State."[69] Among the early settlers in New England the idea of separating the church and state did not seem to have had any acceptance. For many in New England, membership in the church and in the state were practically the same thing.

According to Horton, another reason for the failure of the Plan "lay in the rivalry between two conceptions of the Church,"[70] one being affected by the Evangelical movement, which Horton considers to be both ecumenical and individualistic at the same time, while the other was based on a love for the church and its traditions, especially in the realms of faith and order. Presbyterians were divided by these two viewpoints. By 1831 those who took the second viewpoint felt that there was a danger that the very structure of Presbyterianism, as they knew it, would be changed. In addition, Horton saw the issue of Negro slavery as a hidden element in the failure of the Plan of Union. "Recent studies prove . . . that the Plan failed partly because it tried to yoke those who tolerated slavery with those who did not."[71]

Charles A. Anderson, director for many years of the Department of History of the Office of the General Assembly of the Presbyterian Church in the U.S.A., referring to the failure of the Plan of Union, wrote "that . . . differences of opinion arose with the passage of years, centering around the slavery issue and doctrinal interpretations, and aggravated by intense commercial competition which also affected the Churches."[72]

Whatever the reasons for the demise of this early ecumenical venture, it not only was an interesting experiment but was also a movement that contributed toward the formation of a Board of Foreign Missions that the Presbyterian Church in the U.S.A. could call its own.

Chapter III

PRESBYTERIAN FOREIGN MISSION AGENCIES

The Board of Foreign Missions of the
Presbyterian Church in the U.S.A.

Formation of the Board of Foreign Missions

On June 7, 1837, the General Assembly of the Presbyterian Church in the U.S.A., at its meeting in Philadelphia, adopted a report of the Committee on Bills and Overtures, dealing with an overture from the Presbytery of Salem, concerning the formation of a board of foreign missions.

The first paragraph of the report was as follows:

> RESOLVED, That the General Assembly will superintend and conduct by its own proper authority, the work of Foreign Missions for that purpose, and directly amenable to said Assembly.[1]

The same resolution ordered that the new board was to be styled "The Board of Foreign Missions of the Presbyterian Church in the United States of America," and that the General Assembly was to choose forty ministers and forty elders, to be elected annually for a term of four years. The Board was instructed to make an annual report to the General Assembly.

The Board was empowered to receive the transfer of funds and personnel of any foreign missionary societies existing in the Presbyterian Church, and all properties and funds accruing to the new board, or to be acquired by it, were ordered to be taken in the name of the trustees of the General Assembly. On October 31, 1837, The Presbyterian Foreign Missionary Society (formerly The Western

55

Foreign Missionary Society) transferred its work and assets to the new board. The Presbyterian Foreign Missionary Society then had forty-four missionaries, some of whom had not yet left for their fields. "Eleven . . . were ordained ministers, five were teachers, one was a printer and book binder, and twenty were women. It had under its care three presses, one high school, and two boarding schools. The receipts for the year ending October 15 [1837] were $40,266, and the balance in hand $5,784."[2] The new board established its headquarters in New York and elected the Rev. Samuel Miller, D.D., President, General William McDonald, Vice-President, and the Hon. Walter Lowrie, Corresponding Secretary. During the first year, the receipts of the Board (including an initial balance) amounted to $47,855.61, and the expenditures were $44,405.20. Sixteen missionaries were sent out during the year: ten to India, three to China, and three to work among the American Indians.

The Old School and New School Controversy

The Board of Foreign Missions of the Presbyterian Church in the U.S.A. came to birth under very difficult circumstances, because of the division in the church between the Old School and the New School, beginning in the early 1830's. In addition to the issue of church boards, as compared with support of voluntary agencies, there were differences on questions of doctrine and polity.

The Old School felt that the admixture of Congregationalism with Presbyterianism was unconstitutional and should cease. The Plan of Union of 1801 was referred to by many in the Old School as "Presbygational" and as such was impracticable. The Old School expressed its preference for ecclesiastical agencies for conducting missionary work and evangelistic work.

The New School believed that union with the Congregationalists should continue, and that the Presbyterians should support voluntary agencies such as the American Home Missionary Society and the American Board of Commissioners for Foreign Missions.

With all these serious issues dividing the Presbyterian Church, the New School held the majority in the General Assembly five times between the years of 1831 and 1837, while the Old School held it twice. The New School dominated the General Assembly of 1836, when a resolution to transfer The Western Foreign Missionary Society to be under the care of the General Assembly failed to pass.[3]

In the crucial General Assembly of 1837, the most heated discussions centered around the resolution to exscind The Western Reserve Synod (formed on the basis of the Plan of Union of 1801) from the Presbyterian Church. The groundwork was laid for this action by a resolution abrogating the Plan of Union of 1801, declaring it "unnatural and unconstitutional." In addition to The Western Reserve Synod, the Synods of Utica, Genesee, and Geneva were also separated from the Presbyterian Church. "The Old School majority in the General Assembly of 1837 . . . disowned four synods, as so far Congregationalized that they could not be any longer acknowledged as Presbyterian bodies."[4] Furthermore, a resolution was approved by the General Assembly of 1837 "affirming that the organization and operations of the so-called American Home Missionary Society and American Education Society . . . are exceedingly injurious to the peace and purity of the Presbyterian Church."[5]

The way was now open for the adoption of the report on the formation of the Board of Foreign Missions, to which reference was made at the beginning of this chapter. Following the action of the General Assembly of 1837, the new Board of Foreign Missions held its first meeting in Baltimore in 1838. In a sense, it can be said that the Presbyterian Church as a whole was not ready to support its own Board of Foreign Missions until 1870, when the reunion took place.

The controversy between the Old School and the New School had deep theological undertones. The first theological seminary of the Presbyterian Church in the U.S.A. had been established in Princeton in 1812. When the controversy between the Old School and the New School developed, Princeton Theological Seminary came to be a symbol of the former. " 'Princeton Theology' as it has often been called, has, beyond question, been almost universally prevalent among the Old School. If opposing systems must take a modern nomenclature, there may be no harm in making Princeton and New Haven respectively the synonyms of the Old and the New Divinity."[6] Details concerning the theological aspects of the controversy cannot be given here, our interest being chiefly in the bearing that the schism had on the missionary work of the church.

First of all, let us consider the issue of a separate board of foreign missions, as it related to the Old School-New School controversy. We have already referred to the principle of placing foreign missions (and the same would apply to domestic missions and Christian education) within the mainstream of the life of the church. This principle impinges on the question of the form of church government and is, in a sense, at the heart of Presbyterianism.

The Old School felt that they had to translate into practical terms something that they believed was vital so far as the furtherance of Christ's Kingdom was concerned. "To save their own credit, much more for the glory of God, they [the Old School] must prove that Congregational order was no help to Presbyterianism; that church boards were better than voluntary associations."[7]

Ashbel Green referred in detail to three different types of people in the Presbyterian Church. Regarding the prosecution of foreign missions, the first group considered that an ecclesiastical organization —such as a board of foreign missions—was absolutely essential, and according to their view this would rule out the relationship that had hitherto existed with the American Board. Ashbel Green explained that when the missionary spirit was first awakened in this country, few people had any definite or systematic ideas on the subject, particularly on the best way to promote and conduct such missions. Hence, as examination, experience, and observation developed, many were led to change their opinion. "No inconsiderable number of these who for a time contributed to the American Board, changed their views, and became unwilling to patronize any institution of a missionary kind, which had not an ecclesiastical organization and responsibility."[8]

The second group of Presbyterians agreed with the first one in considering that an ecclesiastical organization was clearly the most Scriptural. However, they felt that it was better to cooperate with the American Board than to remain inactive. "They remarked, that although the American Board was a secular institution in its corporate character, and was brought into existence by the agency and for the special accommodation of congregational and independent churches, yet, for the present, all its concerns were conducted by men of decided piety."[9] The Southern Board of Foreign Missions of the Synods of South Carolina, Georgia, and East Tennessee, as well as the Central Board formed by the Synods of Virginia and North Carolina, were largely to be found in this second group.

The third group believed that no separate ecclesiastical organization was necessary and urged a formal merging of interests and action with the American Board. It was this group which attempted in 1826, when The United Foreign Missionary Society merged with the American Board, to secure an agreement on the part of the General Assembly to continue to use the American Board as one of its missionary agencies. The attempt was renewed in 1831, but again it failed.

A number of outstanding Presbyterians at that time were deeply grieved by the spirit of controversy that prevailed in the church. One such was Dr. John H. Rice, who in the closing months of his life presented the overture at the General Assembly of 1831 in which he declared himself in favor of promoting the true spirit of missions within the church rather than the Presbyterian spirit. This venerable and greatly loved man seemed torn between two opposing points of view. He declared that the Presbyterian spirit had been so awakened that he began "to apprehend that no power of man will ever bring the whole body to unite under what is *thought* to be a Congregational Board," and added, "I will never do anything to injure the wisest and best missionary society in the world—the American Board."[10] There followed a paragraph in Dr. Rice's statement to the General Assembly which has been quoted many times since. He said that "the Presbyterian Church in the United States is a missionary society, the object of which is to aid in the conversion of the world, and every member of the Church is a member for life of said society, and bound, in maintenance of his Christian character, to do all in his power for the accomplishment of the object."[11]

In the previous chapter we noted that the Synod of Pittsburgh created The Western Foreign Missionary Society in 1831. We shall now describe some of the developments that led to this event. In 1826, when The United Foreign Missionary Society was absorbed by the American Board, the Presbyterian leaders, who believed that a church should direct its own missionary program, began to plan with such a possibility in mind. In this respect, the General Assembly of 1831 turned out to be a crucial one.

At that General Assembly, a committee was appointed to confer with the American Board, but it became evident that the Assembly was neither willing to commit itself to the American Board, as far as the future conduct of foreign missions was concerned, nor ready to create a board of foreign missions of its own. "Thereupon, the advocates of a church board decided to wait no longer, and since it was clear that the General Assembly was not prepared to establish one, the Synod of Pittsburgh did so on October 24 of that year [1831] by constituting The Western Foreign Missionary Society."[12]

The Minutes of the Synod of Pittsburgh (1831) contained the following paragraph:

> RESOLVED, 1st. That it is expedient forthwith to establish a Society or Board of Foreign Missions, on such a plan as will admit of the co-operation of such parts of the Presbyterian Church as may think proper to unite with it in this great and important concern.[13]

The center of The Western Foreign Missionary Society's operation was transferred to New York in 1837, and by that time the Society had established work in five mission fields (India, Africa, Smyrna, China, and among American Indians).

Summarizing briefly the controversy that preceded the formation of the Board of Foreign Missions of the Presbyterian Church in the U.S.A., it can be said that it was over the question of how the Christian mission should be pursued. Should this mission, both at home and abroad, be conducted through personal participation in voluntary societies, or should it be entrusted to an agency set up by the church itself? We have seen how the American Board of Commissioners for Foreign Missions was composed not only of Congregationalists but also of Presbyterians. Ashbel Green and Samuel Miller, both strong advocates of a Presbyterian board, were elected members of the American Board. "That Green, who did more than anyone else to further the idea of ecclesiastical missions within the Presbyterian Church, could have been a member of the American Board shows the degree to which Presbyterians were willing to cooperate with Congregationalists."[14]

The debate seemed to point more directly to the issue of whether or not a board of foreign missions should be created within the Presbyterian Church. However, the issue was related also to the Presbyterian Board of Domestic Missions. The difference between the two relationships was that in 1831 the Board of Domestic Missions had been in existence for nearly three decades, whereas the Board of Foreign Missions had not yet been established.

Undoubtedly some of the motivation for forming a separate Presbyterian agency was rooted in denominationalism, which led to the belief that only a Presbyterian agency could truly represent Presbyterian concerns. But it must also be noted that those who believed that the church must have its own board, because only thus could the church express itself as a "missionary society," were unconsciously preparing for events of more than one hundred years later. When independent churches across the world sought a "church-to-church" relationship with The United Presbyterian Church in the U.S.A., the Commission on Ecumenical Mission and Relations was in a position to deal directly with them, as the former boards of foreign missions (prior to 1958) were not.[15] The relationship of those boards was with "missions," but within a few years after 1958 nearly all those missions had been dissolved, and in the meantime a commission, which included "ecumenical relations" had come into being. If the Presbyterian Church in the U.S.A. had never had its own Board of Foreign Missions, the history of the church's missionary involvement and interest might have been quite different from what it actually was between 1837 and 1958.

The Presbyterian Church in the U.S.A. experienced an unprecedented growth during the early years of the 1830's. In 1829 there were 19 synods, 98 presbyteries, 1,491 ministers, 2,158 churches, and 173,329 members.[16] By 1837 there were 23 synods, 135 presbyteries, 2,140 ministers, 2,865 churches, and a membership of 220,557.[17] However, the effects of the controversy in dividing the church into two separate denominations were seen. The support for missions by 1841 came from only half of the churches. As the years went by, the demands for more funds to support the growing number of missionaries overseas, and the developing needs of the work itself, continued to increase. The Annual Report of the Board of Foreign Missions for 1853 said: "More men are wanted. A larger amount of funds is also wanted. Most of our missionary brethren are overworked. Some of them are in impaired and precarious health."[18]

The Separation Between North and South

During the nineteenth century the growth of the church, as well as its missionary program, was influenced by political and social developments. The reason for this is that the church, while seeking to fulfill its divine mission and calling, is an integral part of society. In other words, it is at the same time a divine and a human or social institution, and thus it is subject to the pressures and forces that shape society.

The most serious social issue during the first half of the nineteenth century was the question of slavery. As early as 1767, the Synod of New York and Philadelphia discussed the question, and urged such "prudent methods as would procure eventually the final abolition of slavery."[19] The General Assembly of 1818 condemned the voluntary enslaving of one part of the human race by another, and, in later years, other pronouncements were made on the issue. The feeling against slavery was not confined to the North. "It is a remarkable fact that from 1825 to 1837 there were more antislavery societies in the South than in the North."[20]

The question of whether the Old School was less antislavery than the New School during the years preceding the Civil War is difficult to determine. The claim of the New School that it was antislavery, while the Old School was proslavery, was disputed by leading figures in the latter group. "Sometimes it has been intimated that proslavery tendencies on the part of the Old School were among the most influential causes of the division of 1838. No allegation could be more entirely opposed to historical truth . . . the Assembly of 1835, in which there was a decided Old School majority, appointed a committee to report on slavery; but the Assembly of 1836 in which the New School had altogether their own way, postponed the whole subject indefinitely by a vote of one hundred and fifty-four to eighty-seven."[21]

On the other hand, Charles Lemuel Thompson, writing in 1903, believed that "the New School Assembly was the more positive in its declarations and in 1853 called on the churches under its care in the South to make report of what had been done to purge the Church of this great evil."[22]

The Old School evidently wished to preserve the unity of the church, and so was more prone to condemn evils connected with slavery than the institution itself.

In the years immediately preceding the Civil War, the Old School and the New School alike maintained in good standing congregations, presbyteries, and synods whose members had slaves and were willing to defend the practice. Both branches of the church refrained from making any pronouncements other than those already approved by earlier Assemblies. From 1845 to 1861 the General Assembly (Old School) enjoined the Southern churches to give increased attention to the moral and religious improvement of slaves.

In the New School, developments reached a crucial state in 1857 when the Presbytery of Lexington, Kentucky, gave notice that some of its ministers and elders held slaves on principle, and by choice, believing that the practice was sanctioned by the Bible. The report of the Presbytery of Lexington was condemned by the 1857 General Assembly (New School). In 1858, the Southern synods withdrew from the General Assembly and formed the United Synod of the Presbyterian Church. The Synods of Missouri and Kentucky of the Old School remained united with the Northern wing all through the war. The split came after the war, when they were required to take a public stand declaring that civil disloyalty to the Federal Government was a sin. These synods then joined the Church in the Confederate States of America (later named the Presbyterian Church in the U.S.).

In December, 1861, a Southern General Assembly was convened, the Southern States having seceded from the Federal Union that same year. It can be assumed that, to a large extent, slavery was the cause of the creation of a separate denomination in the South, only in the sense that slavery was the cause of the secession of states from the Union. The name adopted by the Constituting General Assembly of the new denomination was "The Presbyterian Church in the Confederate States of America." In 1865, this was changed to "the Presbyterian Church in the U.S."

Despite the break that precipitated the creation of a new denomination, the Presbyterian Church in the U.S., there was no discontinuity in missionary zeal and commitment in the church. The newly formed Assembly in the South proceeded at once to form an Executive Committee on Foreign Missions. By a happy circumstance, the first Secretary of this committee was Dr. John Leighton Wilson, a man who had served as a missionary in Africa from 1834 to 1853, and from 1853 to 1861, as Secretary of the Board of Foreign Missions of the Presbyterian Church in the U.S.A. A man with great gifts, a wise and talented administrator, Dr. Wilson guided the destinies of the foreign missionary enterprise of the Southern church from 1861 to 1885.

The strained relationships and the wounds of the early years of separation between the two churches, North and South, diminished and gave way in time to cordiality, mutual understanding, and, in many cases, close fellowship. In several countries, missionaries of the two churches worked side by side and in partnership with the same indigenous Presbyterian Church.

The Board of Foreign Missions of the United Presbyterian Church of North America

The early history of the Board of Foreign Missions of the United Presbyteran Church of North America was quite different from that of the Board of Foreign Missions of the Presbyterian Church in the U.S.A. The principal reason for this was, of course, the fact that two denominations, the Associate Presbyterian and the Associate Reformed Presbyterian Churches, merged in 1858, and each of them brought its foreign mission interests and activities into the newly formed church.

In Chapter II we referred to the Covenanters and the Seceders and the two denominations that developed among them. Plans for union between these, the Associate Presbyterian and the Associate Reformed Presbyterian Churches, were first discussed at a convention in Philadelphia in 1845. The main disagreement between the two groups was over minor changes in the Westminster Confession of Faith. In 1852, a United Presbyterian Church was formed in Oregon, and this union proved to be one of the important factors leading to the merger of the two churches in Pittsburgh in 1858. Over a period

Rev. Francis Makemie

Born in Ireland in 1658, educated in
Glasgow, Scotland. Licensed to
preach in Barbados in 1681.
Organized first Presbytery in
America—in Philadelphia in 1706.
Began itinerant ministry in Maryland
and Virginia in 1683.

Rev. Ashbel Green, D.D., LL.D.

Born in Hanover, New Jersey, in
1762. Professor of Mathematics and
Natural Philosophy, and later,
President, College of New Jersey
(now Princeton University). First
President, Board of Directors,
Princeton Theological Seminary.
Moderator, General Assembly,
Presbyterian Church U.S.A., 1824.
Foremost in advocating formation of
Presbyterian Board of
Foreign Missions.

Rev. John Witherspoon, D.D., LL.D.

Born in Scotland, 1722. Educated in Edinburgh. As Presbyterian minister emigrated to America, 1768. President, College of New Jersey, 1768. Was the only minister who signed the Declaration of Independence. Convened first General Assembly, Presbyterian Church U.S.A., 1789.

Hon. Walter Lowrie, LL.D.

Born in Scotland, 1774. Came to America in 1782. Representative, Senate of Pennsylvania, 1811. Elected U. S. Senate, 1816, and later, Secretary of Senate. Secretary, Western Foreign Missionary Society, 1836. First Secretary, Board of Foreign Missions, Presbyterian Church U.S.A., 1837.

of years the two churches, organized mainly in the eastern part of the country, had discovered that they held many beliefs and practices in common, although at times, discussion and differences of opinion marked the negotiations.

The city of Pittsburgh, Pennsylvania, which by 1858 had become not only a strong center of Presbyterianism but also of missionary interest, was chosen as the place where the union of the two churches was to be effected. "On Tuesday, the day before the final ceremony, it rained all day—a gray drizzle such as only Pittsburgh can provide. When Wednesday, May 26, dawned, it was still dark and threatening, but by ten o'clock, the time set for the union to take place, the clouds disappeared and warm sunshine flooded the city. To the commissioners of both Churches, it was a happy omen for the future. God seemed to smile on what they were about to do. . . . With glad hearts, the commissioners set out, led by their moderator and clerk, to meet the men of the Associate Reformed Presbyterian Church. The two long lines of black-coated men met, the moderators linked arms, followed by the professors of theology of the Church seminaries, and the clerks of the two Synods, and after them came, two-by-two in order of precedence, all the rest of the commissioners."[23]

The union of these two churches represented a milestone in church history, and it was all the more notable because the Scots, who largely comprised the membership of the two denominations, were well known for their ability to disagree. They were churches with a marked dissenter tradition, and yet it must be recognized that in the hearts of the dissenters, with their spirit of independence, were always the latent longings for union with other parts of the body of Christ.

Thus, it can be said that the formation of the United Presbyterian Church of North America in 1858 emphasized the two important characteristics of Presbyterianism, namely, a deep concern for unity and a passion for missions.

The United Presbyterian Church of North America inherited a deep interest in, and concern for, foreign missions from both of the uniting churches. At the time of union, six mission stations had been established, three by each church. The Associate Reformed Presbyterian Synod was one of the founders of The New York Missionary

Society, which was formed in 1796, and in 1818 it became a member of The United Foreign Missionary Society. Ministers and members of the Associate Reformed Presbyterian Church were active supporters of the American Board of Commissioners for Foreign Missions from its inception in 1810, and even following establishment of a Board of Foreign Missions after the union of 1858. In 1834, the Associate Reformed Presbyterian Synod asked its congregations to pray, collect funds, and form congregational societies in the interest of foreign missions, in cooperation with The Western Foreign Missionary Society of the Pittsburgh Synod of the Presbyterian Church in the U.S.A. The following year, 1835, the denomination established mission work of its own with the appointment of the Rev. and Mrs. James McEwen to India, where they opened a school and a church in Allahabad. Three years later, due to ill health, the McEwens had to return to the United States, and the mission was abandoned.

In 1842 the General Synod of the Associate Church decided to establish a mission in Latin America, and sent the Rev. Joseph Banks to explore the area. Upon his return to the United States in 1843, he recommended the opening of work in Trinidad, and in the summer of that year, he and the Rev. and Mrs. David Gordon and Miss Beveridge began their labors there. Other missionaries joined them, but the health casualties were such that in 1854 the work had to be left in the hands of a missionary of the Free Church of Scotland, the Associate Church, by arrangement, providing his support. In 1867 the work was turned over to the Presbyterian Church of the Lower Provinces of "British America."

The first successful work by either of the two uniting churches was that begun in Syria in 1843 by the General Synod of the Associate Reformed Church in the West. The Rev. James Barnett and J. G. Paulding, M.D., established the Syria Mission with headquarters in Damascus. Years later, in 1877, the General Assembly of the United Presbyterian Church voted to transfer the mission property to the Presbyterian Church of Ireland.[24] Since the beginning of this work, the property in Syria had been jointly owned by the two missions, and there was an agreement that in the event of one withdrawing, the property would become the possession of the other.[25]

For health reasons, Dr. Paulding made a trip to Cairo, Egypt, in 1853, and at the same time it was felt that in case conditions deteriorated in Syria under the Turks, Egypt might be a haven for the missionaries stationed there. The General Synod not only approved this plan, but also sent the Rev. and Mrs. Thomas McCague to initiate the work in Egypt in 1854. A few weeks afterward, the Rev. James Barnett reached Cairo, having been transferred from the Syria Mission. He was a valuable addition to the mission because he already had a good working knowledge of Arabic, and was able to preach in that language.

The full story of the establishment and development of the work in Egypt has been admirably told in Earl E. Elder's *Vindicating a Vision*. In this book one finds not only an encounter with hardships of many kinds and opposition from Muslims and Copts but also the friendly cooperation and, in times of difficulty and danger, a helping hand from the British residents and officials, the effectiveness of education and medical work in mission program, new ways of reaching village folk, and the continuous search for the most appropriate Christian approach to the Muslim world.

In the introduction to his book, Dr. Elder says: "The great majority of its [the American Mission in Egypt] members have come from the Scotch-Irish ancestry that welded the United Presbyterian Church into being, out of the uniting Presbyterian bodies. But the Christian Reformed Church, the Reformed Church in America, the Presbyterian Church in the U.S.A., and the Associate Reformed Church in the South have also contributed personnel who were appointed to the mission."[26]

The initiation of work in Sialkot, North India, began an important chapter in the annals of the Associate Presbyterian Church, and later of the United Presbyterian Church of North America. One of the great, enduring pieces of missionary literature is the book *Our India Mission*, written in 1886 by the founder of the work, the Rev. Andrew Gordon. The idea of establishing a mission in India in 1853 was conceived when a group of four earnest Christians met with Dr. James Rodgers, pastor of the Associate Presbyterian Church of Allegheny City, Pennsylvania. This meeting was followed by others within the same congregation. In May, 1853, when the Associate Presbyterian Synod of North America met in Pittsburgh, the congregation in Allegheny City, together with a similar one in Pittsburgh, urged the establishment of a mission in India, pledging $600 a year toward its support. The Synod put the names of ten ministers in nomination for appointment as missionaries, but none of them expressed willingness to go. There being no candidates, the matter was dropped until June, 1854, when the Synod met in Albany, New York.

The Rev. Andrew Gordon appropriately called the first chapter of his book, "Go," and proceeded to describe in detail how the call came to him and his wife. The Associate Presbyterian Synod, having taken the decision to open a mission in India, was faced with the problem of finding suitable missionary candidates. The Synod was divided on procedure, some members proposing that a call for volunteers be issued, others feeling that the Synod should choose men whom they judged to be qualified. Advocates of the latter course prevailed. However, when two of the young men who had favored this method of recruitment were chosen, they declined appointment.

Just before adjournment of the Synod, an aged minister, who with difficulty had obtained the floor, read a passage from The Acts describing how Barnabas and Paul were set apart by the Holy Spirit for their missionary work. The Synod thereupon proceeded to vote on two names, only one of which was read aloud, that of Andrew Gordon. The two men, J. T. Tate and Andrew Gordon, were selected by the Synod, but the former withdrew his name. Andrew Gordon, not yet an ordained minister, learned about his appointment after the Synod had already adjourned. He described his reaction in these words: "I do not think I ever would have offered of my own accord to go on a foreign mission. . . . But the whole circumstances of my appointment, unsought and unexpected, gave it to my mind the force and authority of a clear call from the Master. As soon as the announcement was made, there sprung up a positive desire to 'go,' which did very much to make obedience easy."[27] Together with his wife and sister, Andrew Gordon set sail in September, 1854, and arrived there the following year, with instructions "to begin work in North India." Sialkot was selected as the first site of a mission station, and from there the work developed over a wide area.

The Establishment of a Board of Foreign Missions

When the United Presbyterian Church of North America came into being at Pittsburgh in 1858, steps were taken, as soon as possible, to continue the mission work of the two merging churches. At the General Assembly of 1859, requests were received from the General Synod of the Associate Reformed Church and from the Associate Synod that the General Assembly would hear the reports of their Boards of Foreign Missions.

On May 20, 1859, the Clerk of the General Synod of the Associate Reformed Church, which had missions in Syria and Egypt, presented the following resolution to the General Assembly of the new church:

> That the report of the Board of Agency for Foreign Missions for the Associate Reformed Church be made to the General Assembly of the United Presbyterian Church; and that the Assembly be, and hereby is requested to take our foreign missions under their care.[28]

A similar resolution was presented by the Associate Synod, transmitting an action of the General Synod of the Reformed Presbyterian Church in North America, which at that time had missions in Trinidad, India, and California.

The General Assembly took action accepting the offers of the two bodies, and resolved "that said missions be, and hereby are, formally received under the care of this Assembly: their stations, missionaries, funds, and all of their concerns, to be subject to its direction and control."[29] The Committee of Correspondence was requested to open "correspondence with foreign churches."

On May 26, 1859, the Committee on Foreign Missions presented a report consisting of a constitution of the Board of Foreign Missions, and the Board was formally organized in Philadelphia on June 21, 1859. According to the original constitution, it consisted of nine members, appointed for a period of three years, with meetings to be held quarterly. The number of members was later increased to fifteen, and the term of office to five years.

The first report of the Board of Foreign Missions (1860) spoke of having held twelve meetings and seventeen sessions during the year. The report showed that there were twenty missionaries under the care of the Board, distributed as follows: Trinidad, 2; Syria, 5; Northern India, 7; Egypt, 6.[30] We noted earlier that the Rev. Andrew Gordon and his wife reached India in 1855, and established the Sialkot Mission in Northern India. In the few intervening years, a church had been organized, and a boys' school and a school for orphans had been established. In Egypt we saw how the Rev. and Mrs. Thomas Mc-Cague initiated the work in 1854 under the Associate Reformed Church. By 1860, stations had been established in Cairo and Alexandria, and the work had progressed so satisfactorily that a presbytery was formed in Cairo in April, 1860.

The first report of the Board of Foreign Missions made reference to the serious financial situation that it inherited when the Board was formed. For the year 1860, a total of $19,360 was required, and it was estimated that "less than one-third of a dollar for each member in the church in this favored Christian land"[31] would cover it.

In 1860 the Board opened new work in Canton, China, when the Rev. J. C. Nevin was appointed as the first missionary to that country. A second missionary was ready to go, but insufficient funds were in hand. The report stated that "with a treasury in a low state, the Board are constrained to say, and they could do so with tears, Fathers and brethren, help must be had, or this beloved brother now ready, and saying 'Here am I—send me,' cannot be sent! Shall it be?"[32] Mr. Nevin labored for eighteen years and in 1878 the work was transferred to a German missionary society.[33] He continued his missionary work among the Chinese in California.

In time it became evident that the foreign missionary effort of the United Presbyterian Church was concentrated in two countries, Egypt and India. In both of these areas, the majority of the people were Muslims. At the time of the merger of 1958, the work of the Board of Foreign Missions and the women's work of the United Presbyterian Church of North America constituted the largest missionary effort by a single denomination among Muslims.

Women's Work

The record of the history of the foundation and subsequent development of women's work shows how important a contribution the women have made to both home and foreign missions. Indeed, it can be stated without hesitation that had it not been for the vision, the sacrificial efforts, the gifts, and the prayers of the women, the missionary enterprise of the two churches that merged in 1958 would not have become what it is today. In addition to what we have already described, mention must be made of the wide outreach and influence of the World Day of Prayer. At the suggestion of Mrs. Darwin R. James, of New York, president of the Women's Board of Home Missions of the Presbyterian Church in the U.S.A., a special meeting was called in 1887 to pray for home missions. This soon developed into an interdenominational day of prayer for missions in the United States and abroad. The World Day of Prayer not only is observed by women's groups all over the world but it has also prompted sacrificial giving that has been devoted to the production of Christian literature, to the support of Christian colleges, and to many other worthy projects. "The Church owes much to the women who have organized and developed the foreign missionary interest of Presbyterian women. In world vision, in consecration to Christ's service, and in qualities of leadership, many were women of splendid power."[34]

The Role of Women in Society

"The women of the Church," said Dr. Robert E. Speer in 1902, "have been from the beginning among the best friends of missions."[35] During the nineteenth century, the first avenue open to organized womanhood was the Christian church, and it was through its missionary thrust that women were able to give expression to their compassion, their concern for others less fortunate than themselves, their devotion, and their loyalty to the Christian faith.

The home, the nurture and care of children, as well as the status and condition of women, must always have a central place in the program and outreach of the Christian church. A century ago, however, women had to make a place for themselves not only in the witness of the church in foreign lands but also in society itself.

In 1835, Dr. D. L. Child wrote a two-volume *History of the Condition of Women,* covering most of the countries of the world. She said "that the women of the United States have no direct influence in politics; and here, as in England, it is deemed rather unfeminine to take an earnest interest in public affairs."[36] Mrs. Child felt, however, that in no country in the world did women have more freedom than in the United States.

In the mid-twentieth century, the contribution of women to Christian missions overseas, apart from their influence on the home, is most effective in the fields of education and medicine. It was in these same fields, and particularly in education, that women came to occupy a more important position in American society, which undoubtedly prepared the way for their contribution to missions during the nineteenth century. In the early part of that century, "education awakened women to the social and civil subserviency of the female sex."[37] It was in education that the restrictions on women were first loosened, and new areas of opportunity and service were made available. The first high school for girls was established in Worcester, Massachusetts, in 1824, to be followed by another in New York City in 1826. During the first half of the nineteenth century, numerous academies for girls came into being. High school education paved the way for higher education for women and their entry into the teaching profession.

During the Crimean War of 1854, Florence Nightingale initiated the noble tradition of nursing. Just a few years before that time, women entered the field of medicine for the first time, when in 1849, at the Geneva Medical School of Western New York, Elizabeth Blackwell received the first medical degree given to a woman in America.[38] Before that time it was not considered proper for a woman to have anything to do with the human anatomy in the sense that medical doctors have.

The position and the status of women were not as secure in the early nineteenth century as they are, happily today. In the early days of the women's movement "a pastor in Michigan insisted on being present at the women's meetings in his church 'because no one knows what those women would pray for, if left alone.' Another said, 'It will not be easy to find women for officers of the society. For president you must have a fearless, loud-voiced woman; and for secretary one whose husband can write good letters and reports.' "[39]

Motivation for Women's Missionary Activities

In the April, 1871, issue of *Woman's Work for Woman,* the official organ of the Woman's Foreign Missionary Society of the Presbyterian Church, Philadelphia, there appeared an editorial on the two movements among women in the United States at that time. The first movement was for the securing of equal rights with men. "It [the movement] seeks to give to her whatever advantage in the battle for life is supposed to belong to man to afford her the opportunity (and more than this, to lay it upon her as a duty), to push her way into public life, to the polls, and to the rostrum. She is to let no man come between her and any right, which she can fight for and win, no matter how much of womanliness or delicacy she must lose in gaining the victory."[40]

The other movement among women in this country was described as an effort "to take a more active part than they have hitherto done in extending the blessings which they enjoy to their less-favored sisters in heathen lands. These women feel that to the Gospel they owe the place of honor and of dignity which is theirs in this Christian land."[41] The first movement aimed to secure rights for women, the second to render service in the name of Christ.

It is probably true that when women assumed responsibility for a share in the Christian missionary enterprise, not only was much enthusiasm engendered, but also considerable emotion and sentiment. This can be seen in the first editorial of the magazine *Woman's Work for Woman* in April, 1871, one year after the Woman's Foreign Missionary Society was formed, when it began with the following paragraph:

> We come to you, dear friends, amid the perfumed buds of spring —spring in the natural world, and among the nations of the earth. The frost-fetters that have barred for centuries the doors of the Orient, are melting one by one. Of many lands it may be said, "Lo, the winter is past, the rain is over and gone; the flowers appear on the earth; the time of the singing of birds is come, and the voice of the turtle is heard in our land." Truly, it is time for thankfulness and rejoicing. As we look abroad upon the earth, we cannot but exclaim, "Behold, what hath God wrought!"

The editorial went on to remind its readers that it was a time for planting in the Lord's vineyard. In the early part of the nineteenth century, Presbyterian women gave expression to their missionary zeal and interest by supporting work with their gifts and their prayers. In 1835 Mrs. D. L. Child referred to the numerous "female societies" which were largely supported by church women, their funds being raised "by the sale of ingenious articles of their own manufacture."[42]

In the early days, little money circulated in some areas, and business was often carried on by barter. Women contributed by preparing food products or by using flax and wool for weaving, knitting, and sewing, and making goods available to the cause of missions.

Later on, as mission work under the Presbyterian Church in the U.S.A. developed in different parts of the world, women sponsored their own work, sending out women missionaries as teachers, Bible readers, and so on. Indeed, they were encouraged by the church itself to engage in more direct missionary work. The Standing Committee of the Board of Foreign Missions in its report to the 1871 General Assembly of the Presbyterian Church in the U.S.A. said: "The Assembly also recognizes with gratitude to God the effort to organize the women of the Presbyterian Church, for the purpose of sustaining the work of the Board of Foreign Missions, under the direction and control of the Board. The women of the church have always been forward in every good work, both at home and abroad. But their identity with our work among the heathen has hitherto lost much of its power for good by reason of their inability to realize a direct contact with the work of their heart and prayers. They must work, not abstractly, but directly, if they would work efficiently and in accordance with the laws of their nature."[43]

The principal reason or motivation for this activity on the part of the Presbyterian women of those days stemmed from a deep and compelling conviction that women alone could minister to the needs of women in foreign lands. "Woman alone," they said, "can reach woman in her degradation, and can we sit idly at home while there are some of our own sisters and daughters who have so much of the real Christ in their souls, who have gone into the darkness of Pagan superstition to try to bring up those mothers from their ignorance? Let us not be satisfied with doing little."[44]

Women came to see that there was a service in the name of Christ that they alone could render, and the more they learned through firsthand reports from other lands about the condition of women, the more impelling and strong was the motivation and desire for service. Innately sensitive to human need and suffering, and ingenious in ways to raise funds, women were eminently suited to the missionary task of the church.

The motivation for missions can be said to have been strengthened and directed by an increasing knowledge during the nineteenth century of the effects of social systems on the condition of women in the Far East. "It was primarily the *purdah* and the latticed window, the *zenana* and the harem, that roused the women of Christendom to attempt an errand of mercy to their sister-women of the heathen world."[45] They believed that no nation can be great unless, and until, its women are uplifted to a position of respect, security, and rightful consideration. In their own land, the United States, the gospel had given women honor, security, and freedom, and these benefits were derived largely from the gospel. The conscience of Christian women in the Western world was aroused by the condition of women in the East. When it was clear to the former that "no man, whether clerical missionary, or even physician, can carry the Gospel to the jealously-guarded women of Oriental households,"[46] then the urge to engage directly in missionary work became imperative.

Up to this point we have been referring to the place of women in general in the missionary enterprise. From the beginning of missions overseas, wives accompanied their husbands in practically all cases. The situation of single women was quite different. Pierce Beaver has pointed out that the prevailing ideas and prejudices against employing single women in the early years were such that mission boards which did send them to the field were careful not to advertise the fact.[47] As a rule, church members, especially the males, did not think it proper to send a woman out alone to work in pioneer situations, where customs were different, and finding suitable housing presented special problems.

In time, however, single women demonstrated their ability, not only to render valuable service, especially as missionary teachers, but also to cope with the problems we have referred to.

Women's Societies and Boards of Missions

1. *The Presbyterian Church in the U.S.A.* The first official reference to Presbyterian women by the Presbyterian Church in the U.S.A.

was a statement made at the General Assembly of 1811: "We rejoice in the increase of Missionary, Tract and Bible Societies within our bounds, and the more so because there is so much need of missionary exertions in different parts. . . . It has pleased God to excite pious women also to combine in associations for the purpose of aiding, by their voluntary contributions, one or other of the above institutions. Benevolence is always attractive, but when dressed in a female form, possesses peculiar charms. Hard, indeed, must that heart be which can resist the example, or the solicitation of a mother, a wife, a sister or a friend. . . . We hope the spirit which has animated the worthy women of whom we speak, will spread and animate other bosoms."[48]

From providing financial support for existing missionary organizations, Presbyterian women moved to a more direct participation in the work itself. Mission boards were slow to use the services of single women, and it is not surprising that women took things into their own hands and formed their own missionary organizations. "They first supported their denominational missionary organizations fully, and then, having discharged that obligation, they raised sufficient additional funds to send out their own missionaries unhampered by the limitations which the male mind insisted on placing upon women missionaries."[49] These limitations or restrictions were to be found in all the various denominations engaged at that time in mission work. However, there were some outstanding missionaries who believed that women could perform a valuable service on the mission field. "To the Rev. David Abeel, D.D., an American missionary to China, must be conceded the honor of suggesting to Christian women the importance of a distinctive mission for heathen women."[50] Dr. Abeel felt that "heathen homes" were the greatest obstacle to the spread of the gospel. He was also deeply troubled by the status and condition of women in the Far East. "Womanhood itself, synonymous with ignorance and superstition, was trampled under brutal feet. Women throughout the Orient were unwelcomed at birth, unloved and oppressed in life, and unwept at death. . . . Only by the undivided efforts of Christian women aglow with gratitude for their elevation through Christ, could they be approached."[51]

Dr. Abeel made his dramatic appeal to the women of England and the United States, and as a result of his burning zeal for work among women in the Orient, the Society for Female Education in the East was formed in England in 1834, but in the United States, hearts were not yet ready for a similar movement. A society was formed in New York, but it was quietly abandoned at the urgent request of the mission boards. Mrs. Sarah Doremus was the moving spirit in this effort, and largely due to her persistence and faith, there came into existence a quarter of a century later (in 1860) the Woman's Union Missionary Society. In 1879 a book was published under the title *Historical Sketches of Woman's Missionary Societies,* and it was dedicated "to the memory of Mrs. Sarah P. Doremus, the founder, first president, and firm support of the Woman's Union Missionary Society, who, in thought, love, and labor, abounded in every good word and work; whom we regard as the highest representative type of the Christian womanhood demanded and developed by the activities of the nineteenth century."[52]

The Society was nondenominational in character, and it immediately set about its task of engaging directly in missionary work in Burma, India, China, Japan, and Greece. Between 1861 and 1878, it had sent out forty missionaries, employed 165 native Bible readers, established and aided 76 schools, and helped educate 256 girls by special gifts.[53] In eighteen years, the Society had collected over $500,000.

We have given a few facts about the Woman's Union Missionary Society because it opened a way and established a precedent in mission work.

The first Presbyterian women's society was formed in Derry, Pennsylvania, in 1818, and this was followed by one created in Philadelphia. In 1835, the Society for the Evangelization of the World was organized in the First Presbyterian Church of Newark, New Jersey.

Another step toward the formal organization of women's work was the creation of The New Mexico, Arizona and Colorado Missionary Association in New York in 1868, with a Board of Managers composed of responsible and well-known women. At first it concerned itself with work among Indians in the United States, but in 1870, influenced by the union of the Old School and New School denominations, the Association was renamed The Ladies' Board of Missions of the Presbyterian Church, and became an auxiliary to both the Home and Foreign Boards of the church. Nine years later, in 1879, the Board was supporting "42 missionaries, 30 Bible readers, 38 schools and 100 scholarships, and . . . laboring in Syria, Persia, India, China, Siam, Japan, Africa, and Mexico,"[54] in addition to having work among American Indians. In 1883 the Board decided to transfer its Home Mission Department to the Woman's Synodical Committee of Home Missions and to become the Women's[55] Board of Foreign Missions of the Presbyterian Church in the U.S.A., which continued as the principal agency for women's work for several decades.

The impetus created by the union of the two Presbyterian churches of the Old and New Schools in 1870 gave rise to a number of women's societies. One of these, the Woman's Foreign Missionary Society in Philadelphia, formed in 1870, was the first women's society to be organized exclusively for foreign missions. Its official organ, *Woman's Work for Woman,* did a great deal toward bringing the needs of the world to the attention of the church. In 1875, the Society began to publish *Children's Work for Children,* and in 1882 a series of *Historical Sketches of Presbyterian Foreign Missions.*

At the beginning of the twentieth century, the foreign missionary activities of the women of the Presbyterian Church in the U.S.A. were being carried on by seven regionally based boards and societies, all of them auxiliary to the church's Board of Foreign Missions. They were:

1. Woman's Foreign Missionary Society of the Presbyterian Church, Philadelphia. (1870)
2. Woman's Board of Foreign Missions of the Presbyterian Church, New York. (1870)
3. Woman's Presbyterian Board of Foreign Missions of the Northwest, Chicago. (1870)
4. Woman's Presbyterian Foreign Missionary Society of Northern New York. (1872)
5. Woman's Occidental Board of Foreign Missions of the Presbyterian Church, San Francisco. (1873)
6. Woman's Presbyterian Board of Foreign Missions, St. Louis, Missouri. (1877)
7. Woman's North Pacific Presbyterian Board of Foreign Missions, Portland, Oregon. (1888)

In 1908 the Woman's Foreign Missionary Society of Northern New York merged with the Woman's Board of Foreign Missions of the Presbyterian Church, New York.

All these agencies rendered remarkable service for Presbyterian women, and also for the whole church. Not only did these agencies promote missions and enlist the sympathy and interest of countless women across the country, but they also raised large sums of money. During the first fifty years, the total was $17,154,630.45,[56] most of which came from tithes and sacrificial giving.

When these agencies were established, there was evidently a need for women's work to be organized on a regional basis. However, facilities for travel grew, and there was a greater feeling of oneness in the church at large. The time came when it was considered to be in the best interests of women's work, and of the church as a whole, for the various boards to be consolidated.

The unification took place in 1920, and the new Woman's Board of the Presbyterian Church in the U.S.A. was incorporated in the State of New York on November 18 of that year. The headquarters were established in New York, and regional offices continued in Philadelphia, Chicago, St. Louis, San Francisco, and Portland, with their own secretaries. For some time before 1920, the separate boards had confined their efforts to promoting missionary interest in the churches and raising funds for the general mission program of the Board of Foreign Missions, reverting in a sense, to the original purpose of women's groups in the nineteenth century. The united board continued the same practice. In this way, the missionary drive of the women was integrated into the life and structure of the church, rather than being apart from it. Their loyalty to the church's purpose and main responsibility is seen in their attitude toward special or designated gifts. "Pastors and laymen often embarrassed the Board by designating gifts for outside objects and thereby lessening the funds that were available for the obligations that the Board had assumed in the annual appropriations, but the woman's boards were loyal to the objects that were authorized by the Assembly's Board."[57]

The final step in organization was taken in 1923, when the General Assembly consolidated fourteen agencies into four boards—National Missions, Christian Education, Ministerial Relief, and Foreign Missions—a step which also meant that the Woman's Board was merged with the Board of Foreign Missions. Synodical, presbyterial, and local women's societies continued as previously constituted.

In 1924, *Woman's Work for Woman* and *The Home Mission Monthly* were consolidated into one magazine called *Women and Missions.*

2. *The United Presbyterian Church of North America.* Much of what appears in the preceding section concerning the origin of women's work in missions, the motivation, the enthusiasm, and the energy of women, applies also to women of the United Presbyterian Church of North America. As we have seen, this church was formed as a result of a merger of two denominations in 1858. Long before the union, however, the women in the two churches, Associate and Associate Reformed, were active in supporting the missionary cause, and various societies were formed toward this end.

As far as the records show, the first society was the one organized in Xenia, Ohio, in the Massies Creek Church on October 6, 1817. "Not only was this the first missionary society, but as far as we know it was the first women's organization in the Northwest Territory. Perhaps we should add that either the pastor or a member of session met with the women to do the praying."[58] Some years later this society ceased to exist!

"As early as 1838 a women's foreign missionary society was organized in the First Associate Reformed Church of Allegheny. Presumably, there were similar societies in other congregations, but nothing was done to coordinate their efforts in the support of missions."[59] However, the main thrust of women's organized missionary work was to come later in the nineteenth century. By 1879, there were 168 local societies with 5,649 members, and they contributed $12,386 annually to the Boards of the church.[60] Nevertheless, there was no central organization, and the need for this was increasingly felt. The guiding spirit in women's work at that time was Mrs. Sarah Foster Hanna, a woman of remarkable dedication and faith. "Up to 1883, there was no central organization of the missionary societies aside from the peripatetic Mrs. Hanna."[61] Mrs. Hanna presented a memorial to the General Assembly of 1875. "She was granted the privilege of reading it before the Assembly, which was unusual, because the Assembly was reluctant to permit a woman to speak before it."[62]

On May 25, 1883, the Women's General Missionary Society was organized at a meeting held in the First Church, Allegheny. The corporation that was formed had among its purposes "giving aid to various departments of the missionary work undertaken by the other Boards of the church, by supporting educational and medical institutions, and erecting and maintaining buildings necessary for the prosecution of the work in this and other lands. For this purpose it shall receive and disburse all money placed in its charge by auxiliary societies and individuals."[63] In 1886 a Women's Auxiliary Board was formed at the third annual meeting of the Women's General Missionary Society. The Board had the power to nominate missionaries for medical work to the Board of Foreign Missions, it being understood that the entire expense of the medical work was to be borne by the Women's Board. The Women's General Missionary Society supported mission work at home and abroad, and thus played an important role in the total life of the church. Indeed, the Society was without equal in the history of American churches. In time its activities and powers were extended so that they became more or less similar to those of the Board of Foreign Missions of the church. In other words, the Women's General Missionary Society, not only found support for missionaries on the foreign field, but also recruited and appointed missionaries, and owned properties in different countries.

The General Assembly of 1889 agreed to transfer the support of all medical work abroad to the Women's General Missionary Society, though in later years the Board of Foreign Missions also undertook medical work. In addition, the Women's General Missionary Society assumed support of all unmarried women in the foreign fields—a responsibility that it continued to carry throughout its history. A heavy building program was undertaken by the Women's General Missionary Society—schools, colleges, hospitals, and clinics being included in it. United Presbyterian women were greatly interested in education for women in foreign countries. The schools they founded and supported in Egypt and Pakistan, for example, became well-known institutions in those lands.

As in the case of the women in the sister church, the Presbyterian Church in the U.S.A., the United Presbyterian women were eminently successful in raising money for missions. The most dramatic and effective way of doing this was by way of what came to be known as a Thank Offering. The idea as outlined in the April, 1888, issue of the *Women's Missionary Magazine* was that each woman in the church should provide herself with a "mite box" in which to deposit her offerings during the year. "A Committee was appointed to look after 'mite boxes,' and before long we hope to supply mission bands and older members with these silent reminders of blessings received and faults to be overcome."[64] During the first year the amount raised was $5,919, which was a considerable sum in those days. Over the years, this practice became immensely popular among the women of the church, and produced a large part of the funds for missionary work. By 1956 the annual amount reached $315,738.[65]

In addition to raising money, and closely related to it, the promotional aspect of the work was important. The *Women's Missionary Magazine* was the chief organ of publicity from 1887 to 1953, when it changed its name to *Missionary Horizons*. The year 1955 was an important one for women's work in the United Presbyterian Church of North America, and indeed for the church itself. Until then the work was administered by what was known as the Women's Board, and members of the Board acted as staff, each member carrying responsibility for correspondence and administration.

The Annual Report of the Women's General Missionary Society to the General Assembly of 1956 said: "The past year was one of paramount importance in the history of the Women's General Missionary Society. It opened up wider opportunities in United Presbyterian women's work and marks a new development in the Church's life."[66]

The General Assembly of 1955 had directed the Board of Directors of the Women's General Missionary Society and the Board of Foreign Missions to establish a single Board of Foreign Missions which would include women, nominated by the Women's Board. On the new board there were eighteen men and nine women. This administration change was not only significant in its implications, but also simplified the procedures necessary for union with the Presbyterian Church in the U.S.A. three years later.

In 1956 the General Assembly took a similar action assigning responsibility for all home mission work to the Board of American Missions, reorganized to include women members. Thereafter, the Women's General Missionary Society, though no longer administering mission work, continued its program of promotion, missionary education, and support, until 1958, when it united with the National Council of Presbyterian Women to form a new organization called United Presbyterian Women.

The interest of women in missions has not only continued in recent years, but it has been greatly extended. Under the guidance of a National Executive Committee, United Presbyterian Women have carried out a twofold program of missionary education and sacrificial giving, a task begun by the earlier women's boards of both churches. In 1965 they raised $2,307,732 for the church's work.

A Missionary Heritage in Perspective

In this chapter we have attempted to outline the history of the founding and development of the missionary enterprise of the two churches that merged in 1958 to form The United Presbyterian Church in the U.S.A. Vast changes in every aspect of life have taken place in the past one hundred and fifty years, and it must be remembered that a close correlation exists between these changes in the secular world and the development of the Christian church, and more especially the missionary enterprise. Just consider the question of travel. When the first Presbyterian missionaries went to the field, they had to travel in sailing vessels; even in 1863 the journey in a sailing vessel to China took six months, and because of poor food and much discomfort, it impaired the health of the missionaries before they even reached their destination. In the countries they served, railroads were introduced much later in the century, and so, much travel on land was done by animal-drawn vehicles.

When the Presbyterian missionary work began, a large part of the non-Christian world was closed to missionaries. At mid-twentieth century, there is a Christian church in practically every country in the world, although they exist amid serious tensions in many cases. In the early nineteenth century, most people in the United States knew little about these lands or their people, and cared less. Only a few had any information about them, and even that was very limited in scope and depth. Africa was a dark continent, not because of the color of the people's skin, but because its vast interior regions had not been explored and were entirely unknown. Japan was still submerged in medieval feudalism, and Korea was termed the "hermit nation." In Muslim countries, especially in the Middle East, Christians were considered to be "infidel dogs," and feelings toward them were largely hostile. Latin America had just emerged from a period of wars for political independence from Spain, and many parts were very unsettled and backward.

All these conditions and circumstances had a direct bearing on the development of Christian missions, and to realize what actually came about as the nineteenth century unfolded, and then came to a close, is to marvel at the triumph of God's grace. In some places, missionaries labored for years without seeing any results of their work, and they were sustained alone by the power of the Holy Spirit and the courage of their convictions. As time went on, congregations were formed and Christian leaders emerged. Preachers, teachers, and helpers of various kinds had to be trained, and this required the establishment of institutions. Christian missionaries have always believed in education, not only to provide a trained leadership, but also to educate the common people. The contribution in this field, as well as in medical work, can never be fully measured.

As a result of two world wars, as well as the convergence of dynamic social and political forces, new nations began to emerge, and the dominance of the Western nations soon declined. Nationalism became a new religion and the church was not exempt from its influence. "Nationalism is rampant and some of its devotees claim that Christianity denationalizes its converts."[67] Together with racism and anticolonialism, nationalism, although it has some positive aspects, can pose a serious threat to Christianity, which claims to be universal in character.

Added to these new forces, there are the deleterious effects of films that sometimes depict crime and vice in Western nations. "The ravages of foreign liquor were so disastrous in Africa that a tribal chieftain wrote to a former Archbishop of Canterbury, 'Great and good chief of the tribe of Christ, greeting. The humblest of your servants kisses the hem of your garment and begs you to send to him and his fellow servants more Gospel and less rum.' "[68] It is hoped that the African chief did not wish to imply that the Archbishop had been sending rum to Africa.

The fact that imperialism is so closely associated with the West, whether it be territorial or economic imperialism, has also had adverse effects on missions that emanated from the same lands. The point to remember is that the penetration of Western culture into the non-Christian lands has not been an unmixed blessing. The miracle is that Christianity gained as much acceptance as it did in the nineteenth and early twentieth centuries. In the latter part of the nineteenth century, the slogan current among Christian students in the West was, "The evangelization of the world in this generation." Optimism seemed to abound. "The hegemony of Christian Europe was being established over the whole world of heathendom, and European 'Christian' culture was being everywhere desired."[69] In a hundred years or so, the number of converts in non-Christian lands had grown from a handful to over six million, and the church of Christ had taken root in many lands, amid great varieties of language, culture, and social conditions.

Chapter IV

UNITED PRESBYTERIAN INVOLVEMENT
IN ECUMENICAL BODIES

BEGINNING with the nineteenth century, modern Protestantism in the United States has shown an increasingly significant degree of unity through cooperative movements, programs, and organizations. Today, the witness of the Christian church, to some extent, is a united witness in which Christian groups, while retaining their denominational loyalties, can work together in programs and projects. This cooperation is more clearly seen among top denominational leaders than in the local churches.

The various ecumenical bodies to which we shall refer in this chapter are visible forms of cooperation at different levels, created for a variety of purposes. Consistently, Presbyterians have been in the forefront of these cooperative movements, through which they came to know and understand one another and to manifest an over-riding common concern for witness.

In an address on "The Contribution of the Reformed Churches to Christian Unity," delivered in 1952 before the Western Section of the Alliance of Reformed Churches Throughout the World Holding the Presbyterian Order, Dr. Theophilus M. Taylor said: "Through the 19th century the Reformed Church cannot, of course, take all the credit for carrying the ball in the movement toward Christian unity, but it did play an important role. The Reformed churches were moving at least as fast as other confessional groups, if not more rapidly, and I am inclined to believe that Reformed churchmen made the largest single contribution of any confessional group in the total process."[1]

The historical records show that the various cooperative efforts, some of which have developed into important movements of worldwide outreach, began in the hearts and minds of concerned individuals rather than in the courts of the official body of their denomination.

The American Bible Society

Although the American Bible Society cannot be classified as an ecumenical body, in the same sense as the World Council of Churches or the National Council of the Churches of Christ in the U.S.A., yet it has a significant place in the ecumenical movement. It was the first manifestation of Christian unity on a national scale in the United States, and "this primitive experiment along the road of Christian unity was the precursor of many more."[2]

It is difficult for us, one hundred and fifty years after the event, to realize the inertia, and even bitter opposition, that had to be overcome in the formation of the American Bible Society in 1816. It only became a reality because of the vision, persistence, and courage of men like Samuel J. Mills, Elias Boudinot, Gardiner Spring, John M. Mason, J. B. Romeyn, John H. Rice, and other well-known theologians and distinguished laymen of the day. Mills was a graduate of Williams College and Andover Theological Seminary, who traveled widely among the settlers in the West and the South, and made impassioned pleas in the North for a united Bible Society. Dr. Elias Boudinot, who called the Convention that launched the American Bible Society in 1816, and who became its first president, was a distinguished citizen— as president of the National Congress he had signed the peace treaty at the close of the Revolutionary War with Great Britain. Among the sixty-six men who attended the Convention that launched the American Bible Society were many ministers of the Reformed churches and, along with those of other churches, they attended the meetings as individuals, without being representatives from their denominations. These bodies were not yet ready for such a step, in any official way.

During the past one hundred and fifty years many outstanding Presbyterians or Reformed churchmen, along with those of other denominations, have served as officers of the American Bible Society. We shall mention two prominent figures in the earlier years.

The Rev. John M. Mason, pastor of the Associate Reformed Church in New York and provost of Columbia College (now Columbia University), and the Rev. J. B. Romeyn, pastor of the Cedar Street Reformed Church, were among those who attended the Constituting Convention, and upon its organization, became the first two secretaries of the American Bible Society. In 1816, Dr. Mason published a book entitled *A Plea for Sacramental Communion on Catholick Principles* defending the celebration of a joint Communion service in 1810, in which his Associate Reformed congregation and the Dutch Reformed congregation, of which Dr. Romeyn was the pastor, participated, an act that was hitherto unknown in the United States. "As a result of this unprecedented event, Mason, his elders, and his congregation, became the subject of heated debate, and the butt of much criticism and censure, all of which dragged on for years in the Associate Reformed Synod."[3] This incident reveals the kind of attitudes that prevailed in church circles at the beginning of the nineteenth century and lends significance to the fact that these men became corresponding secretaries of the newly formed American Bible Society.

Down through the years the Presbyterian Church in the U.S.A. and the United Presbyterian Church of North America (and now The United Presbyterian Church in the U.S.A.) have been consistent supporters of the American Bible Society. In many countries throughout the world their missionaries have found that the work of distributing the Scriptures in the languages of the nations provides them with a unifying purpose of an unmistakably ecumenical character.

We shall now turn to consider the World Presbyterian Alliance, an organization that has had ecumenical significance since its inception in 1875.

The Confessional Approach to Unity

The World Alliance of Reformed Churches Holding the Presbyterian Order can more accurately be characterized as a confessional body. However, within the context of this chapter, the significance of the World Presbyterian Alliance, as it is generally known, lies in its contribution over the years to the mainstream of the ecumenical movement. In other words, the Alliance presents "the Confessional Approach to Unity."[4]

At a meeting of the Executive Committee of the Alliance held in Basel, Switzerland, in 1951, approval was given to a document that contained these words: "Presbyterians want to bring as their contribution to the ecumenical movement a Presbyterianism which has been scrutinized by the eyes of Christ and purified by the Holy Spirit. . . . It is the true glory of this tradition to seek and promote Christian solidarity and also Church union where the local or national situation demands it. . . . If the great world denominations, the Reformed Churches among them, pursue denominational pre-eminence, they will betray Jesus Christ."[5]

In the Minutes of the General Assembly of the Presbyterian Church in the U.S.A. for the year 1873 and succeeding years, one finds reference to the proposed Alliance in the Index under the heading "Ecumenical Presbyterian Council," clearly indicating that the founders of the Alliance considered the movement to be ecumenical in character or intention.

The writings of the Reformers, particularly of John Calvin, reveal that the concept of an alliance of Presbyterian churches across national boundaries was in their thinking. The Introduction to the *Report of the Proceedings of the First General Presbyterian Council* (1877) begins with these words: "The idea of an Alliance, Council, or Confederation of the Reformed Churches had a prominent place in the minds of the Reformers, and has seldom been overlooked by those whose minds have been impressed with the unity of the Church. In 1561, Beza, at a Conference at St. Germain, urged the necessity of such a Council."[6]

Dr. William Garden Blaikie, of Edinburgh, one of the three organizers of the Alliance, in an article that appeared in 1875, expressed his concern that while Presbyterianism in its several branches had exhibited a remarkable unity, it had "never presented to the world that aspect of unity *as a whole.*"[7] He added, "The Presbyterian system is remarkable for its unity of organization; yet that feature is wanting where it is most natural to look for it."[8]

It might well be asked why such a movement was not founded until 1875 if the will to create it existed at the time of the Reformation. Evidently there were many practical difficulties during the sixteenth century, and as Blaikie puts it, "When the Reformation movement subsided, it [the idea of unity] went to sleep, and for three hundred years it was little heard of."[9]

In 1866, Professor MacGregor, of New College, Edinburgh, in an article entitled "Our Presbyterian Empire," referred to the desirability of holding a Presbyterian Council once every five, ten, or twenty years, alternately in Edinburgh, London, and New York, "at which all the Churches might confer for oecumenical purposes."[10]

On the other side of the Atlantic, Dr. James McCosh, the President of Princeton College, New Jersey, preached a sermon in New York in 1870, in which he spoke of the need for a Pan-Presbyterian Council. Dr. McCosh and Dr. Blaikie later became the principal organizers of the World Presbyterian Alliance.

In 1873, the General Assemblies of the Presbyterian Church in the U.S.A. and the Presbyterian Church of Ireland adopted the following resolution:

> WHEREAS there is substantial unity of faith, discipline, and worship, among the Presbyterian Churches in this and other lands; and whereas it is important to exhibit this more to the Churches and to the world: and whereas a desire has been expressed in various places for closer union among all branches of the great and widely-scattered family of Presbyterian Churches: therefore, resolved that a Committee, consisting of the Moderator of the General Assembly, the Stated Clerk, and the Rev. James McCosh, D.D., LL.D., be appointed to correspond with sister Churches holding by the Westminster Standards, with the view of bringing about an Ecumenical Council of such Churches to consider subjects of common interest to all, and especially to promote harmony of action in the mission fields at home and abroad.[11]

Meetings of representatives of Presbyterian churches were held several times in both Britain and the United States during the early 1870's, that is, before the first meeting of the General Council of the Alliance in 1877. One of these was held in New York in 1873, at the time of the Conference of the Evangelical Alliance. Taking advantage of the presence of Presbyterian delegates from several countries, a meeting of Presbyterian ministers and elders was convened, about one hundred and fifty attending. A committee of thirteen, with Dr. McCosh as chairman, was appointed to correspond with individuals and church bodies to ascertain their feeling with regard to the

formation of a council. The benefits of having such an organization
as outlined by the committee, included the following:

1. It would exhibit before the world the substantial unity, quite
   consistent with minor diversities, of the one great family of
   Presbyterian churches.
2. It would . . . tend to hold up and strengthen weak and strug-
   gling churches. . . .
3. It would enable churches, which are not inclined to organic
   union, to manifest their belief in the unity of the church. . . .
4. Each Presbyterian church would become acquainted with the
   constitution and work of sister churches. . . .
5. It would manifest the proportions and power of the Presbyterian churches. . . .
6. From such a Council . . . there might proceed . . . new im-
   pulses of spiritual life. . . .[12]

Significant meetings of Presbyterian leaders were held on both
sides of the Atlantic in 1874, and more detailed statements of purpose
and policy were issued. There was a clear understanding from the
beginning that a Presbyterian council would not be an authoritative
body, and that it would have no jurisdiction over the churches
represented.

The Constitutional Conference was convened in the English Presbyterian College in London on July 21, 1875, under the chairmanship
of Dr. McCosh, of Princeton College, New Jersey. There were delegates from England, Ireland, Scotland, Wales, France, Belgium,
Switzerland, Italy, Germany, Spain, Canada, and the United States.
A constitution was adopted in which the Alliance was designated as
"The Alliance of the Reformed Churches Throughout the World
Holding the Presbyterian System." The Preamble to the Articles
stated that the time had come for churches holding the reformed faith
to manifest their essential oneness and to promote great causes by
joint action. "In forming this Alliance," the Preamble stated that "the
Presbyterian churches do not mean to change their fraternal relations
with other churches, but will be ready, as heretofore, to join with
them in Christian fellowship, and in advancing the cause of the
Redeemer, on the general principle maintained and taught in the
Reformed Confessions that the Church of God on earth . . . is one
body in the communion of the Holy Ghost, of which body Christ is

the Supreme Head, and the Scriptures alone are the infallible law."[13]

At the first meeting of the General Council of the Alliance, convened in July, 1877, in Edinburgh, Scotland, the Rev. David Inglis, pastor of the Dutch Reformed Church in Brooklyn, referring to the development of Presbyterian or Reformed churches (he preferred the word "Reformed") on the mission field, said that it was important not "to seek to build up in heathen countries Scotch, English, Irish, or American denominations; they ought not to have American Presbyterians or American Reformed or Scotch United Presbyterians, or any other kind of split P's—but a great Church . . . taking its special form and special development from the circumstances of the country in which it was placed. . . . Let their missionaries, and those who might be added to them from time to time among the native converts, build up upon these principles their Chinese Churches, their Japanese Churches."[14]

In these words there is evidence of thinking on some of the problems that mission board leaders in a later period were to wrestle with, problems related to the indigenous character of the church as an essential feature of the ecumenical movement.

During the ninety years of its existence the World Presbyterian Alliance, far from absolutizing its confessional loyalty, or disrupting in any way the broad ecumenical movement, has increasingly been able to "make its own specific contribution to the ecumenical dimension of Christian life and work, in the fulfillment of its mission in the world."

In 1888, an Executive Committee of the Alliance was formed, to care for the business of the Alliance between Councils. This Committee was divided into two sections, the Eastern, with headquarters in Scotland, and the Western, with headquarters in the United States.

While it is true that the ecumenical movement and the confessional movement (Anglican, Baptist, Congregational, Lutheran, Methodist, and Presbyterian) are developing side by side, and that in many instances the same church leaders are to be found in both movements, the broad question of the relationship between them has not been clearly defined. A Dutch theologian, active in the Presbyterian Alliance, discussing the question as to how the concept of confessionalism can fit into the new ecumenical picture, wrote, "It is spiritually and theologically important that in the Reformed Church, confessionalism (that is, the assertion that our confession is the true, or at any rate, the purest Church) is scarcely anywhere regarded as a possible solution to the problem."[15] Berkhof maintains that confessionalism must not become a self-justifying monologue, but that each confessional church—and in this case, the Reformed Church—should enter into serious conversation with other confessional churches, "acting in the name of the *ecclesia catholica.*"[16]

The Cooperative Approach to Unity

In a profound and incisive study that he called *The Unfinished Reformation,* Charles Clayton Morrison claims that "the ecumenical movement in our time is . . . an awakening of Protestantism to the fact that it is the inheritor of an unfinished Reformation."[17] Protestantism has become aware in recent decades that it is "involved in a system which hides the true church" and that "our eyes are being opened to the truth that only the whole church, acting as a united whole, can bear witness to the whole gospel. The world will not believe the gospel which our sectarian churches proclaim."[18]

The phenomena of denominationalism and of the proliferation of sects are well-known characteristics of the American religious scene. The official list is made up of more than two hundred and fifty religious bodies, of which about two hundred and ten are Protestant. It is true that over 90 percent of Protestants belong to roughly fifty denominations, but even that figure is high. Dr. Morrison characterizes the situation by commenting that "the fissiparous tendency which has characterized the whole of Protestantism has run riot in the United States."[19]

Several factors account for denominationalism in this country. The right of private interpretation of the Bible was established at the time of the Reformation, and in the New World it was extended to cover freedom from ecclesiastical control and domination. The denomination itself became a new empirical ecclesiastical reality. The church as such had become the church invisible, and the visible churches came into being.

The second factor was the new spirit of freedom and independence in America with its vast territorial expanse and an ever-moving frontier. The feeling of restraint and confinement of European life was replaced by the psychology of the frontier and a rugged individualism.

A third important factor in the rise of denominationalism was the principle of religious liberty, which found expression in the late eighteenth century in the separation of church and state.

A fourth factor is that of immigration from Europe during the nineteenth century. Lutherans came from Germany, Sweden, and Norway, while Reformed groups came from Holland, Germany, and Hungary. All these language groups established churches on the patterns familiar in Europe, and thus helped perpetuate denominationalism in the New World.

A fifth factor was the Civil War, which not only produced political and social divisions in the country but also split some of the major denominations. This was particularly true in the case of the Presbyterians, Methodists, and Baptists.

"The ecumenical awakening in our time is . . . not an experience alien to Protestantism. It is the resurgence in Protestantism of the ecumenical awakening of the sixteenth century."[20] The reason for this is that while doctrines such as "justification by faith" and "the priesthood of all believers" were of great importance in the minds of the Reformers, they also had a clear and vital conception of the nature of the church. Moreover, they had no desire, at least in the early days of the Reformation, of breaking with the historic church, but rather they were determined to rescue it "from the clutch of an alien regime which had fastened itself upon it and kept it unconscious of its true nature for a thousand years."[21]

Thus the thesis of Morrison's book *The Unfinished Reformation* is that Protestantism in the mid-twentieth century is "becoming aware that its denominational system is a decadent survival of an era that is past."[22]

It is this mood which provides the rationale for the cooperative movement as an approach to unity and an effective expression of the essential ecumenical nature of the Christian church. Christian leaders felt increasingly after the Ecumenical Conference of 1900 in New York, and the Edinburgh Conference of 1910, that the time had come for the different denominations to work together on projects of common interest, without waiting for the consummation of organic union, which is a much more lengthy process. During the twentieth century an extensive program of cooperation among the churches in the United States has unfolded, but not only that, and perhaps preeminently, a missionary effort of vast proportions and ever-increasing variety, has been undertaken to a remarkable degree by the churches working together.

All this did not come about easily or without the intense devotion and labor of many leaders, as well as careful organization and planning. We now turn to a description of the origin and nature of some of the ecumenical bodies which came into being. In all the organizations with which we shall deal, Presbyterians have had a prominent share and the denomination as a whole has lent enthusiastic support.

Referring to the movement for Christian unity, Morrison finds in Presbyterianism a strong sense of the ecumenical church, and feels that it has "not only contributed leadership to this movement [for Christian unity] equal to that of the Episcopalians, but it has gone further in expressions of willingness to subordinate its denominational existence in order to achieve a united church."[23]

Christian organizations do not spring into existence in mature forms. Rather, they develop from the concerns of a few individuals who confer with one another in an ever-widening circle and with deepening interest. This is particularly true of organizations of a cooperative nature. The National Council of the Churches of Christ in the U.S.A. is an example of how different streams eventually came together to form a full, flowing river, this river receiving the water from the various streams but without being just a confluence. The result was, rather, a new body of water, different from all the tributaries that went into it.

The various streams that came together to form the National Council of Churches were:

The Federal Council of the Churches of Christ in America (1908)
The Foreign Missions Conference of North America (1893 and 1911)
The Missionary Education Movement of the United States and Canada (1902)

The Home Missions Council of North America (1908)
The International Council of Religious Education (1922, actually
an outgrowth of a national Sunday School Convention held in 1832)
The National Protestant Council on Higher Education (1911)
The United Stewardship Council (1920)
The United Council of Church Women (1940)
Church World Service (1946)
Interseminary Movement (1880)
The Protestant Film Commission (1947)
The Protestant Radio Commission (1947)

The earliest of these forerunners of ecumenical cooperation was
the Sunday School Movement founded in 1832 when the first national
Sunday School Convention was held in New York. The movement developed slowly and sporadically, and it was not until 1872 that a
permanent national organization was established. In 1907, it became
the International Sunday School Association, and in 1922, The International Council of Religious Education. This movement has rendered
important service to its constituent bodies and to the church in general, in the field of leadership and teacher training and in the preparation of curriculum materials.

The Foreign Missions Conference of North America

If Sunday school work furnished an incentive to interdenominational
cooperation beginning with the nineteenth century, so did foreign missions, but in a much wider sense. The organization of such a movement began in 1893, and for the next eighteen years was called the
Conference of Foreign Missionary Boards of the United States and
Canada before it became The Foreign Missions Conference of North
America in 1911. Later in this chapter we shall emphasize the fact
that the real urge toward Christian unity came from the mission field
itself.

Before proceeding to outline this movement in the United States,
a word needs to be said about the historic Union Missionary Conference held in the Presbyterian Church at Nineteenth Street and Fifth
Avenue, New York, on May 4 and 5, 1854. The occasion was the visit
by special invitation of the Rev. Dr. Alexander Duff, one of the outstanding missionaries to India of the nineteenth century. A public

Mrs. T. C. Doremus
(Sarah Platt Doremus)

Born in New York, 1802. Pioneer in
many civic organizations (New York
Women's Prison Association,
Presbyterian Home for Aged Women,
City Bible Society). Actively engaged
in support of foreign missions. In 1860
was one of founders of the Women's
Union Missionary Society. Served as
its president for fifteen years.

Mrs. Sarah Foster Hanna

Born 1802. Became outstanding
pioneer in women's work, United
Presbyterian Church of North America.
Traveled widely to promote foreign
missions. In 1875 presented memorial
at General Assembly requesting
founding of a women's society, thus
laying groundwork for Women's
General Missionary Society.

Rev. Arthur J. Brown, D.D., LL.D.

Born in Holliston, Mass., in 1856. Ordained by Presbyterian Church, 1883. Secretary, Board of Foreign Missions, Presbyterian Church U.S.A., 1895-1929. Secretary, Ecumenical Missionary Conference, New York, 1900. Missionary statesman, world traveler, author. In 1936 wrote *One Hundred Years*.

Robert E. Speer, D.D., LL.D.

Born in Huntingdon, Pennsylvania, in 1867. Outstanding Presbyterian layman and missionary statesman. Secretary, Presbyterian Board of Foreign Missions, 1891-1937. Moderator, General Assembly, 1927. President, Federal Council of the Churches of Christ in America, 1920-1924. Chairman, Committee on Cooperation in Latin America, 1916-1937. World traveler and author. Was author (or editor) of 67 books.

meeting had been held earlier in 1854, in Philadelphia, at which Dr. Duff was the speaker, and at which committees were appointed to arrange for, and convene, the conference in New York. The circular of the committee that called the convention in New York opened with these words: "At a public meeting of Evangelical Christians interested in Foreign Missions, convened to receive the Rev. Dr. Duff, we were charged with the arrangement of a General Missionary Conference, to aid in combining and judiciously directing the efforts now making for the Salvation of the Heathen—thus illustrating the practical unity of the church, and exciting an increased interest in this holy work."[24]

In the business sessions of the Conference the following questions were discussed:

1. To what extent are we authorized by the Word of God to expect the conversion of the world to Christ?
2. What are the divinely appointed and most efficient means of extending the gospel of salvation to all men?
3. Is it best to concentrate laborers in the foreign field or to scatter them?
4. In view of the great extent of the heathen world and the degree to which it is opened, is it expedient for different missionary boards to plant stations on the same ground?
5. How may the number of qualified laborers for the evangelization of the world be multiplied and best prepared?

Dr. Duff delivered a stirring missionary address in Broadway Tabernacle, New York, and a report of it, which was included in the Proceedings of the Conference, contained the following footnote:

> The Reporter regrets having lost the concluding passage in which Dr. Duff drew a picture of the present ominous state of the world, and the awful judgments that seem to be impending over it.[25]

The organizers of the Convention of 1854 evidently had no intention of founding an organization, and in the call for the meeting they included the following paragraph:

> The Committees disclaim all intention of establishing a new organization, or of interfering with those now in existence, for they believe that at present each branch of the Christian Church can

most efficiently work in the missionary cause, by sustaining laborers of its own appointment.[26]

Four decades were to pass before another interdenominational foreign missionary conference was organized. The Report of the Interdenominational Conference of Foreign Missionary Boards and Committees in the United States and Canada, held in the Presbyterian Mission House, 53 Fifth Avenue, New York, on January 12, 1893, states that the Conference had been called because it had long been felt that "the Foreign Missionary Boards and Committees of the Protestant Churches . . . might very profitably hold a Conference for the discussion of practical questions of missionary policy, and if possible draw nearer to each other in real cooperation in their common work."[27] The Report went on to say that "in the Council of the Presbyterian and Reformed Alliance which was convened in Toronto September 1st [1892], the Standing Committee on Missionary Co-operation was recommended to invite at an early day: *First,* a conference of all Presbyterian and Reformed Missionary Boards in the United States and Canada, for one day's sessions; and *second,* a General Conference of all Protestant Boards and Societies in the two countries for like purposes, and to be convened on the day following."[28]

The Presbyterian Alliance Committee, seconded by the Board of Foreign Missions of the Presbyterian Church in the U.S.A., sent out invitations for both conferences to be held at the Presbyterian Mission House on January 11 and 12, 1893. Dr. F. F. Ellinwood, Presbyterian minister in New York, who in Toronto the year before had voiced the idea of holding these two conferences, became the chairman of both meetings.

Commenting on the Interdenominational Conference of 1893, Dr. Richey Hogg wrote, "When that meeting assembled, it kindled a spark, and the spark produced a flame."[29]

The Conference met the following year at the Methodist Mission House, 150 Fifth Avenue, New York, and was called "The Second Conference of the Officers and Representatives of Foreign Mission Boards and Societies in the United States and Canada." The Conference continued to meet year after year. Topics such as the following were discussed: "The Development of Self-Supporting Churches on the Foreign Field," "Means of Securing Missionary Candidates of the

Highest Qualifications," "The Place of Higher Education in Missionary Work," "Practical Provision for Missionaries in Regard to Stipends, Outfits, Houses, Furloughs, etc."[30]

As the years went by, the name of the Conference became shorter, and by 1898 it was known as the "Sixth Conference of Foreign Mission Boards, United States and Canada." At the Conference of 1897, the proposal to hold an ecumenical conference was approved, and plans were set in motion. This was the famous Ecumenical Missionary Conference held in New York in 1900. During the discussion of the plan to hold this conference, the chairman of the organizing committee, Dr. Judson Smith, said: "Some correspondence that has come to me has contained an objection to the word 'ecumenical' as savoring of ecclesiasticism. As a matter of fact, that word is a very old one and goes back of Roman Catholicism, and there is scarcely any other word, unless we use the term, 'world-wide,' that so fitly expresses exactly what we mean."[31]

The holding of the Ecumenical Missionary Conference of 1900 represented an important step in the history of foreign missions. The secretary of the Conference, and one of its architects, was Dr. Arthur Judson Brown, a secretary of the Presbyterian Board of Foreign Missions. It is estimated that, in all, between 170,000 and 200,000 attended the various meetings that were held in Carnegie Hall, New York. The opening address was given by the President of the United States, William McKinley. For sheer size, outreach, range of topics, and influence, this was the largest and most important conference that had ever been held. "Its agenda was tremendous. Even a bare listing of its subjects (e.g., medicine, education, evangelism, etc.) would require too much space here. In addition, every phase of women's work was also covered. . . . Besides these . . . the Conference included a vast territorial survey of missions, region by region."[32]

In 1911, the Foreign Missions Conference, which had met annually since its inception in 1893, was formally organized as a permanent functioning body known as the Foreign Missions Conference of North America. By the year 1950, when it became a part of the structure of the National Council, the Foreign Missions Conference had grown in importance, with area committees representing the major regions of the world, and functional committees with worldwide programs in audio-visual work, literature and literacy, Christian education, medical work, and agricultural missions. The Foreign Missions Conference was one of the sponsors of Church World Service.

The Federal Council of the Churches of Christ in America

This body, which was formed in 1908, can rightly be considered to be the most important constituent element in the formation of the National Council of the Churches of Christ in the U.S.A., which was consummated in 1950. With the creation of the Federal Council, the Protestant churches in the United States began to play a much more significant role on the stage of world history. The Federal Council, moreover, proved that a movement based on the federative principle, and dedicated to a wide range of activities, both in the United States and across the world, could be an effective instrument for its constituent bodies. In a number of ways it paved the way for the later development that we know as the World Council of Churches. William Adams Brown, one of the architects of the ecumenical movement, said, "It is difficult to exaggerate the importance of the contribution to Christian unity which was made by the formation and development of the Federal Council" and "by its adoption of the federal principle, a precedent was set which was destined to be followed thirty years later in the creation of the World Council."[33]

The idea of establishing an alliance or federation of Protestant bodies in the United States was conceived as early as 1838, when Samuel Schmucker, a Lutheran minister, issued an appeal to the churches "urging an 'alliance' of the several Protestant bodies which would not disturb their denominational organization and would enable them to render united service."[34] In 1846, Schmucker went farther and urged the formation of a united Protestant body that would be part of a world body. Associated with Dr. Schmucker's name is that of the Rev. Philip Schaff, Presbyterian historian and scholar, who later gave a prophetic definition of federal unity as follows: "Federal or confederate union is a voluntary association of different churches in their official capacity, each retaining its freedom and independence in the management of its internal affairs, but all recognizing one another as sisters with equal rights and cooperating in general enterprises, such as the spread of the Gospel at home and abroad."[35]

The World Evangelical Alliance was formed in London in 1846, and an American branch under the name of the Evangelical Alliance came into being in 1873. While the Alliance was effective in bringing Protestants of different denominations together for united action, it was not an organization of representatives of official church bodies. In this type of organization the Federal Council pioneered.

Another organization that had a distinct bearing and influence upon the formation of the Federal Council was the Open and Institutional Church League. "In the Providence of God the honor of pioneer leadership in the steps that led finally to the calling of the historic Inter-Church Conference on Federation, 1905, came on an inter-denominational fellowship organized in 1894 as 'The Open and Institutional Church League.' "[36] The person largely responsible for creating this body was the Rev. Charles L. Thompson, pastor of the Madison Avenue Presbyterian Church, New York, where the opening conference met in May, 1894. Later, Dr. Thompson became Secretary of the Presbyterian Board of Home Missions, and also the chief founder of the Home Missions Council. "Under his [Dr. Thompson's] leadership, social and missionary work received an impetus and inspiring guidance, the influence of which permeated the life of all the Churches of Christ in the United States."[37]

The Open Church League, which was organized by a group of ministers and laymen of the Presbyterian, Methodist, Baptist, and Congregational churches, "stood for open church doors for every day and all the day, free seats, a plurality of Christian workers, the personal activity of all church members, a ministry to all the community through educational and philanthropic, as well as more specific spiritual channels, to the end that men might be won to Christ and His service."[38]

The Open Church League led to the formation of the National Federation of Churches and Christian Workers in 1901, a body whose significance consisted not so much in the type of organization it was as in the outstanding men who belonged to it. At its meeting in 1902, well-known figures, such as Elias B. Sanford, Frank Mason North, Charles L. Thompson, and William H. Roberts, were largely responsible for the appointment of a committee to secure delegates from churches to a meeting to be held in 1905. Macfarland considers that in the minds of such men "the Federal Council of the Churches of Christ in America was born at that moment after years of pregnancy and patience."[39]

The Inter-Church Conference on Federation was held in Carnegie Hall, New York, in 1905, and was presided over by Dr. William H. Roberts, at that time Stated Clerk of the General Assembly of the Presbyterian Church in the U.S.A., and later, Moderator of the same body. Writing about Dr. Roberts in his definitive work on the Federal Council, Dr. Sanford said: "I have never come in contact with a man who could with almost unerring accuracy, in a shorter time, clean up the docket brought to his attention. An authority on all matters connected with the history of the Presbyterian Church (in the U.S.A.), Dr. Roberts has a wide knowledge of ecclesiastical affairs not only in his own church, but in other denominational bodies. For many years he has been an advocate of Christian unity, and his influence has been wisely used in giving the Presbyterian and Reformed Churches leadership in the federation movement."[40]

Sanford refers also to a remarkable group of Presbyterian laymen who took part in the Inter-Church Conference on Federation in 1905. These included such well-known names as Woodrow Wilson, John Wanamaker, Robert E. Speer, John H. Converse, and James A. Beaver.[41]

The Inter-Church Conference on Federation of 1905 was a notable gathering. The addresses, findings of the Conference, and the Constitution of the Federal Council are contained in a volume of 691 pages, compiled by Elias B. Sanford and published under the title *Church Federation*. Never before had such a wide range of topics been presented and discussed in such a representative gathering.

"As a masterpiece of organization and of unity in diversity, the Inter-church Conference on Federation stands out in church history matched only by the contemporary World Council of Churches, of which the Federal Council was a forerunner and in whose building the Federal Council has had an ample share."[42] In this manner wrote Charles S. Macfarland, the creative spirit of the Federal Council, in 1948.

Following the Inter-Church Conference on Federation, three years of planning and organizing were required before the Federal Council actually became a reality. From the beginning, the leaders of the movement made it clear that the Federal Council was to be an evangelical body; while its constitution did not contain a credal statement since it was not an ecclesiastical body, the preamble to the Constitution did state that "the time has come when it seems fitting more fully to manifest the essential oneness of Christian Churches of America, in Jesus Christ as their Divine Lord and Savior."

Among the dominant notes at the 1905 conference were two that became basic concerns of the Federal Council after 1908. These were the challenges of the social order and of international order. In an address on Labor and Capital, the Rev. Wallace Radcliffe, pastor of the New York Avenue Presbyterian Church, Washington, placed the main emphasis on man, whether he be employer or laborer. He said that some have made a narrow and hasty reading of Christ's teaching. "The rich man's camel has been sadly overworked, until I sometimes think he does not even care to look at the eye of that needle. Poets and sentimentalists have perverted as they have insisted upon poverty as a virtue."[43]

Three years later, conditions in the field of labor relations became critical, and the question before the newly organized Federal Council was whether the church should take a stand on such issues. "Up to this time, the only major denominational agency dealing with social or industrial problems was the Presbyterian Department of Church and Labor, of which Charles Stelzle was the superintendent."[44] In a report to the Federal Council by the Committee on Church and Modern Industry, Stelzle made the following points: (1) there is an estrangement between the church and industrial workers; (2) industrial progress has taken the church unawares; (3) many phases of the present industrial conditions cry aloud for immediate remedy.[45] The Federal Council recorded its belief that the complex problem of modern industry can be interpreted and solved only by the teachings of the New Testament. The developments in a new and complex social order demanded the clear enunciation of Christian principles and their effective application.

In the field of international relations the Federal Council was a pioneer. Up to that time no church body had ever dealt with the problems of peace and war. In 1911, the Council established a Commission on Peace and Arbitration, which later became the Commission on International Justice and Goodwill. The Federal Council rendered outstanding service in fields such as race relations, evangelism, and radio broadcasting, and made a contribution in the realms of social service and international peace. Not only during two world wars was the Federal Council called upon to render service in the name of the churches, but also in the postwar periods when men sought eagerly for ways to prevent future wars.

The names of two Presbyterian ministers will always be associated with the Federal Council because of their fruitful service as executives of the organization. They were Dr. Samuel McCrea Cavert and Dr. Roswell P. Barnes. In 1917, Dr. Cavert became an assistant secretary of the newly created General War-Time Commission, and thus began his long and distinguished career with the Council. Dr. Cavert was appointed as one of the two general secretaries of the Federal Council, and in 1930 its chief executive, continuing as such until the merger of the Council into the National Council of Churches in 1950 and serving with great distinction. During World War II the Government of the United States turned to Dr. Cavert for the performance of special duties.

Dr. Roswell P. Barnes, also a Presbyterian minister, served as an executive of the Federal Council from 1936 to 1950. When the National Council was formed, he served as Executive Secretary of the Division of Christian Life and Work (1950-1954) and as Associate General Secretary until 1958, when he was named Executive Secretary in the United States of the World Council of Churches. In 1964, the 176th General Assembly of The United Presbyterian Church in the U.S.A. presented Dr. Barnes with a citation, naming him one of the ecumenical architects of this generation who played a significant role as a Christian statesman in stimulating the pioneer and prophetic spirit in the life and work, and faith and order of Christendom.

The Federal Council became a potent force as an instrument of Protestant and Orthodox Christianity. Its program and interests were so multifaceted that we cannot attempt to deal with them here; the reader will find a number of excellent books on the history as well as the program of the Council. Some local councils of churches existed before the formation of the Federal Council. However, over the years, and under the dynamic impulse of the Federal Council, there was established a network of councils of churches at the local and state levels. Viewed as a whole, this movement can be considered of supreme importance in laying the foundations of the ecumenical movement and enabling the Christian churches to play an important role in today's world in the spirit of unity for Christian service.

Both the Presbyterian Church in the U.S.A. and the United Presbyterian Church of North America were charter members of the Federal Council and gave it their support. Throughout its history, these churches have also provided leadership to the organization.

Other Cooperative Organizations

Other streams of cooperative work that converged to form the National Council were the United Council of Church Women, the Home Missions Council, and the Missionary Education Movement.

One weakness in the early years of the Federal Council was the absence of women in its organization. No women were included among the delegates or speakers at either the 1905 or the 1908 conferences. Charles S. Macfarland, who served for many years as one of the secretaries of the Federal Council, wrote, "We have more than once reminded the reader of the belated recognition by the constituent bodies of the existence of women in the churches, and the more or less consequent neglect of them by the Federal Council."[46]

In 1925 the Council took action, expressing its conviction "that women as well as men should be appointed to represent denominations on the central governing bodies of the Council."[47] At that time, there were twelve hundred councils of women in the country, and conferences on women's organized interdenominational work were held each year. These conferences were a stage in the development of the United Council of Church Women, which was formed in 1940, and in 1950 became part of the National Council of Churches. At a constituting convention held in Atlantic City in 1941, a program was outlined whereby ten million Protestant women could work together at local, state, and national levels, "to do those things that no single denominational group of women can do alone."[48]

The Home Missions Council was formed in 1908 at the same time as the Federal Council, and there was a close cooperation between the two organizations from the beginning. The Home Missions Council carried on an effective program in such areas as race relations among minority language groups, migrant workers, and in home missions, and became a channel of cooperation for the denominations.

At the Inter-Church Conference on Federation in 1905, Dr. Charles L. Thompson, soon to become the president of the Home Missions Council, summed up the development of the idea of cooperation in these words: "A hundred years ago, opinions were often mistaken for conscience, and those who should line up as soldiers—arm to arm and step with step—were often in hostile camps—apparently more given to mutual suspicions and oppositions than to defeating a common foe. That was the day of theological wars . . . continuing well into the middle of the century . . . [when] a somewhat better day [came]. Indifference took the place of hostility. Churches no longer fought each other. They only passed by on the other side."[49] Thompson found that a change had taken place within the previous generation. Churches had begun to feel more kindly toward each other, and denominational comity was the order of the day. In the founding of the Federal Council and the Home Missions Council, a real advance along the road to cooperation and unity could be seen. It was to be Christian cooperation, so that unity might be manifested; it was the marshaling of a common Christianity with a common purpose.

Another stream of cooperative endeavor, of a different nature from those we have been considering, was the *Missionary Education Movement*. Founded in 1902, this movement enabled many denominations to pool their resources for the production of a common literature on both home and foreign mission themes for use in their church constituencies.

Church World Service was formed in 1946 to act for the denominations in meeting widespread human need across the world, and to consolidate the work of various agencies, some of which had been carrying on relief services following World War I, and in the case of Asia, in the 1920's and 1930's.

The National Council of the Churches of Christ in the U.S.A.

Many group consultations, protracted deliberations of intercouncil committees as well as denominational bodies, were held over a period of years before the National Council became a reality. In 1938, the General Assembly of the Presbyterian Church in the U.S.A. sent two overtures to the Federal Council, expressing the hope for "fuller unity in Christian service," and looking toward "means by which the missionary work at home and abroad might be done in greater unity."[50]

In 1940, a Planning Committee was appointed, with representatives of the Federal Council, Foreign Missions Conference, Home Missions Council, International Council of Religious Education, the Council of Women for Home Missions, and the National Council of Women. In 1941, the Missionary Education Movement, the United Stewardship Council, and the Council of Church Boards of Education joined the Committee, and it was convened in April, 1941. The chairman of the Planning Committee was Dean Luther A. Weigle, of the Yale Divinity School, and the secretary, Dr. Hermann N. Morse, Secretary of the Presbyterian Board of National Missions. The names of these two men appear in all the reports of discussion and negotiations, and in the formulation of a constitution and a set of bylaws. In its special issue on the National Council, *The Christian Century* said, "If any men deserve to be known as fathers of the National Council of Churches, Dean Weigle and Dr. Morse are the most eligible for that honor."[51]

The charter membership of the National Council included twenty-five Protestant and four Orthodox churches. In 1963-1964, the National Council structure was reorganized to become effective January, 1965. While the General Assembly, originally meeting every two years and later every three, and the General Board, as an executive body, remained substantially as outlined in 1950, the nature and function of the divisions, departments, and committees were radically changed at various points in order to meet new conditions as well as fresh demands and challenges in a fast-changing world.

Thirty Protestant and Orthodox churches in the United States have membership in the National Council of Churches, and it has four main divisions: Christian Life and Mission, Christian Education, Overseas Ministries, and Christian Unity. The last-named division was created in a major restructuring that became effective in January, 1965. The Council has provision for specialized ministries in such fields as world literacy and Christian literature; radio, audio-visual, and mass communication; medical work; agricultural missions; evangelism; and education. In all, there are seventy-two divisions, departments, and commissions in the National Council, and its programs reach into almost every part of the world.

Few, even in the National Council itself, are aware of the immensely complex machinery that has been created. Dr. Henry Pitney Van Dusen, an outstanding United Presbyterian leader, says that the Council "has been described as 'beyond challenge, the most complex and intricate piece of ecclesiastical machinery which this planet has ever witnessed.' "[52] Dr. Van Dusen goes on to express his admiration for the skill and statesmanship that created the National Council and his "amazement at the ingenuity and imagination which elaborated its structure."[53]

The complexities of organization and structure naturally bring problems concerning first things. One of these is how the Council can be at all times a genuine expression of the churches it represents, and secondly, how it can be a prophetic voice of the Christian conscience with so vast and complicated an organization. The National Council is a council of churches, but as we have noted, it came into existence through the merger of eight interdenominational bodies (with four others joining later). The welding together of the many programs and interests these represented has required the highest form of statesmanship, and in this task the officers of the Council have had the closest cooperation of denominational executives, as well as of ministers and laymen in the churches concerned.

Presbyterians made outstanding contributions not only in the planning process but also in the founding and early development of the National Council. Dr. Glenn P. Reed, Corresponding Secretary of the Board of Foreign Missions of the United Presbyterian Church of North America, was influential in persuading some of the hesitant members of the Foreign Missions Conference to join the Council. Dr. Charles T. Leber, Dr. Hermann N. Morse, and Dr. Paul Calvin Payne, of the Presbyterian Church in the U.S.A, were chairmen respectively of the Division of Foreign Missions, Home Missions, and Christian Education in the first triennium, and as such, were Vice-Presidents of the National Council. Dr. Eugene Carson Blake, Stated Clerk of the

General Assembly of the Presbyterian Church in the U.S.A., was the third president of the National Council of Churches.

It can be said that in the National Council of Churches, thirty Protestant and Orthodox Churches have an effective and powerful instrument for cooperative service and witness, as well as a demonstration of essential unity of purpose and commitment. Obviously, the National Council of Churches can also be considered as an example of the conciliar approach, since it is a council. However, it can be said that the Council exists for the purpose of cooperation among its member boards and agencies. As a council it is a major voice for Protestantism and Orthodoxy concerning many issues in the United States. Its program, reaching out not only in the United States but also across the world, is an outstanding form of cooperation.

The Conciliar Approach to Unity

The World Council of Churches

The conciliar movement finds its greatest expression in the two most important organizations to emerge within the ecumenical movement in the twentieth century, the International Missionary Council and the World Council of Churches. The former, which came into being in 1921, eleven years after the Edinburgh Conference of 1910, was destined to play a creative role for four decades, as the coordinator of worldwide missionary policy, and as the chief unitive symbol of the mission of the church across the world. Its missionary conferences in Jerusalem (1928), Madras (1938), Canada (1947), Willingen, Germany (1952), and Accra, Ghana (1957) are important milestones along the road to Christian unity in mission.

The World Council of Churches, which was founded in Amsterdam in 1948, is the organizational expression of the essential unity of the Protestant and Orthodox churches. While the International Missionary Council was a council of councils, its constituent members being thirty-five councils of churches in as many countries around the world, the World Council is a council of churches or denominations.

From 1948 to 1961 these two organizations existed separately, although many of the same leaders were active in both. From the time of its inception, the World Council of Churches maintained close cooperation with the International Missionary Council, as was shown by the fact that the letterhead of each carried a phrase indicating it was in cooperation with the other. There were those who, having these two organizations in mind, referred to the missionary movement and the ecumenical movement, as if they were two separate movements. However, discerning church leaders realized that the church in the twentieth century was being called by her Lord to mission in unity and that the two could not be separated.

It so happened that the chairman of the International Missionary Council for several of its most creative years was that foremost Presbyterian leader, Dr. John A. Mackay, who had strong convictions concerning the centrality of missionary purpose in the ecumenical movement. Of equal interest was the fact that another outstanding Reformed churchman, Dr. W. A. Visser 't Hooft, was the General Secretary of the World Council of Churches. Dr. Mackay observed that "it is not insignificant . . . that the first General Secretary of the World Council of Churches is a distinguished Reformed Churchman from Holland."[54]

In February, 1966, Dr. Eugene Carson Blake, Stated Clerk of the General Assembly of The United Presbyterian Church in the U.S.A., was elected by the World Council of Churches as its General Secretary, to succeed Dr. Visser 't Hooft, at the end of the year.

These three churchmen have a profound sense of the mission of the church in the world today and of the essential character of the church. Around the concepts of the nature of the church and of its task, and sensing the need to work closely together, a Joint Committee of the International Missionary Council and the World Council of Churches was formed. As a culmination of these efforts, the two bodies merged into one in 1961, and the interests, concerns, and activities of the International Missionary Council were continued under the newly formed Division of World Mission and Evangelism of the World Council of Churches.

The World Council of Churches is the culmination of a process by which the ecumenical movement gathered strength and became organizational and institutional. Two mainstreams of thought, represented by the Faith and Order Movement and the Life and Work Movement, intertwined and closely related with the impetus and passion of the missionary movement, were largely responsible for this development. The Faith and Order Movement dealt mainly with theological considerations, while Life and Work came out of a deep social concern. "It is . . . not surprising," says Visser 't Hooft, "that it was at the International Missionary Conference at Edinburgh in 1910 that Bishop Charles Brent received the impulse to found the movement for church unity (Faith and Order), and that the strongest initiatives for church unity come from the younger Churches."[55]

The Edinburgh Conference of 1910 was an important ecumenical event. Three movements, which eventually gave both content and direction to the ecumenical movement, originated there. They were the International Missionary Council and the Movements of Faith and Order and of Life and Work. At Utrecht, in 1939, representatives of the two movements, Faith and Order and Life and Work, met and drew up a constitution for a World Council of Churches. The International Missionary Council, while remaining a separate organization until it became part of the World Council in 1961, was in close relationship with the latter for many years before then.

The First Faith and Order Conference was held at Lausanne, Switzerland, in 1927. This was the first time since the church was divided into East and West in the eleventh century that all branches of the church except the Roman Catholic came together to consider questions of Faith and Order. Lausanne was followed by the Conferences at Edinburgh in 1937, and Lund, Sweden, in 1952. The aim of these conferences was not so much to reach a consensus on faith and order, but rather to allow representatives of churches to confer on all matters pertaining thereto, exploring differences and reaching fuller understanding of one another's viewpoint and position. Questions regarding such aspects of faith as the place of tradition, Scripture and the Creeds, the nature of the ministry, diverse ways of celebrating the Sacraments of Holy Communion and Baptism, and forms of worship were topics for discussion at these conferences. At its meeting in Amsterdam in 1948, the World Council appointed a Commission on Faith and Order to continue the work already accomplished.

A parallel movement took place in the area of Life and Work. What Bishop Brent was to the Faith and Order Movement, Archbishop Söderblum of Sweden was to that of Life and Work. Along with three American churchmen, Frederick Lynch, Henry Atkinson, and Charles Macfarland, Söderblum worked for six years to organize the Stockholm Conference in 1925. There was a growing conviction among church leaders that unresolved differences in faith and practice should not prevent churchmen from seeking Christian solutions to the outstanding social, economic, and political problems of the time. At Stockholm, the Universal Christian Council of Life and Work was established, with headquarters at Geneva.

The Stockholm Conference was followed by another important gathering at Oxford, England, in 1937. At Stockholm, the emphasis was on the work of the individual in bringing about social reform; at Oxford, the delegates, conscious of the disintegration of modern society, the collapse of moral standards, and the growing menace of international conflict, called upon the churches themselves to mobilize their spiritual resources to combat injustice, cruelty, and hate. A joint proposal was put to the Oxford Conference of Life and Work, and the Edinburgh Conference on Faith and Order, both held in 1937, to merge in the formation of a World Council of Churches.

The two world conferences, one on Life and Work in Oxford, and the other on Faith and Order, held in Edinburgh in August, 1937, represented broad areas of concern of the Protestant churches that ultimately came together in one body, the World Council of Churches. These conferences were of great importance, for they were the basis for the formation of this ecumenical body.

The Department of Church Cooperation and Union, in its report to the General Assembly of the Presbyterian Church in the U.S.A. (1938), said, "The climax of the two World Conferences centered in the proposed World Council of Churches."[56] The report proceeded to give the details of the Constitution of such a council. World War II intervened and the actual formation of this body was postponed until 1948.

However, the Provisional Committee carried on a number of important ministries during World War II, and immediately afterward, so that, by 1948, it already had an experience and a record upon which to draw.

The mood of the inaugural assembly of the World Council of Churches at Amsterdam in 1948 is expressed in the oft-quoted words of the message of the Conference: "We are divided from one another not only in matters of faith, order, and tradition, but also by pride of nation, class, and race. But Christ has made us His own, and He is not divided. In seeking Him we find one another."[57] These words contain a basic underlying truth concerning the ecumenical movement, particularly in its maximum organizational expression, the World Council of Churches. On the one hand is the divine imperative of unity in the church through Christ, and on the other, are a recognition, a disunity, and a disagreement concerning the nature of the church. If there were no disagreement, there would in all probability be one church. Thus the World Council of Churches is a form of compromise between complete integration of churches and denominational separateness, between the deep desire to be one and the inability to overcome the many obstacles to organic unity. Firmly convinced of their unity in Christ and of the urgency of seeking to fulfill that unity in and for mission, churches or denominations have felt impelled to come together in a conciliar movement, without relinquishing their basic denominational identity.

The creation of the World Council of Churches was a new venture in the history of the Christian church. Never before had such a diverse group of ecclesiastical bodies been brought together, with different nationalities, cultures, languages, and theological viewpoints. Soon after it came into being, Dr. W. A. Visser 't Hooft, its General Secretary, said: "The World Council is like a new kind of ship, on its maiden voyage, on an uncharted course, to an unknown destination, with an untried crew that does not even speak the same language, and the trip is being made at a time when the storm at sea is the worst that man has ever known. However, the symbol used by the World Council of Churches is a little boat on a tossed sea with the Cross for a mast. That Cross represents the victory of God over man and his evil, and that Cross gives the people of the Churches of the world abiding hope."[58]

The World Council of Churches has insisted that it is neither a church nor *the* church, and it is significant that negotiation toward organic union has never been a condition for membership.

The membership of over two hundred churches in ninety countries includes most of the great Christian traditions: Protestant, Anglican, Orthodox, and Old Catholic. At the New Delhi Assembly in 1961, Eastern Orthodox membership increased and Pentecostal churches were accepted as members for the first time, demonstrating once more that the Council transcends both theological and social boundaries, and that its membership covers a broad spectrum regarding theology, liturgical practices, the sacraments, ordination, and church order.

The supreme legislative body of the Council is the Assembly, which meets every six or seven years. The chief policy-making body is the Central Committee, which has one hundred members, the largest regional group in the Committee being from the United States. In addition, there is an ad interim Executive Committee of fourteen members, plus officers, which meets twice a year.

Programs are carried on through four divisions: World Mission and Evangelism (formerly the International Missionary Council); Inter-Church Aid; Refugee and World Service Studies; and Ecumenical Action and Studies. There are also three Commissions: the Commission of the Churches on International Affairs; the Commission on World Mission and Evangelism; and the Commission on Faith and Order.

The United Presyterian Church in the U.S.A. is a member of the World Council of Churches and is represented on most of its committees and commissions. Two United Presbyterians were appointed at New Delhi (1961) by the World Council, to serve on its Central Committee.

The integration of the International Missionary Council with the World Council at New Delhi greatly strengthened both the Council and the ecumenical movement as well. It has brought missions into the center of ecumenical thought and activity. The merger was the formalization of a close relationship that had existed ever since the World Council was formed. This was emphasized by Visser 't Hooft,

General Secretary: "Thus the ecumenical movement of the Churches and that of the missionary enterprise are bound up with each other. . . . We must work to ensure that the ecumenical movement of the Churches grows more and more evangelistic, and that the missionary movement grows more ecumenical."[59]

The Regional Approach to Unity

Paradoxically, at a time when the concept of one world is emerging, the reality of the region is assuming more and more significance. There is a sense in which the people of diverse nationalities within a region are bound together by racial origins, cultural backgrounds, and very often a common outlook. The existence of the region must also be taken into account in the life of the church and the development of its mission to the world. We shall refer in this section to the regional ecumenical organizations related to the mission of the church in Asia, Africa, the Middle East, Europe, and Latin America. These organizations which have emerged represent the regional approach to Christian unity in mission and are the regional embodiment of the ecumenical movement.

At first glance, a regional movement might appear to be fracturing or segmenting the ecumenical movement and the ecumenical ideals. This danger is generally recognized, but it is highly questionable whether regional councils will prove to be disruptive. A Baptist leader from Burma wrote a chapter titled "East of New Delhi: Regionalism or Centralism?" in a book called *Unity in Mid-Career*. One section of the chapter bears the heading "Healthy Universalism Presupposes a Healthy Regionalism."[60] "True regionalism and true ecumenicity do go together, and in history we must contend with the tension between regionalism and 'ecumenicity' because of the tendency on the part of both to become false."[61]

We shall now refer to the regional movement as it has developed in the major areas of the world.

Asia. The East Asia Christian Conference is the foremost regional expression of the ecumenical movement outside North America. Until recently, and because of the strength of the Christian churches in the West, the one overall organizational expression of the ecumenical movement, the World Council of Churches, was, to a large extent, dominated by Western leaders. This was, perhaps, quite natural. Efforts were made by the World Council of Churches to include leaders from the younger churches in positions of influence and responsibility. These same leaders rather resented being considered as representatives of "younger churches." U Kyaw Than, from whose writing we have quoted before, said: "One can imagine the irony of a situation where a youngish Western churchman introduced to an audience a hoary ecclesiastic from Asia as a 'younger churchman' from one of the newer nations! Yet it is the way most of the churchmen from Asia are regarded by those in the West, and only a limited number of the alert among them realize that there are in Asia churches such as those along the coast of Malabar in India, which trace their history back to the apostolic days, long before Columbus discovered America or England first heard the Gospel."[62]

It is therefore quite understandable that Asian Christians feel they know the problems that their churches face better than those who belong to another culture. This does not mean that the East Asia Christian Conference was established as a countermove against Western domination of the ecumenical movement. Rather, able Asian Christian leaders are seeking to develop a responsible regionalism within a global context. The Foreword to the report of the preparatory meeting of the first East Asia Christian Conference held at Prapat, Indonesia, in 1957, expressed the feelings of Asians in these words: "Thus we may nurture the sense of partnership and solidarity. Thus we may develop a regional ecumenism not circumscribed by narrow sectionalism, nor limited in initiative, on the one hand, nor on the other by overall control and direction from outside the region."[63]

Another factor that led to the formation of the East Asia Christian Conference was the feeling of isolation that the churches had. The leaders knew more about the churches in the countries from which the missionaries came than they did about other Asian churches. The sense of a regional "belonging" developed as Asian leaders met and got to know one another in missionary gatherings, such as Jerusalem (1928) and Madras (1938). It was at Madras that these leaders talked with one another about the need for a regional ecumenical secretariat. The war intervened and delayed the maturing of ideas and plans.

In 1949, the year after the formation of the World Council of Churches, that body and the International Missionary Council jointly sponsored an East Asia Christian Conference at Bangkok, Thailand. The Conference recommended the appointment of a person who would serve as an "ecumenical ambassador" among the Asian churches. Dr. R. B. Manikam, who was appointed as the Joint East Asia Secretary of the International Missionary Council and the World Council of Churches, served with distinction and effectiveness from 1950 to 1956. Valuable regional conferences were held in Asia on Christian Literature, Home and Family Life, and Theological Education. Dr. Manikam helped to initiate new forms of cooperation, as well as to strengthen the bonds among church leaders.

However, as Dr. Mackay has pointed out: "There is little doubt . . . that the luminous regional idea, which was envisioned at Bangkok . . . would have succumbed before the forces of ecumenical centralization but for one providential circumstance. That circumstance was the vision and zeal of the late Charles T. Leber. Charles Leber was a dedicated ecumenist, who, at the same time, was committed to the principle of granting to the 'younger' Churches complete autonomy in the management of their own affairs and the shaping of the Christian mission in their own countries . . . [and who] with the full support of his own mission board, the Board of Foreign Missions of the Presbyterian Church in the U.S.A. stimulated the creation of the Asia Council on Ecumenical Mission."[64] There was concern among some mission board and ecumenical leaders about this Council, but due to Dr. Leber's efforts, and with "the support and statesmanship of Leber's distinguished successor, Dr. John Coventry Smith, and others like him, the regional idea triumphed, and a new chapter was written in the pursuit of Christian unity."[65]

On July 23, 1954, an East Asia Consultation on Ecumenical Mission was convened in Hong Kong by the Board of Foreign Missions of the Presbyterian Church in the U.S.A., under the leadership of Dr. John Coventry Smith, then Associate General Secretary of the Board. Present were representatives from Korea, Japan, Thailand, the Philippines, and Hong Kong. The participation of other boards was sought, but the way could not be worked out at the time.

Prior to the Consultation, the Board of Foreign Missions of the

Presbyterian Church in the U.S.A. had taken action, part of which reads as follows:

> We have now come to a stage in the development of the missionary movement of the Christian Church and of the relation of the churches to one another when attention must be focused upon the obligation of all the churches, "older and younger," to accept their responsibility for the ecumenical mission of the church, and thereby express their unity with one another in the worldwide missionary task.
>
> Pursuant, therefore, to the policy of the Board toward strengthening and enlarging the ecumenical mission of the churches, and after exploration with representatives of churches here and abroad and interdenominational agencies, the Board voted to initiate consultations toward constituting regional committees on ecumenical mission in order to further the ecumenical idea and strategy, *with the hope that there may emerge central ecumenical administration on an interdenominational and worldwide basis.*[66]
> (Italics added.)

When the Consultation was convened, the chairman explained that there had been a number of requests from various lands for fraternal workers from other than the traditional missionary-sending countries. In addition, churches in East Asia were increasingly desirous of giving expression to their sense of mission by sending fraternal workers themselves to other countries.

The representatives at the Consultation made a detailed study of those requests and how they could be met. An East Asia Interim Committee on the Mission of the Church was set up. The following year (1955), an organizational meeting of the Asia Council on Ecumenical Mission was held in Hong Kong. Representatives attended from:

Church of Christ in Thailand
United Church of Christ in the Philippines
United Church of Christ in Japan
American Board of Commissioners for Foreign Missions
United Christian Missionary Society
Methodist Missionary Society (London)
Hong Kong District Association of the Church of Christ in China
Board of Foreign Missions of the Reformed Church in America
Board of Foreign Missions of the Presbyterian Church in the U.S.A.

There were some observers from Methodist, Presbyterian, and Baptist Churches in other Asian countries, as well as from the National Council of Churches in Indonesia.

The Consultation spent a good deal of its time drawing up a Statement of Principles, which included an understanding of the ecumenical task and the procedures to accomplish it.

The 1955 Consultation opened the way for the one convened in Bangkok, Thailand, in March, 1956, by the International Missionary Council and the World Council of Churches, and this, in turn, paved the way for the Conference at Prapat, Indonesia, in 1957. The Batak Church invited the International Missionary Council and the World Council of Churches to call the Consultation.

An indication of the dynamics of the ecumenical movement in Asia is that both the first Consultation in Hong Kong in 1954 and the Prapat Conference in 1957 put the chief emphasis on evangelism. The theme of the Prapat Conference was "The Common Evangelistic Task of the Churches in East Asia." Both President Sukarno and the Minister of Religious Affairs of Indonesia addressed the Conference. Speaking as a Muslim, the Minister said that Christianity could not be considered as a foreign religion in Asia, since it was born in Asia and it had its place in Asian life. The Conference opened with a mammoth gathering of more than fifty thousand people in Liberty Square in Pematang Siantar, which gave evidence of the strength of the Christian movement in Sumatra.

Some maintained that the Prapat Conference was an "ecclesiastical Bandung." In other words, they felt that the Afro-Asian Conference of Bandung in 1955 was to the political world what Prapat was to the Christian world. However, as U Kyaw Than pointed out, "it was unthinkable in the Christian world that a conference should be called to form a fellowship of 'colored' Christians in Asia over against the other Christians in the West."[67] He went on to emphasize that the spontaneous inclusion of the churches of Australia and New Zealand was ample proof that the main consideration behind the dimensions of the movement was a common regional concern, and not race.

What the Asian churches were saying in effect, as they met at Prapat, was that the Christian churches in Asia have a vitality and a dynamic role as a movement that has become indigenous, and that they are not just appendages of the churches of the West. Prophetic statements by leaders of the ecumenical movement in global terms tend to become academic and abstract, compared with the challenge of the churches of East Asia as they find themselves in the midst of resurgent non-Christian religions.

At Prapat, the East Asia Christian Conference, as a regional entity, became a reality. The Secretariat consisted of an outstanding and internationally known Asian leader, Dr. D. T. Niles, as Secretary, and a foremost Christian leader from New Zealand, the Rev. Alan A. Brash, as Associate Secretary and Secretary for Inter-Church Aid. Later, a third member was added to the Secretariat when U Kyaw Than, a distinguished Baptist layman in Burma, was appointed Associate General Secretary.

The inaugural assembly of the East Asia Christian Conference was held at Kuala Lumpur, Malaya, May 14-24, 1959, the title of its report being "Witnesses Together." The East Asia Christian Conference is not a regional council of the World Council of Churches; it maintains a close relationship with the latter, but is an autonomous organization.

Africa. The All Africa Conference of Churches was conceived as a regional organization at Ibadan, Nigeria, in 1958, and became a reality at the meeting held in Kampala, Uganda, in 1963. At the Ibadan Conference there were two hundred representatives from twenty-five countries, the most representative gathering of African Christians ever held up to that time; it was dominated by Africans. Speaking to the delegates of the Inaugural Assembly of the East Asia Christian Conference in Kuala Lumpur, Malaya, in 1959, Sir Francis Ibiam, Chairman of the All Africa Conference of Churches, referring to the Ibadan meeting, said: "For the first time in known history, the Churches in Africa had an opportunity to 'discover and love one another, to speak to one another, and to learn something from one another.' In that atmosphere, charged with vision, and inspired by high ideals for Christian service, the Church in Africa woke up from its slumber, so to speak, and realized with great force and intensity the tremendous tasks and responsibilities which were hers in the evangelization of the peoples of Africa."[68]

At the Ibadan meeting, a Provisional Committee of ten was set up to consult with Christian councils and agencies in Africa, with a view to organizing a permanent body. Dr. Donald M' Timkulu became the first secretary. Between the Ibadan meeting and the Kampala one, a period of four years, he traveled widely throughout Africa, conferring with church leaders, learning as well as inspiring.

The Inaugural Assembly at Kampala was larger and more representative than the Ibadan meeting. There were three hundred and fifty delegates from one hundred churches in forty countries; the meeting was truly a milestone in the history of the African churches. The theme of the Conference was "Freedom and Unity in Christ." There was a frank facing of realities as delegates discussed one of the topics, "The Selfhood of the Church in Africa," and it was recognized that after centuries of Christianity in the continent, the churches had not attained selfhood. The pattern of establishing missions had followed largely the colonization pattern of the European powers, control being exercised from the home base. Fettered by the shackles of foreign forms, traditions, and patterns, the church "has not yet developed an intelligent recognition of her tasks. She deals in foreign, prefabricated theology. She is a personality which has not yet begun to do her own creative thinking."[69]

The purposes of the Conference (already known as AACC) included the following: to keep before the churches and national councils the demands of the gospel pertaining to their life and mission, for evangelism, witness in society, service, and unity; to provide a common program of study and research; to encourage closer relations; to assist in leadership training; and to collaborate with the World Council of Churches and other appropriate agencies.

When Dr. M' Timkulu became the director of the Mindolo Ecumenical Centre in Kitwe, Northern Rhodesia, in 1964, S. H. Amissah, an able teacher from Ghana, succeeded him as General Secretary of the All Africa Conference of Churches. A strong organization has been built up, with Commissions on the Life of the Church; Social, National and International Responsibility of the Church; Literature and Mass Communication. By the end of 1964, fifty-six churches and councils from twenty countries had become members of the All Africa Conference of Churches. Among them are Presbyterian churches in South Africa, East Africa, Ghana, West Cameroun, Ruanda, and Equatorial Guinea (Río Muni). The official organ of the All Africa Conference of Churches is the *AACC Bulletin,* which appears in English and French three times a year. Three important conferences have been held under the auspices of the new organization, the first on Christian Education, the second on the Christian Home and Family Life, and the third on Women's Work.

Europe. The Conference of European Churches was formally constituted on October 5-9, 1964. The meeting was held on board the MS *Bornholm* in the Kattegat, in order to include representatives from East Germany. The fourteen delegates from that country were required to get permits from the Allied Travel Board to travel to other countries in Europe, a procedure which East Germany would not allow. Two hundred and fifty delegates from twenty-one countries attended the constituting assembly. The Conference of European Churches is the first of its kind in Europe. Like the regional organizations in Asia and Africa, it is autonomous, but closely related to the World Council of Churches. A statement by the newly appointed secretary of the Conference said, "United in the activity of the Conference of European Churches are some 70 churches from all European countries, except Albania and Bulgaria."[70] Not all these churches were members of the World Council of Churches.

Near East. At a triennium meeting of the Near East Christian Council, held in Cairo, Egypt, in 1964, this body became the Near East Council of Churches, and as such, has served as a regional ecumenical organization with a full-time national executive secretary, beginning May, 1965. The change in name of the Council may seem slight, but it signified both growth and development. In 1927, a Missionary Council of West Asia and North Africa was formed, and soon after changed its name to the Near East Christian Council. It was composed of both churches and missions. The new body is a council of churches, which are increasingly assuming responsibility for the outreach of the mission of the church in communities where they are found, and in neighboring ones. In other words, a Christian council of churches and missions has now become a council of churches, with those bodies assuming full responsibility.

The churches that comprise the membership of the new Council are:

Coptic Evangelical Church (Egypt)

Armenian Evangelical Union

National Evangelical Union (Lebanon)
National Evangelical Synod of Syria and Lebanon
Episcopal Church of Jordan, Syria, and Lebanon
Church of South Arabia
Evangelical Presbyterian Church of Iran
Syrian Orthodox Church
Episcopal Church of Egypt
Lutheran Church of Jordan
Methodist Church of North Africa
Episcopal Church of Iran

The Near East Council of Churches has a Commission on Outreach and Witness and, in addition to the regular members of the Council, the following bodies are represented:

Near East Mission of the United Board for World Ministries
United Mission in Iraq
Action Chrétienne en Orient
American Mission in Egypt of The United Presbyterian Church in the U.S.A.
Arabian Mission of the Reformed Church in America
American Mission in Iran of The United Presbyterian Church in the U.S.A.

Latin America. The remaining area of the world, Latin America, is not so far advanced as the others in the development of a regional ecumenical organization. It was thought by some that such an organization would emerge from the Second Latin American Evangelical Conference in Lima, Peru, in 1961, but it was evident that the time had not yet come. One factor impeding the formation of a regional organization is the preponderance of faith missions and conservative groups, which have their suspicions about interchurch cooperation and the ecumenical movement. The Evangelical Confederation of Brazil, through the Evangelical Union of Latin America, invited the Evangelical churches of Latin America to attend the Third Latin American Evangelical Conference, in Brazil in 1969.

In recent years progress was made in bringing the Presbyterian churches in Latin America into closer relationship when the Commission on Presbyterian Cooperation in Latin America was created at a conference of representatives of churches, held at Campinas, Brazil, in 1955. The organization came to be known as CCPAL, these being the initials of its name in Spanish (Comisión de Cooperación Presbiteriana en América Latina). In 1965, the name was changed to Association of Presbyterian and Reformed Churches in Latin America. The main purpose of the organization is to enable the Presbyterian churches in Latin America to face many common problems together, and in some cases, to engage in united programs affecting the life and work of the churches in the various countries. Although this movement operates within the Presbyterian family in Latin America, rather than across denominational lines, it is not antithetical to the ecumenical movement as such. It promotes greater understanding among the churches and a desire to cooperate wherever possible.

The Student Movement

The story of the rise and development of ecumenical bodies, and indeed of the ecumenical character and drive of the missionary movement in the late nineteenth century and early twentieth, would not be complete without some reference to the student movement in the Christian enterprise.

Four organizations were largely responsible for the upsurge of missionary interest among university students both in Great Britain and the United States. They were the Young Men's Christian Association, the Student Christian Movement, the Student Volunteer Movement, and the World Student Christian Federation. Each contributed in its own way to the recruitment of many thousands of volunteers for work under existing foreign mission boards, and in some notable cases, they have supplied the leadership for the ecumenical bodies. To cite just a few examples, we have men like Visser 't Hooft and Mackie in the World Council of Churches; there was Paton in the International Missionary Council; and more recently, Niles in the East Asia Christian Conference. Then there was the towering figure of John R. Mott, whose name will be forever associated with the beginnings and the growth of all four of the organizations we have mentioned. Dr. John R. Mott became the outstanding chairman of the International Missionary Council, and was one of the foremost planners of the World Council of Churches.

In personal interviews with W. Richey Hogg in 1947 and 1948, John R. Mott and J. H. Oldham agreed in affirming that "the *real* story behind the growth of international missionary cooperation was not the preceding missionary conferences, but the development of the international Student Christian Movement."[71] Mott called the Student Volunteer Movement and the World Student Christian Federation " 'practice games in weaving together the nations and communions'— practice games in which they prepared Mott and others for the broad international and interdenominational thinking and planning without which Edinburgh (1910) and the International Missionary Council would have been impossible."[72]

An outstanding event in the history of the student movement was the international Christian student conference held at Mount Hermon, Massachusetts, in July, 1886. Organized by the Inter-Collegiate Young Men's Christian Association movement of the United States and Canada, it lasted for four weeks, and was attended by two hundred and fifty-one students from eighty-nine colleges and universities. During the first two weeks, the subject of missions was not mentioned in the regular sessions of the conference. Robert P. Wilder, from the College of New Jersey, and destined to become one of the great leaders of the student movement in his day, called together a group of twenty-one students to pray that the spirit of missions would pervade the conference. A few days later a moving address on missions was delivered by Dr. Arthur T. Pierson, editor of the *Missionary Review of the World,* and a week later, a gathering which came to be known as "the meeting of the ten nations" was held. Brief addresses were given by three sons of missionaries and ten students from different states. Before the conference closed, one hundred students had offered themselves as volunteers for missionary service. This number was later increased, so that, as a result of the Mount Hermon Conference, nearly half of the students decided to enter missionary service. Robert P. Wilder and John N. Dorman, both of Princeton, visited one hundred and sixty-seven institutions throughout the United States and Canada in one year, and over two hundred students became volunteers. In 1888, the Student Volunteer Movement for Foreign Missions was organized, and during succeeding years and decades this organization was a powerful force for enlisting some of the ablest young men and women for the missionary cause. Its watchword was "the evangelization of the world in this generation." A large percentage of Presbyterian and United Presbyterian missionaries were recruited in this way.

The establishing of the World Student Christian Federation in 1895 has been characterized as "one of the most important single contributions to the modern ecumenical movement,"[73] and Dr. Visser 't Hooft, the General Secretary of the World Council of Churches, believes that "the WSCF *was* and *is* the doorway to ecumenism."[74] He further states that "the WSCF and the International Missionary Council, both of which owe their creation largely to Dr. Mott, more than any other organizations, brought to birth the World Council of Churches."[75]

John R. Mott was one of the hundred charter members of the Student Volunteer Movement. It was he, more than anyone else, who shaped the policies and gave continuous leadership to the movement. Mott presided at the first ten quadrennial student conventions held across the country. He and Robert E. Speer,[76] the former a Methodist, the latter a Presbyterian, and both laymen, became the apostles of the world mission of the church, kindling the flame of missionary devotion and passion for a whole generation of students. "Speer moved men by his fervent eloquence, because it welled from the depths of a soul as Christlike as it was brilliant. Mott moved men by his combination of logical argument, daring challenge, and burning sincerity."[77]

Dr. Mott's name will always be associated also with the Y.M.C.A., which, like the World Student Christian Federation, is interdenominational and interconfessional in its membership, but is not under the control of the churches. As president of the World Alliance of Y.M.C.A.'s, Dr. Mott took part in official consultations of leaders of Orthodox churches and Y.M.C.A. leaders in 1928, 1930, and 1933, and the agreements reached in these meetings helped clear the way later for Orthodox churches to join the World Council of Churches.

Dr. Mott is therefore recognized as a pioneer in laying the foundations of the modern ecumenical movement. In the title of a book dedicated to his memory as a great missionary leader and statesman, he is referred to as "the architect of cooperation and unity." Dr. Mott had a vision of the world, and all of his decisions were made in the light of this. He demonstrated effectively the principle of federating national organizations, as contrasted with the plan of bringing together individuals, as was the case with the Evangelical Alliance in the nineteenth century. The ecumenical movement owes a great debt to the vision, the tireless efforts, as well as the widespread and profound personal influence, of John R. Mott, characterized by one of his biographers as "John R. Mott: World Citizen."[78]

Presbyterian Participation in Ecumenical Bodies

In what ways have Presbyterians participated in the ecumenical bodies to which reference has been made in this chapter? As we ask this question we would include the Presbyterians with whom we are in close fellowship and with whom we maintain ties and relationships of one kind or another. We have referred to individual Presbyterians who have played leading roles in the founding of some of the ecumenical bodies, and to others who have served in official capacities.

In the United States, it can be said, that Presbyterians, both before and after the merger of 1958, have been in the forefront of all these movements and organizations. The ecumenical ideal of bringing to bear the whole gospel through the whole church to the whole world makes demands on every segment of the Christian church in the use of its resources, spiritual, financial, and in personnel. In one way or another, The United Presbyterian Church in the U.S.A. is fully committed to the support of the ecumenical bodies we have mentioned. The financial contributions are for both the structure of organizations, such as the World Presbyterian Alliance, the National Council of the Churches of Christ in the U.S.A., and the World Council of Churches, and their programs, particularly of the National Council of Churches and the World Council of Churches. The tendency is for programs such as literature and literacy, audio-visual work, agricultural missions, and social work to be carried on as well-coordinated enterprises through the instrumentality of these two bodies, for there seem to be no valid reasons why work in these areas, and in addition that of Church World Service, should be carried by denominations in competition with one another.

The participation in ecumenical bodies by some Presbyterian

churches with which the Commission on Ecumenical Mission and Relations has close ties and relationships in Asia, Africa, the Middle East, and Latin America is not so complete or enthusiastic. In some areas, particularly in Latin America and Korea, as well as to a lesser extent in Africa, Presbyterian churches are critical of the ecumenical movement, and of the World Council of Churches, in particular. With strong evangelical motives and conservative theological outlook, they do not subscribe wholeheartedly to socially oriented programs undertaken by the church, and they fear that the World Council of Churches is leading its members to union with the Roman Catholic Church.

The General Assemblies of some Presbyterian churches, in Brazil and Mexico, for example, have taken action saying that they will not join or become members of any interdenominational body, an action that some regard as providing a rationale for not becoming members of the International Council of Christian Churches, an ultraconservative body. These attitudes on the part of a number of Presbyterian groups pose some problems for the Commission on Ecumenical Mission and Relations. The Commission on behalf of The United Presbyterian Church in the U.S.A. recognizes the right of a sister Presbyterian Church to remain outside the World Council of Churches. Moreover, such an action should not influence the relationship between the churches. However, where the World Council of Churches has a program related to the national council in the same country, then the problem arises. It is more and more evident that freedom for both churches to act within the context of their own convictions must be preserved. Patience, wisdom, and Christian grace are required at different levels if appropriate solutions for these and similar problems are to be found.

Interdenominational Projects Initiated by Presbyterians

Through the planning and efforts of the former Board of Foreign Missions of the Presbyterian Church in the U.S.A., a major contribution has been made in the fields of mass communication and the training of missionary personnel, respectively. The organizations to which we refer are the Radio, Visual Education and Mass Communications Committee (known as RAVEMCCO) and the Missionary

Rev. William Brennan Anderson, D.D., LL.D.

Born in Illinois, 1868. Missionary to India under Board of Foreign Missions, United Presbyterian Church of North America, 1897. Associate Secretary of the Board, 1914-1916, and Corresponding Secretary, 1916-1938.

Rev. John A. Mackay, D.D., Litt.D., LL.D., L.H.D.

Born in Scotland, 1889. Missionary to Peru under Free Church of Scotland, 1916-1925; founded its work in that country. Lecturer under Y.M.C.A. in Latin America, 1925-1932. Secretary for Africa and Latin America, Presbyterian Board of Foreign Missions, 1932-1936. President, Princeton Theological Seminary, 1936-1960. President, Presbyterian Board of Foreign Missions, 1944-1950. Moderator, General Assembly, Presbyterian Church U.S.A., 1953. President, World Presbyterian Alliance, 1954-1959. Chairman, International Missionary Council, 1947-1958. Author of *The Presbyterian Way of Life, Ecumenics,* and several other works in English and Spanish.

Rev. Charles T. Leber, D.D.

Born in Baltimore, Maryland, 1898.
Served as pastor in Presbyterian
Church U.S.A. Secretary, Board of
Foreign Missions, 1936-1952, and
as General Secretary, 1952-1958.
First General Secretary, Commission
on Ecumenical Mission and Relations,
1958-1959. Died 1959.

Orientation Center at Stony Point, New York, both of which function within the National Council of Churches.

RAVEMCCO

The greatly increased use made of radio and other mass media of communication during World War II, together with new and enlarged opportunities to spread the gospel in the postwar period, led some boards of foreign missions to take definite steps to utilize these media, and particularly radio broadcasting, on a wide scale across the world. The Board of Foreign Missions of the Presbyterian Church in the U.S.A. was one of these. In 1947, it established an Audio-Visual Office, with S. Franklin Mack as Secretary. In that year, also, Dr. Mack was named Secretary of a World Radio Committee of the Foreign Missions Conference of North America (later to be called the Division of Overseas Ministries). In 1948, he was asked to lead a team to survey ten Asian countries, to gather information on the possibilities of developing mass communication programs. The team traveled thirty-seven thousand miles, and its report laid the groundwork for the creation of RAVEMCCO as a functional committee of the Foreign Missions Conference of North America, which replaced the World Radio Committee in 1948.

RAVEMCCO was lodged administratively in the Audio-Visual Office of the Presbyterian Board in New York, with Dr. Mack as Acting Executive Secretary. Through this arrangement, RAVEMCCO could devote all the funds it raised to the program itself. In 1951, Dr. Mack became Executive Secretary of the Broadcasting and Film Commission of the National Council of Churches. His successor in the Audio-Visual Office of the Presbyterian Board, the Rev. W. Burton Martin, directed the program of RAVEMCCO for a number of years along with responsibilities to his own board, RAVEMCCO paying the Presbyterian Board part of the service cost for a number of years, beginning in 1952 and continuing until RAVEMCCO was able to function with its own administrative budget in 1956.

For the initiation of broadcasting programs overseas, the Board of Foreign Missions of the Presbyterian Church in the U.S.A. had the intention of refraining from setting up any permanent work of its own. The Presbyterian-related station DYSR at Dumaguete in the

Philippines is an example of this. Financed and initiated by the Presbyterian Audio-Visual Office, this station before long became interdenominational, functioning under the auspices of the National Christian Council of the Philippines, and receiving substantial grants from RAVEMCCO.

Believing profoundly in the service that mass communication through radio broadcasting could render to the Christian cause, the Board of Foreign Missions of the Presbyterian Church in the U.S.A. provided outstanding leadership through some of its missionaries, in addition to that given administratively in New York. The Rev. Otto DeCamp in Seoul, Korea, the late Dr. Henry Mack in Dumaguete, Philippines, and Dr. Robert McIntire in Brazil are just three examples.

Latin America was the first major region among the mission fields to develop audio-visual programs. This came about as a result of a survey of Latin America carried out by Dr. Clarence W. Jones in 1945, and sponsored jointly by World Radio Missionary Fellowship and the Committee on Cooperation in Latin America. Dr. S. Franklin Mack was named chairman of the Committee's Sub-committee on Radio and Visual Education, and a program involving $150,000 was outlined. In 1948, Dr. Manuel G. Aldama was named field secretary of this committee. In August, 1950, the Annual Report of RAVEMCCO stated that "Latin America has the distinction of having the only area secretary for audio-visual work."[79] In 1950, an important stage in the development of audio-visual work in Brazil was reached when Presbyterian missionary Robert McIntire offered to organize the recording studio in São Paulo, using the equipment sent out by the Committee on Cooperation in Latin America. Out of this effort there developed the Audio-Visual Center, known as CAVE, with a diversified program of radio broadcasting and the preparation of radio programs, filmstrips, and films.

In 1965, the Commission on Ecumenical Mission and Relations, through its Office of Mass Communications Overseas, headed by the Rev. Frederick R. Wilson, was related to a vast network of mass communications centers around the world, contributing funds and personnel through RAVEMCCO. Mr. Wilson also acted as treasurer of the World Association for Christian Broadcasting.

The Missionary Orientation Center

In the mid-1950's, what was then termed "The New Day" had serious implications for the preparation of missionaries, as far as mission boards were concerned. The withdrawal of missionaries from Communist China during the period 1949-1951 had an impact upon the whole question of missionary training. How could missionaries in China have been prepared for a new, revolutionary situation? It soon became apparent that the traditional form of preparation—academic skills, theological training to some extent at least, and language—was not sufficient. A new type of experience, involving adjustment of attitudes, a reexamination of relationships, an awareness of the nature and demands of a revolutionary world and a group-oriented learning process, seemed essential for missionary service in a fast-changing world. Ideally, a missionary going from the United States to a less developed country would need all the information he could acquire about the area he was to serve, including the history and culture of the people. However, essential as all this was considered to be, it was felt that it was even more important that missionaries should be given the opportunity to learn to adjust to new situations, to grow, and to become channels of service. For some young Americans, fresh from college or seminary, with a sureness of purpose and convinced that they had most of the answers to life's problems, it might be difficult to emphasize humility and the ability to learn from colleagues in a group-thinking process.

"In his preparation, it is not the information that a missionary acquires that will make him effective. It is what he becomes. He does not need further specialization. He needs a comprehensive orientation that will help him to understand the rest of the world from within its own frame of reference and understand himself, his cultural conditioning, and his values. His faith must grow into a living reality as he faces the challenge of other faiths and discovers the inner springs of his own motivation and the deep needs of mankind."[80]

Mission boards began to experiment with new forms of training and preparation. In 1955, the Board of Foreign Missions of the Presbyterian Church in the U.S.A. established what it called a Study Fellowship, using the facilities at Hartford Seminary. The program from the beginning was to be a flexible one, of special orientation, ecumenical in spirit, and organized for Christian community living. In 1956, the Study Fellowship was moved to Mount Freedom, New Jersey, where space was rented in a hotel during the fall each year.

In 1959, the Board of Foreign Missions of the Presbyterian Church in the U.S.A. completed buildings on its property at Stony Point, New York, and established an Ecumenical Training Center there. As in the previous experiments in Hartford and Mount Freedom, this was to be a center where approved missionary candidates could receive special training, and at the end of a five months' period, their qualifications for missionary service would be evaluated and if satisfactory, the candidates would be appointed to a specific country overseas.

In 1959, the Division of Foreign Missions of the National Council of Churches, at its meeting in Atlantic City, invited interested denominations to explore the possibility of establishing an interdenominational missionary training center. The Methodist Church had been studying orientation programs both in Europe and the United States, and the United Presbyterian Church had experimented in a new training program as we have already indicated.

Six denominations formulated a Basis of Agreement, and an approach was made to the United Presbyterian Church to find out whether it would consider selling its buildings and facilities at the Ecumenical Training Center in Stony Point to a Board of Managers for a Missionary Orientation Center. An agreement was soon reached, and the Center opened under the new name in 1961, the Commission on Ecumenical Mission and Relations being one of the co-purchasers of the land and buildings at Stony Point. A statement drawn up for the missionary participants contains this paragraph: "The Missionary Orientation Center program has been carefully designed to prepare you for effective Christian service in a revolutionary world, amid circumstances that may well demand resources you never dreamed you possessed." The six denominations participating in the Missionary Orientation Center are the United Church of Christ, the Disciples of Christ, the Evangelical United Brethren, The Methodist Church, the Reformed Church in America, and The United Presbyterian Church in the U.S.A.

Chapter V

THE PRESBYTERIAN SEARCH FOR WHOLENESS

WE have already referred to the United Presbyterian concept of the wholeness, or integrity, of the church as being basic to the ecumenical movement of our time. During the nineteenth century and up to the present time, two formative aspects of the ecumenical movement have been of fundamental importance: the unitive movement and the changing concept of the mission of the church. In this chapter, we shall deal with the Presbyterian search for unity, it being understood that it is part of the larger concept of the wholeness of the church, to which The United Presbyterian Church in the U.S.A. endeavors to make its ecumenical witness.

The words "wholeness" and "integrity" convey the real meaning more precisely than unity, which for some connotes institutionalism, but the usage of wholeness and integrity in this context is not common, and they might not be clearly understood. Whenever we use the word "unity" in this chapter it is in the sense in which it is employed in the New Testament. For example, there is the phrase, "Till we all come in the unity of the faith."[1] Both Jesus and Paul frequently expressed the idea of unity as that of "being one" or belonging to one body, and it is this spiritual oneness or wholeness which we have in mind.

The Search for Unity

The word "unity" is a simple one in common use, and yet, as is sometimes the case with the simplest things, its full meaning is not easy to grasp. When we refer to unity in the Christian sense, it would seem necessary to consider the connotation of the word to get a clear understanding of what is meant.

Some Christians are rather wary about using the word "unity," because for them it connotes church union and the idea of one great united church. Such people usually are critical of the ecumenical movement, because it seems to them to be headed in this direction, toward the establishment of one great superchurch. A sense of unity in Jesus Christ may result in church union, but it does not necessarily do so. "It is unfortunate that, in the minds of many people, Christians and non-Christians alike, the Church's unitive function is regarded as exhausting the connotation of 'ecumenical,'" says Dr. John A. Mackay.[2] However, he maintains, the pursuit of unity must be regarded as a major responsibility of the Christian church everywhere.

"To immediately conclude that this movement [the ecumenical movement] means eventually one great united church everywhere, is not justified from either a Biblical or theological viewpoint."[3] The purpose of the ecumenical movement is neither organization nor union, but rather to seek unity in Jesus Christ, realizing that that unity will find expression in cooperative agencies, and at times in church union, when these come under the guidance of the Holy Spirit.

What, then, is unity? One dictionary defines it as "the state of being one; singleness; absence of diversity; concord; harmony; uniformity."[4] In 1957 a group of distinguished churchmen attended the Faith and Order Conference at Oberlin College, and for a whole week discussed the theme "The Nature of the Unity We Seek." Out of this conference came many insights and fresh degrees of understanding concerning Christian unity.

We might consider the dictionary definition as the secular understanding of unity, and the report of the Oberlin Conference as expressing the meaning of Christian unity. The main difference in the viewpoints is with regard to uniformity and the absence of diversity. Reference was made to both of these concepts several times at Oberlin, but one is of particular interest. Principal J. Russell Chandran, of the Church of South India, said that "the basis of Christian unity is neither uniformity, nor even the reduction of diversities, but our oneness in Christ. It is in Christ that all diversity of God's gifts in creation can be held together without causing division or disunity."[5] It is the claim of the Christian church that its concept of unity includes a deep, spiritual dimension which is absent, in the sense in which we are using the words, from the secular concept. The Oberlin report stated that "our unity is in Christ who commissions us to go into the world; nowhere else than in Christ do we find unity, or can we hope to find it as completely."[6] The report added that to be real, unity must express itself and be made visible, and that "the unity we seek is the diversity in unity that allows place for various forms of worship, polity, interpersonal relations, and service."[7]

The Faith and Order Conference at Oberlin defined Christian unity as "the broad community of faith and devotion and ethical norms common to professing Christians throughout the world, on the basis of which individuals coming out of widely separated churches can have fellowship with one another."[8] Church unity as distinguished from Christian unity refers to "all forms of unity that involve the Church or the parts of a church, or churches, in their character as distinguishable communities with some institutional structures."[9]

The principle of Christian unity is found in the teachings or sayings of Jesus, as recorded in the Gospels, and in Paul's writings. Jesus' priestly prayer was "that they [the believers] all may be one; as thou, Father, art in me, and I in thee, that they also may be one in us; that the world may believe that thou hast sent me. And the glory which thou gavest me I have given them; that they may be one, even as we are one."[10] Paul takes up the theme, and emphasizes the givenness of the oneness of Christ's followers. "There is one body, and one Spirit, even as ye are called in one hope of your calling; One Lord, one faith, one baptism, One God and Father of all. . . ."[11] It should be noted that Paul does not say that there ought to be one body, one Spirit, etc. He says, there *is* one body and one Spirit.

The unity of Christians cannot be contrived, nor can it be organized into existence. It is not a human achievement; it is a gift of God. Unity among Christians is related to both calling and mission. "Unity grows," said Dr. Visser 't Hooft at Oberlin, "as we realize that we share in one call, and begin to fulfill our mission together."[12] Christian unity is a profoundly spiritual experience and quality of life in terms of relationships, and can only come about by a deep commitment to Christ. That is why Paul refers to Jesus Christ as the chief cornerstone of the spiritual habitation in which we are all built together. Without the chief cornerstone the building collapses, and its oneness is shattered. Speaking to a group of ministers in Louisville, Dr. Elton Trueblood said that "the secret of unity is altitude. At the foot of the mountain you may be far apart, but at the pinnacle you are together."[13]

So far we have been considering Christian unity in general, or in principle, as it applies to all Christians. We must now ask how much unity has been achieved by Presbyterians, or in what ways have they expressed their sense of unity or wholeness. At Oberlin, Bishop Angus Dun, in his opening statement as Chairman of the Faith and Order Conference, said: "There has been widespread agreement that the unity God wills for his Church is a *manifest* or visible unity, not something hidden."[14] Ultimately it involves faith and order, life and work, as the Christian churches have already testified.

The Sense of Unity Among Presbyterians

"Churches in the Reformed tradition have, with some minor exceptions, been consistently 'ecumenical' in outlook, in the spirit of Calvin, who abhorred schism and longed for the restoration of unity in the Church."[15]

Calvin saw the church under two aspects, the visible church and the invisible church. He felt that Rome identified the two, with no room for the invisible church. "The Invisible Church, the community of the chosen, is one," said Calvin. "Her unity is given in Christ."[16] In his famous *Institutes*, he wrote: "By the unity of the Church we must understand a unity into which we feel persuaded that we are truly ingrafted. For unless we are united with all other members under Christ our head, no hope of the future inheritance awaits us."[17] Thus Calvin believed that the church in reality is one across all national and local boundaries, according to the preaching of the Word and the administration of the Sacraments. As to the relation between the invisible and the visible church, Nijenhuis believes that "the unity of the Invisible Church is a given reality, a gift granted in Christ. But the unity of the Visible Church . . . is also a goal to be reached,"[18] and he maintains that "the concept 'ecumenical,' in the three meanings that have been mentioned—the original, geographical one; the classical, ecclesiastical one; the modern one—fully apply to the work of Calvin."[19]

In the two Presbyterian communions that merged in 1958 to form The United Presbyterian Church in the U.S.A., the sense of unity has grown and developed since they were first established in the United States. "The history of the United Presbyterian Church [of North America] has been distinctly a story of union activity. This child of church union has been interested in church union ever since its formation in 1858. In the 88 years since 1858 [i.e., 1858-1946], there have been only 24 years in which there were no union activities. During the first 50 of these years, 1858-1908, the United Presbyterians were favorably inclined toward union. Ten times during that interval, church union, involving the United Presbyterian Church of North America, was voted on, and only once was the negative vote cast by the United Presbyterians."[20]

The same striving for unity can also be seen in the Presbyterian Church in the U.S.A., beginning with the nineteenth century. From then on, the ecumenical outlook, and the sense of unity in both communions, found expression at two different levels, the intraconfessional and the interconfessional. These are only two forms of Christian unity, but they are important ones. We shall consider both of them in this chapter.

Presbyterians have a profound sense of the sovereignty of God and of his essential oneness. "Presbyterian dedication to the cause of Christian unity and cooperative effort is founded in theological conviction regarding the nature of the Church."[21] Christian unity is in the will of God, and it is part of his plan of redemption. Bishop Johannes Lilje, of the Evangelical Lutheran Church of Germany, addressing the delegates at the Oberlin Conference, said: "The fundamental unity of the Church is something very different from formal uniformity. There must be a unity which goes far beyond our attempts to organize. . . . This [real unity] has to do with the very nature of the Church. . . . This Church [the One Holy Catholic Church] exists and by her very nature she can only be one. . . ."[22] Presbyterians subscribe to a belief in the holy catholic church of the creeds.

Incentive to Unity from the Younger Churches

As we discuss this important topic, it must be remembered that the missionary thrust of the past few centuries was one of the factors that helped provide the passion and motivation for unity in the twentieth century. In the previous chapter we have referred to some of the great missionary conferences, beginning about the middle of the nineteenth century, and we saw how the yearning for unity emerged time and again.

In similar fashion, and yet even more insistently, the same note was struck in conferences of missionaries (with nationals sometimes included) in India, Japan, China, Africa, and Latin America. In a series of such conferences, held in North India in 1855, 1857, and 1862, there was manifested "the united action of Christian men who pray, confer, and work together, in order to advance the interests of their Master's Kingdom."[23] In a conference held in South India in 1858 one delegate was heard to say that "denominational controversies may elicit truth in the West, but elsewhere they produce 'nothing but evil.' "[24]

Faced with the challenge of non-Christian religions, missionaries felt the urgency of some form of unity among the churches more than did the churches in the West. At a conference held in Madras in 1902, a recognition on the part of both missionaries and Indian Christians that a unity in spirit, which already existed, was actively demanding an outward expression became the dominant note of the gathering. The Madras Conference of 1902 exercised considerable influence upon the nature and direction of the Edinburgh Conference of 1910, which, as we have seen, was a landmark in the quest for unity and cooperation.

During the latter half of the nineteenth century and the early years of the twentieth, important conferences were held in India, China, Japan, Africa, and Latin America, and in all of them, in varying degrees, the need for cooperation and unity was stressed. A typical one was the General Conference of Protestant Missionaries held in Tokyo, Japan, in 1910, a conference attended by four hundred and fifty missionaries from forty-two societies, and fifteen Japanese guests. "They directed much of their attention to cooperation, comity, and church union and passed a resolution urging all Christians to pray and labour for 'corporate oneness.' "[25]

In a later chapter, reference is made to the united churches that were formed in Japan and the Philippines. In addition to these, there are The Church of Christ in China (Hong Kong Council), The Church of South India, The Church of Christ in Thailand, and The United Church of Northern India. This movement toward church union in Asia exercised considerable influence on church leaders in Europe and the United States.

Brief History of Efforts Toward Union

It is only natural that the first efforts put forward by the Presbyterians of the two communions we are considering should be at the intraconfessional level, that is, within what is known as the Reformed and Presbyterian family. Neither denomination felt that unity should be pursued for its own sake. The concern has always been for unity if it seemed that the time had come to unite, and more important still, if it was abundantly clear that such a move would further the cause of Christ in the world.

A perusal of the historical details of union efforts since 1870 reveals the many talks, conversations, negotiations, plans, statements, and resolutions that took place in almost bewildering fashion. Some might question the validity of this enormous expenditure of time and effort by committees, presbyteries, and General Assemblies. However, the church historian, Wallace N. Jamison, feels that "all the seemingly fruitless conversations, the plans of union, the endless negotiations of the past were not wasted. Instead, they contributed to the growth and maturity of the Church. Horizons were broadened by contacts with other denominations, and some of the harshness of the Scottish highlands has been mellowed by the years. Even more important, behind these events there is discernible the gentle hand of Providence."[26]

The history of church union negotiations reveals a variety of causes for failure and frustration. They include different kinds of mistakes in voting procedures, conflicting viewpoints, property rights, social practices, doctrinal questions, denominational pride, and the fear of being "swallowed up" by a larger denomination and losing the identity of one's own group. The record also shows how important a role has been played by editors of church magazines, as plan after plan has come before the church constituency for consideration. The question of interpretation sometimes was crucial. During the negotiations from 1907 to 1910 between the United Presbyterian Church of North America and the Presbyterian Church in the U.S.A., "twice the editors of *The United Presbyterian* and *The Presbyterian Banner* gave precisely opposite reports and interpretations of the same action. There was difference of opinion as to whether McClurkin's famous speech of March 2, 1908, was pro-union or anti-union. Each editor hailed Mc-Clurkin as the champion of his particular view."[27]

The discussions and negotiations concerning church union among members of the Presbyterian family in this country cover a period beginning in 1859 down to the present time. Sometimes only two denominations were involved in the discussions and plans, at other times there were three, four, or five.

As we have already noted, the United Presbyterian Church of North America came into being in 1858. The following year, an invitation came from the Presbyterian Church (New School) to begin correspondence with the United Presbyterian Church, but the invitation was turned down by a blanket action of the United Presbyterian General Assembly of 1859. Eight years later, a real effort toward union was initiated. "On April 15, 1869, the joint committee for Presbyterian-United Presbyterian union met, but the meeting was poorly attended. Little was accomplished because of failure to agree on the point of psalmody."[28]

The reunion of the New School Presbyterians and the Old School Presbyterians in 1870 to form one denomination after thirty-two years of separation, caused such a degree of elation on the part of the Rev. Dr. Musgrave, a Presbyterian U.S.A. minister, that in a statement he made at the Old School General Assembly he appealed to the United Presbyterians to come in the new, enlarged Presbyterian Church, even though their denomination could not see its way clear to unite. Dr. Musgrave also made some humorous references to the practice of singing psalms instead of hymns in the United Presbyterian Church of North America. His statement had been reported in the *Pittsburgh Gazette* of November 11, 1868, and reproduced in *The Evangelical Repository and United Presbyterian Review* of 1869. His remarks evidently caused considerable irritation among the United Presbyterians, and one editor wrote, "If he thinks that United Presbyterians can be induced by such means to leave their own church, and join his, we can tell him that he little knows the stuff of which they are made."[29]

The breach between the two denominations began to widen, but both General Assemblies decided to start all over again when they met in 1870, and a joint committee was appointed. At its first meeting the following year, it was apparent that the two churches could not get together, and when the two General Assemblies met again "the responses showed that each saw clearly that no one can ride two horses moving in opposite directions."[30] By the year 1873 union efforts, for all practical purposes, had been terminated. The period from 1869 to 1872 was not propitious for union between the two churches. Not only were there the question of psalmody and serious differences in orthodoxy, but also the Presbyterian Church in the U.S.A. was busily engaged in strengthening unity within itself after the Reunion of 1870, and the United Presbyterian Church of North America was negotiating also with the Reformed Presbyterian Church, which had remained outside the union of 1858. Between 1887 and 1905 there were three periods when such efforts involving the Reformed Presbyterians were made, 1887-1888, 1890-1891, and 1901-1905.

During one of these periods, in 1904, the Reformed Presbyterian General Synod was also negotiating with the Presbyterian Church in the U.S.A. and the Reformed Church in America. None of these efforts was successful, and the principal barrier was the view of the state held by the Reformed Presbyterians. They could neither vote nor hold public office because "the national constitution makes no reference to Christ as the Head of our government."[31]

During the same period, from 1874 to 1909, the United Presbyterian Church also tried to woo the Associate Reformed Synod of the South. A joint committee was set up and a formal plan of cooperation was agreed on in 1875, involving exchanges of ministers and cooperation in home mission and foreign mission fields. However, the process of achieving union was slow because of distances and delays in correspondence. The United Presbyterian Church sent down an overture to the presbyteries in 1887, and the vote was overwhelmingly favorable. The Associate Reformed Church, however, was increasingly cool to union. The disparity in size was a factor, and they wanted to retain their name and their property rights, but the main stumbling block was the discrepancy of viewpoint on slavery and secret societies.

In the early part of the twentieth century, two unions took place within the Reformed family, one involving the Cumberland Presbyterian Church and the other, the Welsh Calvinistic Methodist Church. The former united with the Presbyterian Church in the U.S.A. in 1906, and the latter in 1920.

The Cumberland Presbyterian Church had arisen one hundred years before in response to the pressing needs of the frontier. Drury considers it to be "one of the most amazing chapters of Presbyterian history in the United States."[32]

In the early 1800's the Presbytery of Cumberland, in the Synod of Kentucky, was divided between the Revival and Anti-Revival parties, as a result of the great revival of 1800. The Revival Party, in its desire to meet the growing needs of the frontier, "insisted on ordaining men who did not meet the educational standards of the Presbyterian Church."[33] The issue became a serious one, and the Synod of Kentucky dissolved the Presbytery of Cumberland in 1806. In 1810 the Revival Party formed an independent presbytery and took the name of Cumberland Presbytery. This strongly evangelistic group grew, and by 1813 a Synod was formed, and later, a new denomination, the Cumberland Presbyterian Church, came into being in 1829, with the organization of a General Assembly. The denomination grew, not by means of any organizational drives, but because "the spiritual destitution of the frontier was answered by zealous Cumberland laymen and clergy who had soul-saving experiences with Christ and yearned to share their convictions with others."[34]

By 1906, when the Cumberland Presbyterian Church united with the Presbyterian Church in the U.S.A., it had 17 synods and 114 presbyteries,[35] but not all of these went into the union. "In 1904, 68,000 of the 198,000 Cumberland Presbyterians refused to join in the union with the Presbyterian U.S.A. Church and remained a separate denomination."[36]

The Welsh Calvinistic Methodist Church had its origin in Wales as a result of the Wesley–Whitefield revival of the eighteenth century. In accordance with Whitefield's theology, which was Calvinistic, the denomination was "Presbyterian in doctrine and polity, but Methodist in its conception of the spiritual life."[37] Welsh immigrants in the United States established a church on similar lines, and by 1869 a General Assembly was organized. In 1920 the leaders of the denomination reached an agreement with the Presbyterian Church in the U.S.A. on union of the two denominations. At the meeting of the General Assembly of 1920, it so happened that Dr. William H. Roberts, the Stated Clerk of the Presbyterian Church, was able to address the delegates of the Welsh Presbyterian Church in Welsh, since he was the son of a prominent leader of that church.

In 1907 a serious approach to union of the United Presbyterian Church and the Presbyterian Church in the U.S.A. was made when memorials from 113 presbyteries came to the General Assembly of the latter, urging that steps toward union be taken. The Moderator of the General Assembly of the United Presbyterian Church, however, gave expression to his reluctance in the matter when he said, "If union were to take place, some great fundamental principles would have to be carefully safeguarded, and we [the United Presbyterians] would likely want to carry our Psalm books under our arms."[38] A joint committee held some meetings, but it was soon evident that the United Presbyterian representation felt they had no clear mandate from their church to discuss organic union. They were willing to discuss a closer federation. The negotiations, however, between the two churches failed, and among the causes of this failure were the questions of psalmody, doctrine, and the fear of absorption. In addition, a new factor appeared, namely, the opinions of influential personalities in the United Presbyterian Church, who opposed union. One tangible result, nevertheless, was the appointment by that church of a Permanent Committee on Inter-Church Relations. "It was one of the first churches to take this important action, and subsequently it served as a pattern for many other denominations in this regard."[39]

In the period from 1912 to 1915 interest developed in union between the United Presbyterian Church of North America and the Presbyterian Church U.S. The General Assembly of the latter church, at its meeting in 1912, appointed a committee to confer with a similar committee of the other church, and the basis of union was formulated in December of the same year. Some confusion arose from the agreement not to print the document until the time of the General Assemblies in

May, and it was alleged that Presbyterian U.S. magazines were using a basis different from the one agreed upon in the joint committee. S. M. Spencer, the editor of *The United Presbyterian,* felt that the time for adequate consideration of such an important matter would be too short. "Hasty marriages bring much business to the divorce court. The United Presbyterian Church, the smaller of the two, may well be considered the lady in the case, and I can conceive of her saying to Mr. Southern Presbyterian, 'I like your looks well enough; I hear many good things said of you; reports say you are active in business; fervent in Spirit; serving the Lord; but really, I don't know you very well; we have just been introduced; I'm not sure I like you well enough to marry you; you might not like me very well either; for I am somewhat peculiar; and so don't rush me too fast; and while we are waiting, I can enjoy a bit of courting; and in the end may like you all the better for it.' "[40]

In 1914 the General Assembly of the Presbyterian Church U.S. voted to send the Plan of Union to the presbyteries without comment. The United Presbyterian General Assembly of the same year refused to send the Plan to the presbyteries, and there the matter ended. Among the reasons for this, differences in views regarding the social responsibility of the church were prominent. Thomas P. Hay, representing the Southern point of view, maintained that the church was exclusively a spiritual organization with responsibility only for the spiritual welfare of its people. He recognized that according to the United Presbyterians, the church must act as a leaven in a sinful world. Thus the leaders of that church expressed their views on political issues and were active in their opposition to vice and corruption. There were also differences in viewpoint on the race issue between the northern and southern churches.

In 1926 the General Assembly of the United Presbyterian Church of North America appointed a Committee on Closer Relations with the Southern Presbyterian Church. "The advantages of a union of all members of the Presbyterian family, if a satisfactory Basis of Union can be drawn, require no argument."[41] In 1929 the Moderator of the Presbyterian U.S.A. General Assembly, Dr. Cleland B. McAfee, said "We are out for all kinds of union with all followers of Christ."[42] Even the secular press was publishing articles on the increased interest in religious unity. The Presbyterian Church in the U.S.A. was negotiating with the Episcopalians, the Methodists, and the Southern Presbyterians. Other churches, such as the Disciples, Congregationalists, and Baptists, were also considering how to effect closer relations.

In 1926 the General Assembly of the Southern Presbyterian Church appointed a Committee on Union and asked the United Presbyterians to do the same. There were many personal contacts among leaders of the two denominations, and in 1928 the issue of union came to a vote in both Assemblies. The Southern Assembly voted strongly to approve the report of its Committee and to send the Basis of Union to the presbyteries. However, in the United Presbyterian Church of North America the matter was handled differently. The Committee on Closer Relations did not recommend sending the Basis of Union to the presbyteries, but merely asked for authorization to continue its efforts. Although sentiment for union was generally favorable, the action of the United Presbyterians was interpreted in the South as being unfavorable, and prospects for union quickly diminished. In 1930, the General Assembly in the South voted down an overture to continue negotiations, and the Committee was discharged. One new factor emerged: the United Presbyterian Church of North America became interested in a larger union, the prospect of which overshadowed the union of only two churches.

In 1930 the supreme judicatories of Presbyterian and Reformed churches in the United States took action on organic union. The General Assembly of the Presbyterian Church in the U.S.A., the General Synod of the Reformed Church in America, the General Assembly of the United Presbyterian Church of North America, and the General Assembly of the Presbyterian Church U.S., all gave their approval to the proposal and instructed their committees to prepare a plan of union.

In 1934, however, three of these bodies had withdrawn from the plan, leaving only the Presbyterian Church in the U.S.A. and the United Presbyterian Church of North America. In that same year a vote was taken on the floor of the General Assembly of the latter church not to send the plan to the presbyteries.

In 1938 the General Assembly of the Presbyterian Church in the

U.S.A. accepted an invitation from the Presbyterian Church U.S. to explore the possibilities of union. During World War II the respective Committees on Interchurch Relations of the two churches continued to meet, and the first plan of union was printed in 1943.

The Presbyterian search for unity was not confined to members of the Reformed family. It should be noted at this point that over a long period of time many forces were at work leading in the direction of closer cooperation and union. Discussions and conferences, both formal and informal, were held from time to time, and helped prepare the climate for further efforts. In 1937 two conferences served to stimulate the participating bodies to consider such efforts. They were the World Conference on Life and Work at Oxford, England, and the one on Faith and Order at Edinburgh in 1937.

It is, therefore, not without significance that within a few months of the holding of these two important conferences, the General Convention of the Protestant Episcopal Church should issue an invitation to the Presbyterian Church in the U.S.A. to join in a declaration leading to a union of the two denominations.

In June, 1938, the General Assembly of the Presbyterian Church in the U.S.A. received this invitation through its Department of Church Cooperation and Union, and declared its intention to cooperate with the Protestant Episcopal Church in the study and formulation of plans for union. There followed conferences, committee meetings, and reports over a period of years, and in 1942, at a joint conference of leaders of the two churches, approval was given to drafts of several documents for study by presbyteries and dioceses. One of these documents was called "Basic Principles Proposed for the Union of the Presbyterian Church in the U.S.A. and the Protestant Episcopal Church in the U.S.A.," and the other was entitled "Suggested Cooperative Arrangements During Negotiations for Organic Union." Over the next few years, reports were made to both churches whenever their governing bodies met. A new Basis of Union was formulated for submission to the respective churches. At its meeting in Philadelphia in September, 1946, the Episcopal General Convention did not give its approval to the proposed plan, but voted to continue negotiations, and to prepare a statement for the Lambeth Conference of 1948 before making any commitment.

The outcome was reported to the Presbyterian U.S.A. General Assembly of 1947. The Basis of Union, therefore, was never submitted to a General Assembly for vote. Relationships continued to be cordial and friendly, but it did not prove practicable to resume negotiations, and hopes for the union began to diminish.

An analysis of the negotiations and the relative positions of the two churches reveals that there were a number of reasons why union failed to materialize. Perhaps chief among these was the question of ordination and the historic episcopate. In the Basis of Union, provision was made for the continuation of the episcopate, and especially in relation to ordination. The problem arose concerning the 9,000 Presbyterian and 7,000 Episcopal ministers, and mutual recognition of their ordination, or reordination. It was thought at the time that a formula had been found, but evidently there was not complete understanding of its meaning and implications when the Episcopal Convention took its vote to postpone approval. The same problem of ordination and the episcopate had been previously faced in discussions involving the possible union of Anglican and Presbyterian Churches, in South India, Canada, and Ceylon.

It is not known whether in 1947 the Presbyterian Church in the U.S.A. was ready or not to accept the episcopal form of church government with the office of a bishop as an important element. Traditionally, Presbyterians have not favored the episcopal form of government, their concept of authority in the church being different. As the question of union of the Presbyterian Church in the U.S.A. with the Protestant Episcopal Church in 1946 never came up for a vote in the former church, and since the latter had demonstrated it was not yet ready for such a step, it can be assumed that the time for union had not yet arrived.

During the 1940's there were renewed attempts at union among members of the Reformed family. In 1944, the Moderator of the General Assembly of the United Presbyterian Church of North America, in an address to the church leaders gathered in Muskingum College, Ohio, said: "Church Union! Yes, we believe in it, when it comes as the evident moving of the Spirit of God upon the Church. . . . Is the time not ripe for a full consideration of a definite basis of union of our Church with the Southern Presbyterian Church and the Associate Reformed Church of the South . . . and possibly the Dutch Reformed Church? . . . It is for us as United Presbyterians to take the initiative in the matter."[43] An approach was made to the Presbyterian Church U.S., but it was discovered that that church had just opened negotiations with the Presbyterian Church in the U.S.A. A three-way negotiation was not favored by the United Presbyterians at that time. Efforts by these churchmen to open negotiations with the Associate Reformed Presbyterian Church in 1944 were also unsuccessful. One reason was that the Southern Church had no committee with authority to carry on talks about union. In addition, the matter of discontinuing the use of psalms instead of hymns in services of worship was still pending.

Following this period, one of its most vigorous and hopeful efforts at union was made by the United Presbyterian Church of North America. Representatives of that church met with those of the Reformed Church in America in 1944 and exchanged reports on educational institutions, church publications, missions, Bible school work, and young people's work. After receiving statements on the theological position of their respective churches, an article dealing with beliefs and aims was drawn up. In 1945 committees were set up and among the topics discussed were seminaries, colleges, social questions, and doctrinal standards of the two churches. While the two committees were in joint session in 1946, a letter was received from the Presbyterian Church in the U.S.A., inviting three members of each committee to discuss union with that church, but the invitation was rejected, as possibly jeopardizing the union of the two churches already negotiating.

There followed a period of protracted discussions and negotiations; studies of many aspects of church life, church polity, liturgy, and doctrine were made, while articles for or against union appeared in magazines of the two denominations. In 1946 the supreme judicatories of both churches voted to set up a joint committee to draft a plan of union. The United Presbyterian General Assembly of 1949 directed each of the presbyteries of the church to vote on the overture on union with the Reformed Church at its first regular meeting in 1950.

The Plan of Union (United Presbyterian Church of North America and the Reformed Church in America) was sent down to the presbyteries and classes of the two churches in 1949. It was overwhelmingly approved by the presbyteries of the United Presbyterian Church of North America. But in the Reformed Church in America classes it received only about a 51 percent vote (three-fourths vote in three fourths of the classes being required for approval). In the Eastern portion of the Reformed Church in America, classes (New York, New Jersey, Pennsylvania, etc.) approved by about two thirds, but the Midwest section, more conservative and largely a result of Dutch immigration only one hundred years ago, defeated it. In the United Presbyterian Church of North America the vote in the presbyteries on any question was a simple majority of the popular vote in all of the presbyteries, provided that two thirds of the presbyteries voted.

The negotiations to which we have just referred undoubtedly had some bearing on the union of the United Presbyterian Church of North America and the Presbyterian Church in the U.S.A., which was consummated in 1958.

In May, 1950, the General Assemblies of the Presbyterian Church in the U.S.A. and the Presbyterian Church U.S. officially approached the United Presbyterian Church of North America with "an invitation to unite with . . . [them] in . . . [their] program of acquaintance and cooperation and in the plan of union which [they] are jointly developing."[44] The invitation also went to other members of the Reformed family. A Plan of Union of the Presbyterian Church in the U.S.A. and the Presbyterian Church U.S. had been in preparation over a period of ten years.

The Union of 1958

For decades, as we have seen, churches in the Reformed family had been vigorous in their attempts at union, sometimes two of them being involved, at other times three or four. A few facts seem to emerge from the record of the many activities during those years. The first is that of perseverance amid setbacks, frustrations, and disappointments. In the various denominations there were degrees of preservance, but it was present in all of them. Coupled with this was a determination to find a way, convinced that it was God's will that a way be found. The second fact is that the road to church union is a difficult, and often, a tortuous one, and as the various judicatories and committees traveled along that road in Christian fellowship and deepening understanding, they learned much by experience. A great deal that was learned could only be acquired that way; it was not in the textbooks or in church constitutions. As each attempt failed, some new lesson had been learned, some way of avoiding certain pitfalls had been discovered. A third fact is that an immense amount of thought and energy has gone into union efforts in recent decades.

In the early 1950's the participants in the negotiations did not know what would be the precise outcome of their efforts, and all those which preceded them. Looking back over the records, particularly the reports of permanent committees to the General Assemblies, one can discern a new spirit, a new confidence running through them.

One interesting development took place at the beginning of this period. The Permanent Committee on Inter-Church Relations of the United Presbyterian Church of North America reported to the General Assembly in 1951 that "at the suggestion of our ad hoc committee, the joint conference recommended to the General Assemblies of the Northern and Southern Churches (Presbyterian U.S.A. and U.S.) the appointment of two women each, to their permanent committees."[45] The inclusion of women in these discussions was one more indication of the increasing role of women in the church.

The invitation to join in a Plan of Union was sent by the Presbyterian Church in the U.S.A. and the Presbyterian Church U.S. to the Associate Reformed Presbyterian Church, the Cumberland Presbyterian Church, the Evangelical and Reformed Church, and the Reformed Church in America, in addition to the United Presbyterian Church of North America. It soon was apparent that of all these, only the United Presbyterian Church was giving serious consideration to the proposal. It thus became a trilateral discussion among the United Presbyterian, the Presbyterian U.S., and the Presbyterian U.S.A. churches, when the General Assembly of the United Presbyterian Church agreed in 1951 to accept the invitation of the other two churches.

It is interesting to note that in 1915, Arthur Judson Brown wrote that "growing fellowship between the Presbyterian Church in the U.S.A., the Presbyterian Church in the U.S., and the United Presbyterian Church of North America, justifies hope that Presbyterians will yet see that 'U.S.' and 'U.S.A.' are the same thing, and that the 'United'

Presbyterians will ere long be ready to do what their name implies."[46]

Three subcommittees with responsibility for the negotiations were set up respectively by the Permanent Commission on Interchurch Relations of the Presbyterian Church in the U.S.A., the Permanent Committee on Cooperation and Union of the Presbyterian Church U.S., and the Permanent Committee on Inter-Church Relations of the United Presbyterian Church of North America. The General Assemblies of the three churches approved the reports of their respective committees in 1951. A Joint Negotiating Committee of the three churches, with six members from each one, was set up. In early September of that year the informal voting in the presbyteries of the United Presbyterian Church on "General Presbyterian Reunion," following the distribution of *The Plan of Reunion* (1949 edition), drawn up by the other two churches, revealed a seven to one favorable majority.

The next step was the drafting of a new three-way Plan of Union, using the 1949 plan as a basis. This new document was issued in 1954 under the title "The Plan Providing for the Union of the Presbyterian Church in the United States of America, and the Presbyterian Church in the United States, and the United Presbyterian Church of North America, as The Presbyterian Church of the United States." The document runs to 315 pages and consists of four main divisions:

1. Certain important introductory, supplementary, and historical material;
2. The Categorical Question on which to vote;
3. A contract of union (15 Concurrent Declarations); and
4. A Constitution for the United Church, consisting of the Confession of Faith and the Larger and Shorter Catechisms, the Directory for Worship, the Form of Government, and the Book of Discipline.

Under the Presbyterian system, questions of such import as church union are sent down from the General Assembly to the presbyteries for their approval. Accordingly, the overture containing the Categorical Question on Union and the Plan for Union itself was sent down in 1955. The requirements for voting on church union differed in the three churches. In the Presbyterian Church in the U.S.A., two thirds of the presbyteries had to approve by a majority vote in each case. In the Presbyterian Church U.S. three fourths of the presbyteries had to give their approval. In the United Presbyterian Church of North America it was necessary to have a majority of the popular vote, provided that two thirds of the presbyteries participated in the voting. The result of the voting in the three churches as reported to the 1955 General Assemblies was as follows:[47]

Presbyterian U.S.A.

Affirmative	255 presbyteries
Negative	1 presbytery

Presbyterian U.S.

Affirmative	42 presbyteries
Negative	43 presbyteries
Tied	1 presbytery

United Presbyterian
(with at least two thirds
of the presbyteries reporting)

Affirmative	946 persons
Negative	531 persons

Thus it was clear that the vote was favorable in the Presbyterian Church in the U.S.A. and the United Presbyterian Church, and negative in the Presbyterian Church U.S. Inasmuch as the vote was on the three-way plan, a new proposal would have to be presented, if the other two churches wished to proceed with a plan for union.

The Chairman and Secretary of the Permanent Committee on Cooperation and Unity of the Presbyterian Church U.S., in a letter to the Permanent Commission and the Permanent Committee of the other two churches, expressed their keen disappointment that the Plan had been defeated in the Presbyterian Church U.S. They noted that "in spite of organized and continued opposition, seventeen General Assemblies [of the Presbyterian Church U.S.] have steadfastly kept open the door to Presbyterian union."[48]

The report to the 1955 General Assembly of the Presbyterian Church in the U.S.A., in its analysis of the negative vote in the Southern Church, said that friends of union in that church pointed out that more presbyteries voted for union than against it, and that the negative votes were against any plan of union, and not just that particular one. Moreover, the report went on to say that "the campaign against union has been waged in the atmosphere of strong feelings about the Supreme Court's decision on segregation in schools . . .

with a persistent misleading attack on the Presbyterian Church in the United States of America as 'Northern,' 'unorthodox,' 'centralized in administration,' 'too large,' 'unspiritual,' and with an attack on their own General Assembly's statement in 1954 against segregation. . . ."[49]

In March, 1955, by general agreement, the committees of the Presbyterian Church in the U.S.A. and the United Presbyterian Church of North America proceeded with the preparation of a two-way plan. In 1956, the General Assembly of the Presbyterian Church in the U.S.A. approved the report of its Permanent Commission, recommending that the two-way plan be approved for transmission to the presbyteries. Much of the three-way plan was used in the two-way plan, the principal changes being in the Concurrent Declarations, the Form of Government, and some of the introductory and supplementary material. The United Presbyterian Church in its General Assembly of 1956 took a similar action, and the way was now clear for the two church bodies to take one of the most far-reaching decisions either had ever taken.

The Permanent Commission on Interchurch Relations of the Presbyterian Church in the U.S.A. reported to the General Assembly of 1957 that, as of May 20, 1957, of the church's 250 presbyteries, 234 had voted "Yes" and none had voted "No" on the question of union with the United Presbyterian Church of North America, as contained in *The Plan of Union,* thus exceeding the requirement that two thirds of the presbyteries approve. It was similarly reported to the 1957 General Assembly of the United Presbyterian Church of North America that, as of May 20, 1957, a vote on the Plan of Union had been taken in 61 of the church's 65 presbyteries, and that in these presbyteries 1,010 persons had voted "Yes" and 755 had voted "No," thus exceeding the Constitutional requirement that at least two thirds of the presbyteries vote, and that a majority of all votes cast be in the affirmative.

Thus the Plan of Union was adopted by both General Assemblies in 1957, and appropriate steps were taken working toward the consummation of union in May, 1958.

The Blake Proposal

Since 1958, the most important development in the area of church union was the proposal made by Dr. Eugene Carson Blake, in a sermon preached in Grace Episcopal Cathedral in San Francisco on December

4, 1960, at the time of the triennium meeting of the National Council of Churches. The proposal called upon The United Presbyterian Church in the U.S.A., the Protestant Episcopal Church, The Methodist Church, and the United Church of Christ to consider seriously organic union. Three important factors were present in this gesture toward union. The first was that Dr. Blake was the Stated Clerk, that is, the chief permanent officer of the United Presbyterian Church; the second was that Bishop James A. Pike of the Episcopal Church had foreknowledge of the proposal, and after it was made, gave it his endorsement; and the third was that representatives of member churches in the National Council were just about to meet. There was a further element in the picture that is not without significance, and that was the wide press coverage given to the proposal, and the immediate impact it made upon the American people.

In his book *Ecumenics*, Dr. Mackay calls the episode "the dramatic approach to unity."[50] Contributing to the element of drama were the form, manner, and circumstances in which the proposal was made, but perhaps more important still, from the point of view of the drama of the situation, was that the impression was given, particularly to the secular world, that "for the first time in American Church history, a serious proposal was being made for Church union,"[51] which, of course, was not the case.

Following the Blake Proposal, a Consultation on Church Union came into being, and to the four churches mentioned by Dr. Blake in his sermon in 1960 have since been added the Disciples of Christ, the Evangelical Brethren, the Presbyterian U.S., and the African Methodist Episcopal churches, making eight all together.

On January 24, 1965, Dr. Blake preached a second sermon in Grace Episcopal Cathedral in San Francisco, and his topic this time was "Second Thoughts on Church Union." The phraseology might suggest that Dr. Blake was having second thoughts on his proposal, in the popular sense in which the phrase is used, but such was not the case. On the contrary, he called on American churchmen to redouble their efforts toward Christian unity. The "thoughts" were concerned with the theological and organizational problems that might prevent union, if no solution for them were found. "Church union delayed," he said, "is church union denied."[52] Dr. Blake referred to three pitfalls that must be avoided. In the first place, he said: "We must be against any church union which is established at the expense of truth. . . . A union produced by compromising convictions is not according to the will of Christ."[53] The second pitfall is "the attitude held by some churchmen that the Christian Church, through union and multiplicity of members ought to become powerful enough to dominate any state, society, or culture."[54] Thirdly, Dr. Blake warned that "we must be against any church union that would in any way threaten the ecumenical movement, or diminish the obligation to continue to cooperate with all Christian Churches in their common witness to the Lordship of Jesus Christ."[55]

The union of the churches mentioned in this proposal is part of their unfinished task as they walk along the road to Christian unity, and the United Presbyterian Church is a vital part of this movement.

Before 1958, discussions and negotiations toward church union were carried on by the Permanent Commission on Interchurch Relations and the Permanent Committee on Inter-Church Relations, of the respective churches. The functions of these bodies were transferred to the Commission on Ecumenical Mission and Relations in 1958. It is not the task of the Commission, however, to negotiate actual church union. Its function, rather, is that of cultivating relationships with other communions, up to the point of negotiation of union itself. If this stage is reached in any particular instance, then a special committee will be appointed to carry on negotiations.

Church leaders are quick to point out that organic union of churches must not be an end in itself. Two aspects of this are important for our discussion. Dr. Eugene Carson Blake, speaking in Grace Cathedral, San Francisco, in 1965, pointed out that "church union must never be thought of as a substitute for, or an alternative to ecumenical cooperation of all Christian Churches. . . . The kind of church union which alone we dare to press for, is one which is recognized clearly as supplementary to all other manifestations of Christian unity."[56]

In the second place, unity without mission misplaces the emphasis and even robs unity of its real meaning when applied to the Christian church. Dr. Mackay expresses the close relation of unity and mission in these words: "Unity . . . is never so real or so Christian as when it is fulfilled in mission. For it is in mission, and only in mission that individual members of the community achieve true stature, when each discovers his place within the whole and becomes equipped to play his part worthily. When this happens, the work of the Church's leaders is not in vain, for then Church members as 'God's people' do not learn merely to 'enjoy religion' or to have a 'wonderful time' together, but are 'equipped for work in His service.' "[57]

Chapter VI

THE FORMATION OF THE COMMISSION
ON ECUMENICAL MISSION AND RELATIONS

IN this chapter we shall attempt to describe the developments and events that led to the creation of the Commission on Ecumenical Mission and Relations, and we shall outline the place it occupies in the ecumenical era.

The Rise of the Younger Churches and Their Place in the Worldwide Mission of the Church

The nineteenth century saw the development of the missionary movement as a vast enterprise with increasing momentum and scope, reaching into all corners of the earth. As the mission program and work unfolded, thousands of devoted missionaries from Europe, the United States, Canada, and Australia went forth into many lands and baptized converts into the Christian faith, according to Christ's injunction. Early in this development, congregations were formed in mission lands, and Christian pastors and workers began to be trained.

The younger churches grew and increased in number during the era of colonization and took on certain aspects of that period. Missionary literature of the nineteenth century in Europe and the United States contains references to "native" churches and "native" pastors, and as late as 1904 Gustav Warneck in his *Outline of a History of Protestant Missions from the Reformation to the Present Time* refers to the conversion of the "heathen" to the Christian faith. When missionaries used the terms "native churches" and "native Christians," resentment developed among Christians in mission lands, for the use of the word "native" not only tended to remind them of their subject status in a

157

colonial relationship, but also made them feel inferior to those of the "enlightened West."

In the twentieth century, the term "native churches" gave way to the more acceptable one of "younger churches." By 1928, when the Jerusalem Missionary Conference was held, the term had come into more common use. However, even this term raises objections in the minds of some, particularly in Asia, for it suggests a certain immaturity on their part, and seems to give the impression that leaders of these churches have not yet attained the maturity and wisdom of the older churches of the West. The latter, on the other hand, feel that the term "younger churches" implies youthful virility and a sense of hope and expectation for the future. No other more appropriate term has been suggested, and so we shall use it with the understanding, however, that it is recognized as not being a perfect way of describing these churches. Some churchmen use the term "sister churches," but its use has not become general.

During the nineteenth century it became evident that some congregations which had developed under the tutelage of missionaries were striving for their independence. Many of them now had their own pastors, but there was a feeling that the congregation had not achieved a life of its own. Members could not say that their church was theirs, when they could not support it financially.

The achievement of self-support has been a long, painful process, because of the low standard of living of the majority of the members of churches, and as funds from missionary sources were usually available. The simplest definition of self-support included paying the pastor's salary and the operating costs of the local church. Even with this minimum, J. Merle Davis, who contributed more than anyone else to the study of this aspect of the younger churches, estimated in 1945 that, after one hundred and fifty years, "of the 55,000 organized Protestant churches of mission lands, it is probable that not more than thirteen or fifteen percent are self-supporting."[1] Merle Davis insisted that the development of a congregation in relation to the economic and social structure of its environment required much more study and attention than had been hitherto devoted to it, and his own books on the subject made an outstanding contribution to what can be called the strategy of the Christian mission.

However, the idea of developing independent churches on the mission field, as self-governing, self-supporting, and self-propagating, is not a new one, although its translation into practice and its implications were not seen fully until modern times. Pierce Beaver maintains that Rufus Anderson, who served as secretary of the American Board of Commissioners for Foreign Missions from 1823 to 1861, was "the first genuine theoretician of the mission in the United States, and he dominated missionary thought for the next hundred years."[2] Anderson's ideas and mission policies greatly influenced Robert E. Speer, who served as Secretary of The Board of Foreign Missions of the Presbyterian Church in the U.S.A. from 1891 to 1937, and became one of the foremost missionary statesmen of his time.

Anderson's main concern was to avoid confusing Christianity with Christian civilization of the West and to base mission policy on the Pauline method of churches independent from foreign control. Dr. Anderson was a pioneer in advocating the importance of having indigenous churches, and central in his thinking was what we would call the missionary obligation of the church, or the church as a missionary community. Using "the three self's" formula, Anderson believed that a church which is self-supporting and self-governing from the beginning, will be self-propagating. "The apostolic model shows the relationship of the three factors."[3]

While Anderson was a pioneer in this type of mission policy as far as American missions overseas were concerned, Henry Venn, Secretary of the Church Missionary Society, held similar views and he formulated these in the following statement:

> Regarding the ultimate object of a mission, viewed under its ecclesiastical result, to be the settlement of a native church under native pastors upon a self-supporting system, it should be borne in mind that the progress of a mission mainly depends upon the training up and the location of native pastors; and that, as it has been happily expressed, the "euthanasia of a mission" takes place when a missionary, surrounded by well-trained native congregations under native pastors, is able to resign all pastoral work into their hands, and gradually relax his superintendence over the pastors themselves, till it insensibly ceases; and so the mission passes into a settled Christian community. Then the missionary and all missionary agencies should be transferred to the "regions beyond."[4]

There have been some among the missionary ranks who seemed willing that the younger churches should achieve self-support and that they should even be ultimately self-governing, but who drew the line at what came to be called "devolution," that is, the turning over of the churches to the national Christians. Richey Hogg expressed this difficulty well in these words: "Missionaries in conference invariably were concerned for the welfare of the younger churches: they should be self-governing and self-supporting. Yet independent status for these churches was always viewed as belonging to the future. When any enthusiast suggested devolution or missionary withdrawal as being shortly feasible, his voice was drowned out by a crescendoing chorus of caution. Missionary work was a long-time enterprise."[5]

At the Jerusalem meeting in 1928, Dr. Cheng Ching-Yi, speaking on behalf of the Chinese delegates, said that two views regarding the development of indigenous churches seemed to prevail. One was almost a Utopian view of the Christian movement. "Others look upon it with a great deal of doubt and misgiving, fearing that the young church in the mission field may go astray and create something that is quite different from historical Christianity, thus losing the essentials of the Christian religion."[6] Dr. Cheng felt that neither view was correct, and that the indigenous church was nothing more than a normal, healthy growth of the Christian church in any land. An indigenous church in China, as defined by the Chinese delegation at Jerusalem, was "a Christian Church that is best adapted to meet the religious needs of the Chinese people, most congenial to Chinese life and culture, and most effective in arousing in Chinese Christians the sense of responsibility."[7]

Changing Concept of Mission Policy and Strategy

The Jerusalem meeting of the International Missionary Council, held in 1928, marked the beginning of a new era of relationships between "older" and "younger" churches, and set the pattern for a reexamination of mission policy and strategy. Not only was prominence given to the two terms, "older churches" and "younger churches," but for the first time a major gathering turned its attention to the mission policy and strategy demanded by the new status of relationships be-

Rev. John Coventry Smith, D.D., LL.D., D.H.L. (Tokyo)

Born in Canada, 1903. Ordained by the Presbyterian Church U.S.A., and served as a missionary in Japan, 1929-1940. Secretary for East Asia, Board of Foreign Missions from 1948, and Associate General Secretary from 1952. Succeeded Dr. Leber as General Secretary of the Commission on Ecumenical Mission and Relations in 1959. Traveled to conferences in many parts of the world in the interests of the church and the ecumenical movement.

Rev. Theophilus M. Taylor, Ph.D.

Born in Cedarville, Ohio, 1909. Professor of New Testament Literature and Exegesis, Pittsburgh-Xenia Seminary, 1943-1962. Vice-Chairman, Committee Negotiating Three-Way Union, 1954. Secretary, Joint Drafting Committee, Joint Conference on Church Union of the Presbyterian Church U.S.A. and the United Presbyterian Church of North America. First Moderator, General Assembly, The United Presbyterian Church in the U.S.A. (1958), and first chairman of the Commission on Ecumenical Mission and Relations, 1958-1962. Elected Secretary of the General Council of the General Assembly (UPUSA) 1962.

Rev. Donald Black, D.D.

Born 1920. Ordained in the United
Presbyterian Church of North America
in 1945, and served in a pastorate
until 1954, when he became
Executive Secretary of the Board of
Foreign Missions. Associate General
Secretary, Commission on Ecumenical
Mission and Relations, 1958- .

tween what had been long regarded as "sending churches" and "receiving churches."

At the Edinburgh Conference of 1910 there were only a handful of "non-Western" delegates. Seventeen came from India, Burma, China, Japan, and Korea, but significantly enough, "these non-Occidentals . . . came under the quotas of Western missionary societies."[8]

The eighteen years between the Edinburgh Conference of 1910 and the one held at Jerusalem in 1928 evidently brought about great changes in the way the older churches regarded the younger churches. The call that went out in 1927 said, "The Jerusalem meeting will afford an opportunity for the first time for any considerable number of representative leaders of the younger churches which are the outcome of modern missionary efforts to meet in intimate fellowship with representatives of the older churches of Christendom, and to consider together how the relations between these churches may be made mutually most helpful."[9] At Jerusalem the delegates from Asia, Africa, and Latin America enjoyed equality with those from Europe and North America, both in status and in numbers. It was a new experience for delegates from fifty younger churches to feel that the findings and messages of the Conference were theirs, as much as those of the Western delegates, and also that their intellectual integrity and standing were given full recognition. This was a new development in the Christian missionary movement.

An entire section of the Jerusalem Conference was devoted to the study of the younger churches and the report of the discussions and findings fills one entire volume, *The Relation Between the Younger and Older Churches*.[10] Consideration was given to what is meant by terms such as "autonomous churches" and "indigenous churches," the relationship of missions and missionaries to indigenous churches, mutual relationships, finances, devolution, Christian unity, and missions.

If self-support and self-government of the younger churches were felt to be important, so was their independence. Dr. Cheng made it clear at the Jerusalem meeting that Christianity was "regarded by non-Christian Chinese as a foreign religion."[11] He, as well as other Oriental leaders, was anxious for Christianity to become "indigenized" or "naturalized" so that the Christian church could be truly the church.

While the younger churches sought independence, they did not want to sever all ties with the older churches, nor did they desire to live in isolation. Both at Jerusalem in 1928 and at Tambaram, India, in 1938, expression was given to the desire for missionaries to continue serving their churches as these assumed a greater share of the responsibilities of the work. However, it was understood that, increasingly, positions of authority in the church structure would be filled by "nationals." Younger church leaders felt that the Christian fellowship with the "mother church" depended to a large extent on continuing some form of relationship, and that Christian statesmanship would be required from the time of the Jerusalem Conference on, if these relationships of younger churches to older churches, and to missionaries, were to be worked out satisfactorily. Thus, the Jerusalem Conference brought into focus for the first time the whole question of the development of the younger churches, and the need to study new patterns of working together, and of mutuality, and to discover new forms of partnership.

Problems of self-support, leadership training, the creation of indigenous literature, and the role of educational institutions, all assumed new importance in the discussions at Jerusalem. Mission strategy became more church centered, since some of the younger churches were rapidly achieving maturity. Ten years later, at the Tambaram Conference in India, it was no accident that the theme of the Conference was the Worldwide Mission of the Church, and the consolidation of the younger churches as essential members of the worldwide Christian community. "Jerusalem symbolized uniquely the emergence within Protestant Christianity of a world church in process of achieving spiritual unity through devotion to a common commitment."[12]

At the Edinburgh Conference of 1910, there was a sprinkling of representatives from overseas, and they were there more as "show pieces" than anything else; at Jerusalem (1928) 25 percent of the delegates were from younger churches and were advisers on mission policy and strategy; at Madras (1938) half the delegates were from younger churches and were there as equals with churchmen from the West. In a generation, the younger churches had taken their rightful place alongside the older churches of the West in the total task of the Christian church.

With their enhanced status, the younger churches, far from desiring to isolate themselves, sought new relationships with other churches across the world. Through such bodies as the World Presbyterian Alliance and the World Council of Churches, younger Presbyterian churches have been enriched by contacts and acquaintance with leaders of other Christian churches.

The ecumenical movement and the shape of the ecumenical era began to be much more meaningful as the younger churches and the older churches worked out new patterns of relationships, and as younger churches took their place on a basis of equality and respect in the worldwide mission of the church.

The Mohonk Consultation

In the early 1950's The Board of Foreign Missions of the Presbyterian Church in the U.S.A. began to use the phrase "a new day." Board members and staff felt that it described the new situation which was developing among the younger churches as they began to take their place alongside the older churches in the carrying out of the mission of the church in a changing world situation. In a world fraught with despair and foreboding, Christian leaders of both older and younger churches saw the hand of God in the swiftly moving events of the time.

Significantly enough, the Board asked Dr. Richey Hogg, a Methodist professor of world Christianity in the Perkins School of Theology, Dallas, Texas, to write the official account of the Mohonk Consultation of 1956. This appeared in book form, with the title *New Day Dawning*. Those who attended the Mohonk Consultation experienced the exhilaration, the hope, and the brightness embodied in that phrase, "New Day Dawning."

At its meeting in February, 1955, The Board of Foreign Missions of the Presbyterian Church in the U.S.A. took an action of which the following is the first paragraph:

> In view of the "New Day" in the mission of the Church, it is the judgment of the Board that we must make clearer our objectives and relationships during the coming years, seeking counsel both at home and abroad.[13]

In preparation for the Consultation, the Board sent out five leading questions:

1. Looking ahead for five years beginning in the fall of 1956, what will be the *program* in each area with which the Board is associated, including the definition and emphasis of ecumenical mission, evangelistic advance, Christian education, theological training and the training and participation of lay church workers, medical work, scholarships, broadcasting and films, literature and literacy, industrial evangelism, the Christian approach to Communism, social services, etc.?

2. What should be the *relationship* of the Board and its missionaries and fraternal workers to the Church during the five-year period, and beyond?

3. What will be the best use of *present* American personnel and funds in the five-year program?

4. What will be the need for *additional* American personnel and funds, if available, during the five years, and how and where would they be used?

5. What will be the things that *must* be done, though some other things now being done or hoped for cannot be done, if the five-year program is not supported sufficiently from indigenous sources, by the Board, or by other world agencies?[14]

Answers to these questions were prepared on each field by leaders of the churches in consultation with the field representatives, who were asked to present the summaries at the Consultation.

It should be noted that the questions covered a wide area of considerations in two broad fields, program and relationships. The two are closely intertwined, because the program of the churches inevitably involved relationships between church leaders and missionaries, churches and the Board of Foreign Missions, as well as between the missionaries and the Board.

The answers to the five questions provided the Board with thorough documentation of existing programs as well as challenging proposals for long-range planning, as in partnership the Board and the younger churches prepared to move forward together.

Invitations went to fifteen churches overseas to send delegates, and the Board asked other nationals and some missionaries and fraternal workers to participate as consultants. Board and staff members, field representatives and executives of the General Council of the Presbyterian Church in the U.S.A. and other Presbyterian world mission boards completed the number in attendance. The Board of Foreign Missions of the United Presbyterian Church of North America was represented by its Executive Secretary, Dr. Donald Black.

It was not a large gathering, as world gatherings go, there being only 129 persons in attendance. They met for ten memorable days, from April 22 to May 1, 1956, at Lake Mohonk, New York. Twice before in the twentieth century, the Presbyterian U.S.A. Board of Foreign Missions had called conferences to discuss mission policy, once at Princeton, New Jersey, in 1920, when 106 missionaries were invited to confer with the Board and staff to face some of the opportunities in world evangelization, and again in Lakeville, Connecticut, in 1931, when seventy missionaries and nine nationals, from seven of the younger churches, met with fifty representatives of the church in the United States.

The Mohonk Consultation differed from these two previous meetings inasmuch as it was centered around the attendance of twenty-two nationals from fifteen younger churches. Word had gone out from the Board to these representatives, saying, "We want you to tell us what to do." This was a new element in mission board policy and strategy, and was appreciated by the overseas delegates as an essential part of the "new day."

The Mohonk meeting can be described as a consultation, rather than a conference. The Board report on the meeting said: "It was a working Consultation. Speeches were outlawed, except for the few which were extemporaneous, short and sweet. Discussion—the exchange of ideas—was the order of every day."[15]

A five-year program did come out of the Consultation, and, in time, proved of great value in the ongoing work of the churches concerned. New opportunities and avenues of service opened up as the delegates discussed the shape of things to come. Priorities and emphases were established in all fields, two of the foremost being evangelism beyond the church, and the recruiting, training, and use of leaders. During the study of the program of evangelism, the delegates noted that today more people can be reached with the gospel message in one hour than were reached in the whole of the first century of the Christian era. In addition to radio, television, films, and literature as modern means of mass communication, drama and fine arts were considered as of growing significance in communicating the gospel.

Besides these two priorities, two other emphases were highlighted: the undergirding of the life of the church through stewardship education and church extension and taking the gospel to the community through rural reconstruction, community services, cooperatives, and mobile medical agencies.

We have already noted that the Jerusalem meeting in 1928 gave special consideration to the whole question of relationships between the older and the younger churches, between the mission board as a sending agency and the church overseas as a receiving agency, as well as relations between missions and churches.

As far as the Presbyterian Church in the U.S.A. was concerned, the Mohonk Consultation witnessed the process of growing independence and achieving maturity on the part of the younger churches coming to fruition. The Consultation took decisive action concerning the integration of missionary work with that of indigenous churches around the world, so that these churches might increasingly determine policy and administer the work within their borders. Recognizing that while the situation differs from country to country, but that the desire for church-mission integration as a means of sharing in a common task existed in all fields, the Consultation recommended that "in every area concerned, the Church, the Mission and the Board plan together a step-by-step program whereby the goal will be achieved within a definite time limit, preferably within the five-year period under consideration by the Consultation."[16] It was recognized that while there was no uniform or final pattern of integration, there was a common goal. However, the Consultation also said that "this goal is not the sole criterion of achievement and maturity in the Christian Church. In fact, there are other aspects of the work that are more important. But at the present moment, under the conditions that exist across the world, we believe the time has come to demonstrate in a visible way our essential oneness by planning full integration."[17]

In retrospect, perhaps even more important than the programs that were discussed or planned was the effect which the Consultation had on those who participated in it. They experienced an enriching world

Christian fellowship, not only in the discussions themselves and in committee work but also in personal contacts, sharing insights, knowledge, and experience with those of other lands and races.

All those in attendance at the Consultation were impressed with the story told by Kyung Chik Han, pastor of a 4,500-member congregation in Seoul, Korea, but no one more than Dr. José Borges dos Santos, of Brazil. Both Han and Borges were Moderators of Presbyterian churches, both were bundles of human energy and spiritual dynamism, both had faced obstacles and problems of many kinds, and both came from countries where the Presbyterian church had experienced phenomenal growth. The Moderator of the Brazilian church, however, was not quite prepared for the kind of story he heard from the lips of the Korean Moderator.

Pastor Han did not tell his life story at Mohonk, but a few facts will help to fill in the picture of this extraordinary man. He was born into a non-Christian home in a village in North Korea. His father was a Confucianist, but he sent his son to a Christian school. There he was introduced to the Bible, and at the age of fourteen he became a Christian through the preaching of a Korean evangelist. Later he attended Union Christian College in Pyenyang for four years. He spent the next six years in the United States, first at the College of Emporia, Kansas, and later at Princeton Theological Seminary. Stricken with tuberculosis, young Han spent the next two years in the Albuquerque Sanatorium. Regaining his health, he decided to return to Korea. The depression had set in and Han had few resources, but he managed to work his way across the United States. Whenever he was helped in any manner by someone along the way, he took down the name and address of the person, and when he reached Korea he wrote over one hundred and twenty letters to thank all these people for their kindness and courtesies. This episode gives an insight into the character of the man. How many would have taken the trouble to do what he did? But Han loved people, and this is the key to his successful ministry.

Han taught in a Christian college for one year, and then became pastor of a Presbyterian church near the Yalu River in North Korea. By 1935, the congregation had grown to 1,500. Then came the Second World War, and Han was thrown into prison by the Japanese, for they considered him to be pro-American. He was later released from prison but forbidden to preach. After the war he went south with twenty other young people, and settled in an abandoned Shintu temple in Seoul. The little congregation of refugees began to grow rapidly, and by 1949 a church building was erected, the members contributing toward the cost with money, clothing, wedding rings, and the labor of their hands. The following year, Han was holding three services each Sunday and was engaged in many other community activities during the war. The Korean War came in 1950 and Seoul was overrun by the Communist army. Han's church was occupied by the troops and he himself fled south with other refugees. With the tides of war and armies alternately advancing and retreating, Han returned to Seoul, only to have to flee south once more. After the war ended he settled again in Seoul where, to his relief, he found that his church had been spared in the bombing of the city.

Han told the delegates at the Mohonk Consultation about the trials and tribulations of his people during the war years when their land was devastated and millions of people were rendered homeless. Five hundred pastors had lost their lives in 1950, and members of churches were scattered and impoverished. Before World War II, Seoul had thirty Christian churches, but not long after the Korean War there were four hundred. The Korean Church, in addition, maintained missionaries of its own in Japan, China, and Thailand, and three hundred Korean Christian chaplains were serving in the armed forces. Within a few years after the Korean War, the Presbyterian Church doubled its membership and in one seminary alone, Dr. Han told how five hundred students were supporting themselves. It is no wonder that the Moderator of the Presbyterian Church of Brazil, the leader himself of a great church, was impressed. "Borges thought he had known Christian devotion and sacrifice in Brazil. But Han's plain, factual statements were eye-openers. Striking, almost overwhelming, they were something new to report back to the churches in Brazil."[18]

The delegates from Latin America were much impressed as they listened to those who came to Mohonk representing united churches in Japan, the Philippines, India, Thailand, and Hong Kong. The Latin American churches had just established the Commission on Presbyterian Cooperation in Latin America, an important step leading to greater understanding among members of the Presbyterian family in that area. There was deep satisfaction that this much had been achieved, for misunderstandings and suspicions still existed, and in certain countries there was little desire for cooperation or for any relationship with the ecumenical movement. As the Latin Americans listened to the delegates from united churches in Asia, they were puzzled by two leading questions. In the first place, they wanted to know how much the former Presbyterian churches in the various countries had lost when they merged with other denominations. The answer was given in a simple and forthright manner—they lost nothing; by uniting with others they were enriched. In the second place, the Latin Americans wondered whether the Board of Foreign Missions in New York had not lost interest and withdrawn its support. On the contrary, they were assured, the Board had shown greater interest in the work than ever before. It was further explained that this was in line with Board policy as can be seen in the following paragraph:

> The historic policy of the Board as approved by the General Assembly has been (1) to build up independent national Churches holding the Reformed doctrine and the Presbyterian polity; (2) to encourage the union of all allied Protestant Churches in a given area into one Church of Christ, with its own statement of doctrine and polity. The Board reaffirms this policy and would encourage the missionaries to help make effective these unions and to seek still larger and more comprehensive unions of all Protestant Churches into one branch of the Ecumenical Church for each area.[19]

One of the delegates at the Consultation was Mrs. Kazuko Miyagi, an ordained pastor in the Japanese Church. According to Mrs. Miyagi, there were sixty women pastors in the church, and they could engage in the same kind of activities as the men. The question of women in the ministry provided some moments of good humor at the Consultation. Earlier in the discussions a pastor from Cameroun, Africa, had stressed the need for married couples rather than single men in the mission in Africa. Quoting Scripture, he said, "It is not good for man to be alone." When the question of women in the ministry was being discussed, Pastor Meye said that he understood that the matter was coming before the General Assembly of the Presbyterian Church in the U.S.A. and, as a commissioner from the Cameroun Synod,[20] he would speak in opposition to the proposal. Dr. Andrew Thakur Das gave the answer that provided appropriate humor for the occasion. "Why, Mr. Meye," he said, "if women are not ordained, there would be only men in the presbyteries—and *'it is not good for man to be alone.'* "[21]

The message of the Consultation on Ecumenical Mission at Mohonk contains this significant paragraph:

> In our consultation, as we have planned for the future, we have had borne in upon us this great truth: the privilege of a sending mission belongs to every Church, irrespective of nationality, culture or financial ability. Therefore, we call upon Churches everywhere to share both in carrying the Gospel across frontiers, and in welcoming fraternal workers from other Churches to help win their own peoples to Christ. We are committed to ecumenical mission.[22]

The Formation of the Commission

Having outlined briefly the rise of the younger churches, and having referred to the Mohonk Consultation as an evidence of this development in the Presbyterian family of churches across the world, we shall now consider the factors that led to the formation of the Commission on Ecumenical Mission and Relations.

Of great significance was the assistance that Presbyterians in the United States were able to render the churches which had suffered so much in a devastated war-torn Europe in World War II. In 1943 the General Assembly of the Presbyterian Church in the U.S.A. took the necessary steps to meet the need for restoration and rehabilitation in Europe after the war. A Restoration Fund was set up and, over a period of time, more than twenty-five million dollars was raised by the denomination.[23] Not only was there great destruction of property and loss of life in Europe during World War II, but the organizational life of the churches was also disrupted and weakened. The Board of Foreign Missions of the Presbyterian Church in the U.S.A. worked in close relationship with the Provisional Committee of the World Council of Churches, and after 1948, with the Council's Department of Reconstruction and Inter-Church Aid. The lives of many pastors and church workers were saved from starvation at the end of the war; transportation was furnished pastors to enable them to visit parishioners scattered during the war years; refugee or exiled pastors and church workers were helped financially; relief was brought to millions of displaced persons; church buildings were restored so that congregations could again worship together.

Americans, whose country had been spared the ravages of war, responded generously to meet the emergency in Europe. Not only were the relief funds of great importance, but also the spirit of reconciliation that enabled Christians belonging to countries so recently alienated by war to draw more closely together. During the war years the lines of communication among Christians in enemy countries had been kept open. Christian fellowship had been maintained. Funds had been raised by the International Missionary Council in allied countries to help "orphaned churches," which had formerly been related to German mission agencies, to maintain their work. The spirit of reconciliation among Christian churches played a leading role in healing the wounds of war. However, the problems of administering relief were not solved overnight; millions of refugees were living in despair and misery for several years after the war. The experience of Christians from many lands, working together to restore a war-torn Europe, was an important factor leading to the organization of the World Council of Churches. There was visible proof that the churches could act together, transcending their denominational differences.

The Board of Foreign Missions of the Presbyterian Church in the U.S.A. was so impressed by the importance of the new form of interchurch service that in 1949, while it retained the legal name of the Board, it described its task as "Foreign Missions and Overseas Interchurch Service" on its letterhead. Relationships between the Board and Protestant churches in Europe were broadened to include the sending of carefully selected personnel for specific tasks. Dr. Benjamin Bush was named as the Board's representative in Europe to coordinate these relationships with the Reformed churches in France, Belgium, Hungary, and Czechoslovakia, the Waldensian Church in Italy, the German Evangelical Church, and the mission work in Spain and Portugal.

Dr. Bush's visiting card gave his title as "a Secretary of The Board of Foreign Missions of the Presbyterian Church in the U.S.A.," and when he first visited people at the headquarters of the Reformed Church of France, their initial impulse was to refer him to the Paris

Mission Society. However, his assignment was not that of a mission board executive in a mission land, in the accepted sense of the term. Here were old, established ecclesiastical bodies, and the usual church-mission relationship was out of place. The relationship was a fraternal one between one church and another. Thus it was necessary to find a term that would describe those who were sent by The Board of Foreign Missions of the Presbyterian Church in the U.S.A. to help in the work of restoring and rehabilitating the disrupted and disorganized church life of long-established church bodies. The term was "fraternal worker."

During the 1950's, the integration of missions with churches took place in a number of Asian countries formerly regarded as mission lands, and the term "fraternal worker" was applied to personnel of the Board of Foreign Missions working with those churches. Later on, the term was used generally in all fields. There were some who felt it was a mistake to discard the time-honored designation of "missionary." The term had acquired a deep emotional and evangelistic symbolism over the decades, and it was only natural that, for some who were strongly attached to the great missionary enterprise, to discontinue the use of the term "missionary" was unthinkable. How could you have a missionary enterprise without missionaries? Those who would ask this question, however, fail to recognize the realities of the new day, and especially the great event of our time—perhaps the greatest —namely, the emergence of the worldwide Christian community and the existence of self-supporting, self-governing, and self-propagating churches in traditionally mission lands.

A Christian missionary is one who is sent, one who has a mission to preach the gospel. A foreign missionary was one who was sent to a foreign country with just such a purpose. When missionaries first went out from the United States, they were preachers and teachers, organizers and administrators. Then churches were established, preachers were trained; the number of church leaders capable of administering church affairs increased. In time, therefore, both the role and the relationship of the missionaries changed. It is true that a person commissioned by the United Presbyterian Church is one who is sent to another country, but his assignment, when he arrives, is different from that of a missionary, and his relationship is to a church body rather than to a mission. Interestingly enough, in its commissioning service for new personnel going overseas the Commission uses both terms, "missionaries" and "fraternal workers." Perhaps it is not stretching terminology too much to say that a person is commissioned as a missionary, but arrives on the field as a fraternal worker.

We have seen how the immediate postwar period occasioned the addition of a phrase to describe the Board's task, namely, ". . . and Overseas Interchurch Service," and that the term "fraternal worker" was used to designate personnel who participated in the work of restoration in an ecumenical relationship with the churches in Europe. We have seen, also, that before long, the term "fraternal workers" began to be used in other areas as well, in Asia, Africa, the Middle East, and Latin America, along with the term "missionary."

Another development proved to be significant. The Christian missionary enterprise was no longer viewed as only a thrust from west to east. To symbolize this additional direction of missionary activity, The Board of Foreign Missions of the Presbyterian Church in the U.S.A. made it possible for personnel to come as fraternal workers from France, Germany, the Philippines, India, Japan, and Brazil to the United States, some to engage in a ministry in a local church, others to serve on the staff of the Board of Foreign Missions.

In the early 1950's there was a growing feeling among Board members and staff that the name "Board of Foreign Missions" was no longer adequate to describe the agency of the Presbyterian Church because of the changes in the world situation since World War II.

The 1954 General Assembly of the Presbyterian Church in the U.S.A. approved "the request of the Board that its General Secretary [Dr. Charles T. Leber] be permitted to convey to the General Assembly something of the new conception of the Board's work [described in the leaflet A New Day Has Come], and the history of its search for a name adequate to that conception, especially stressing the relationship of the mission of the church to the ecumenical movement. The Board invites suggestions from churches as to a new name, particularly as to the effectiveness and adequacy of the term 'The Ecumenical Mission.' "[24] A mimeographed paper called "Re: A New Name for the Foreign Board," issued by the Board of Foreign Missions in 1955, said:

> The historic Christian mission has achieved a global status. With
> a Church now rooted in every nation, with few exceptions, each

Church making its contribution to the other and to the other's
nation, the center of gravity moves from "foreign missions" to the
ecumenical Church in a dynamic revolutionary mission. "Foreign"
and "missions" are outdated. The ecumenical mission of the
Church is united Christian faith and love in action in this new
day, each Church participating according to its genius and resources. Christian advance no longer is measured by the number
of American or Western missionaries sent, and they in turn do
not presume educational and spiritual superiority to Christians of
other lands. Our American Church will send out more workers,
far more than now, but those who represent us are in new ecumenical relationships. Christian workers go from Church to
Church across the world. Some come to the U.S. from overseas.
The Christian mission is no longer only a one-way, horizontal
thrust from West to East. It is the united building of the world
Christian community in which Christian workers representing various Churches and nations are advancing together toward evangelizing both functional and geographical areas. How shall we
think and speak of the mission of the Church today? *Ecumenical*
is the word.

In 1955 the Board voted to use the term "Ecumenical Mission" on its
letterhead, retaining, however, the legal name of the Board of Foreign
Missions.

The General Assembly of 1956 voted to delay any action on the
proposed change, in view of special circumstances involving "a re-
study of the structure and relationships of the Board of Foreign
Missions."[25] In November, 1956, the Board voted to recommend to the
General Assembly that the name of the Board be changed to "Board
of Ecumenical Mission of the Presbyterian Church in the U.S.A."

In April, 1957, the Board voted that in the event that the proposed
structure paper prepared by the Board were not approved by the
Standing Committee on Foreign Missions, the President and General
Secretary of the Board be allowed to present the request to the Gen-
eral Assembly that the name be changed to "Board of Ecumenical
Mission of the Presbyterian Church in the U.S.A."

In May, 1957, the General Assembly requested the Stated Clerk,
the Board of Foreign Missions, and the Permanent Commission on
Interchurch Relations to initiate jointly such procedures as would lead
to the establishment of a commission to be known as the "Commission
on Ecumenical Mission and Relations."

One question that arose was whether the united church, which was soon to be formed, should have one agency dealing with work overseas, which in the light of recent developments meant a relationship with autonomous church bodies, and at the same time have several committees whose task was that of relating the church with other ecclesiastical bodies and with ecumenical bodies. In other words, the question of interchurch relations came up for fresh discussion in the setting of an emerging united church body. The church in the late 1950's was seen as engaging in mission with other churches across the world, but was also conscious of the fact that this very mission involved ever-increasing and vital relationships which could be described as ecumenical. The task was not only one of ecumenical mission, but also of ecumenical relationships as well, and the two were closely related. In the meantime, plans for the merging of the two churches (the Presbyterian Church in the U.S.A. and the United Presbyterian Church of North America) at Pittsburgh in 1958 were maturing. As we pointed out elsewhere, rather than change the names of the Boards of Foreign Missions of the two churches, an entirely new body was created, the Commission on Ecumenical Mission and Relations.

At its meeting on April 21-22, 1958, The Board of Foreign Missions of the Presbyterian Church in the U.S.A., on recommendation of the Special Committee on Consolidation, voted: "That the name of this Board be changed to 'Commission on Ecumenical Mission and Relations of The United Presbyterian Church in the United States of America.'"[26] The phrase "the name of the Board be changed" had to be used in order to fulfill legal requirements. The Board action also stated that the change would not become effective unless and until the change of name were approved by the General Assembly. In May, 1958, the General Assembly approved the establishment of the Commission on Ecumenical Mission and Relations.[27]

Five agencies came together at Pittsburgh in 1958 to form the new body, the Commission on Ecumenical Mission and Relations. They were: the Board of Foreign Missions and the Permanent Commission on Interchurch Relations of the Presbyterian Church in the U.S.A.; the Board of Foreign Missions, the Permanent Committee on Inter-Church Relations; and the Committee on Ecumenical Affairs of the United Presbyterian Church of North America.

Much thinking, study, and planning went into the formation of the

Commission, and many executives of the five agencies were involved in this process. It would be possible to name many who from the beginning have made an outstanding contribution to the missionary work of the two former boards, and thus laid an essential foundation for the development leading up to the union of the two churches and the formation of the Commission on Ecumenical Mission and Relations in 1958. A statement that was approved by the General Assembly at which these acts were consummated begins with the following significant words: "By the gracious providence of Almighty God, we who formerly were two Churches of the same tradition are no longer two but one. We give heartfelt thanks to God for those who have prayed and labored for this day, many of whom, having died, saw its fulfillment only from afar."[28]

Names such as the Honorable Walter Lowrie and his son, John C. Lowrie, are written indelibly in the annals of foreign missions. Walter Lowrie was the first Secretary of The Board of Foreign Missions of the Presbyterian Church in the U.S.A., serving from 1837 to 1868. His son, John C. Lowrie, as was noted earlier in this book, served first as a missionary in India under the Western Foreign Missionary Society from 1833 to 1836, when ill health forced him to leave. In 1838 he joined the staff of the Board and served for a period of fifty-four years, until 1891.

In more recent times, two men stand out for their extraordinary service, not only to foreign missions under the Presbyterian Board, but also to the missionary enterprise in general. The first of these was Robert E. Speer, who joined the staff of the Board of Foreign Missions in 1891 as a successor to John C. Lowrie. Dr. Speer served the Board for forty-six years. He was one of the greatest and most eloquent exponents of foreign missions in the modern world. A onetime Moderator of the General Assembly of his church, a world traveler, renowned orator, and author or editor of sixty-seven books, Dr. Speer was regarded by his contemporaries as preeminent in his day as a missionary statesman and an administrator, but more especially as a man of Christian integrity and character, and one who could sway great audiences and lead many to give their lives for full-time Christian service in the mission of the church.

In 1895, four years after Dr. Speer joined the staff of the Board of

Foreign Missions, Dr. Arthur Judson Brown became one of its secretaries. From that time on, he and Dr. Speer served as senior secretaries of the Board for more than three decades. Born before the Civil War, Dr. Brown lived to the ripe age of 106 and was acclaimed not only as one of the great missionary figures of his day but also as one of the architects of the ecumenical movement. As we have noted already, Dr. Brown was the secretary of the great Ecumenical Conference of 1900. Dr. Speer and Dr. Brown, as senior secretaries of The Board of Foreign Missions of the Presbyterian Church in the U.S.A., guided its destinies for nearly half a century, putting the imprint of their personalities on the Board during the most formative period of its history.

While it is true that neither Dr. Speer nor Dr. Brown used the word "ecumenical" with any frequency, both were completely dedicated to interdenominational cooperation and to the ideal of unity for mission. Truly, it can be said that these two extraordinary statesmen by their own efforts helped lay the foundations of the ecumenical movement of the twentieth century.

During the crucial 1950's, four men played a decisive role in bringing the Commission into being. They were Dr. John A. Mackay, the philosopher; Dr. Charles T. Leber, the prophet of the "new day" and the man of vision and drive; Dr. John Coventry Smith, the negotiator; and Dr. Donald Black, the administrator.

Dr. John A. Mackay, then President of Princeton Theological Seminary, was also president of The Board of Foreign Missions of the Presbyterian Church in the U.S.A. until 1951, and continued as a member of the Board for some years afterward. As president of the International Missionary Council from 1947 until 1958, and president of the World Presbyterian Alliance from 1954 to 1959, Dr. Mackay took part in discussions on the nature of the ecumenical movement and was influential in the thinking of many ecumenical leaders.

In an address he gave at a meeting of the Foreign Missions Conference of North America in Atlantic City, New Jersey, in 1928, Dr. Mackay spoke of the word "ecumenical" as used by Count Keyserling, and gave it a spiritual interpretation. Then, during the 1930's, at the Conference on Church, Community and State of 1937, he used it in such a way that he was instrumental in popularizing the word in the sense in which it is now used in ecclesiastical and missionary circles.

In his book, *Ecumenics: The Science of the Church Universal,* Dr. Mackay says that "it [the Oxford Conference of 1937] restored to currency the term 'ecumenical,' which it enriched with a new connotation that embraced the mission of the Church and the unity of the Church as integral facets of the 'Ecumenical Movement.' "[29]

We have also noted that an event of great significance in ecumenical history was the merger of the International Missionary Council and the World Council of Churches at New Delhi in 1961.

Over a period of many years, and in relation to the several organizations in which he played a leading role, Dr. Mackay never ceased to emphasize the centrality of the mission of the church in the ecumenical movement, and that church unity in itself was not enough. During the discussions in The Board of Foreign Missions of the Presbyterian Church in the U.S.A., the voice of Dr. Mackay was a prophetic one, and he provided much of the philosophical thinking that underlay the plans to create the new body which emerged in 1958 as the Commission on Ecumenical Mission and Relations.

Dr. Charles T. Leber, General Secretary of The Board of Foreign Missions of the Presbyterian Church in the U.S.A., and, until his death in 1959, the first General Secretary of the Commission, was a man of vision and dynamic personality, a man with deep evangelistic commitment. It is probably true to say that no one had more to do with the creation of the Commission than he did. During the last ten or twelve years of his life, the "ecumenical" became his major passion, the guiding star of all his thinking.

The dominating purpose of his life was to help the church to look ahead and anticipate developments in the world. If anyone lived with his eye on the future, it was Charles T. Leber. Rather than wait for things to happen, and then have the church respond to the situation in some improvised way, he tried to foresee events and trends, and urged the church as a missionary agency to prepare boldly and adequately. Like Dr. Mackay, he was personally involved in many ecumenical organizations, including the World Council of Churches, the International Missionary Council, the National Council of Churches, and the World Presbyterian Alliance. In all of these he gave dynamic leadership and inspiration for the main task, the mission of the church in the world today.

Dr. Leber never actually served on the field as a missionary of the Board, but he traveled widely in all continents and, being a missionary at heart, entered dynamically into the life and thought of the church in country after country.

An incident that occurred in the early part of Dr. Leber's career as a Board executive throws light on his personality, his faith, and his unconquerable spirit. In 1936, soon after he became a member of the staff, Dr. Leber accompanied his senior colleague, Dr. Cleland B. McAfee, on a visit to the Japanese consul in New York. Dr. McAfee had responsibility for the work in Japan and Dr. Leber was about to succeed him. Dr. Leber was unfamiliar with Japanese psychology and knew very little about the "shrine question" which, at that time, was a matter of deep concern to the church. "We found the little Japanese official in his swank suite, high up over Central Park. He was very gracious in his reception, but behind the cordial exterior one could feel austere severity. . . . As the interview progressed, my fascination turned to brooding. What power, pomp and circumstance the . . . Japanese [official] symbolized. . . . I thought of how meager the material resources were which supported my friend and myself in contrast to the wealth and might of empire behind the Japanese. What could so little do in its feeble impact upon so much? . . . Had I foolishly thrown my life into futility? A flood of doubts swept over me . . . made me feel very, very small."[30]

Upon the termination of the visit, Dr. Leber, full of foreboding and misgivings, went to a lunch counter at a nearby hotel. As he was leaving, he noticed a Japanese in a corner of the restaurant and he stopped to speak to him. He was Toyohiko Kagawa, a leader already known around the world. In those few moments with this great, yet humble Christian, Dr. Leber rediscovered something that was confirmed innumerable times later, namely, that "the only hope for Japan, America, or the world is in the faith which made and holds Kagawa. . . . Only the Kingdom of God, by the redeeming, creative force of the Christian mission which brought forth Kagawa will produce the new man and the good society which are a prerequisite to a better day."[31]

Thus it was, at a later date, in an article published just before the World Council of Churches Assembly at Evanston in 1954, that Dr.

Leber enunciated his own fundamental faith when he wrote: "The ecumenical movement and the missionary enterprise are essentially one and the same. The proof of this unity in history is illustrated by the origin of the ecumenical movement. It did not emerge as something separate, but as the inevitable development of missionary life and work."[32]

Dr. Leber addressed hundreds of audiences across the United States on the theme of the ecumenical mission of the church, and never tired of telling them about the great fact of our time, namely, that the Christian mission has achieved global status, that there is an organized Christian church in all except three countries, each church making its contribution to the others, so much so that the center of gravity has shifted from "foreign missions" to the ecumenical church in a revolutionary world. He reminded his audience that Christian churches across the world are looking to one another within the context of a new, dynamic "togetherness" in mission. In the early 1950's, Dr. Leber referred to this as the "new day"; later on he called it the ecumenical mission of the church.

Dr. Leber was a dynamic personality, with deep commitment to the mission of the church and to the cause of Christ in a confused, bewildered world. He also had a sense of the dramatic. In his writings and addresses he would make a liberal use of poetry, and at the Mohonk Consultation in 1956, it was he who proposed that the Board make much more use of drama and the fine arts in the presentation of the gospel. Incidents during his travels and situations at General Assembly meetings lent themselves to dramatization. At the first General Assembly of The United Presbyterian Church in the U.S.A. (1958), the moderators of Presbyterian churches from five countries, Korea, Cameroun, Brazil, Pakistan, and Egypt, stood on the platform alongside Dr. Theophilus Taylor, Moderator of that memorable General Assembly. The few words spoken by the moderators from overseas had to be interpreted into English, but what they said was not so dramatic as the fact that they were there as a living demonstration of the worldwide church of Jesus Christ. In his accustomed way of expressing himself, Dr. Leber said, "Oh, the immeasurable miracle of the world-wide Christian Church in ecumenical mission!"[33]

At the Mohonk Consultation in 1956, Dr. Leber particularly emphasized the value of drama in the presentation of the gospel, and his continuing interest during the years which followed the Consultation was largely responsible for the establishment of the Barn Playhouse at Stony Point, New York, in 1959. The Playhouse, which was inaugurated only two months before Dr. Leber's death, is a reminder of his devotion to drama as a means of presenting Christian truth. Sponsored by the Commission on Ecumenical Mission and Relations, the Barn Playhouse offers training in dramatic presentation to both missionaries and Christian workers overseas. During the first seven years of its existence, the Barn Playhouse produced fifty-five plays.

With his keen sense of the dramatic, his deep compassion for suffering humanity, and a recognition of the evils of social injustice, he often spoke of the need for the Christian church to understand and further what he called the Christian revolution. "The world's deepest tragedy," he said, "is that we turn to war to bring about change because we will not use the better way. If only we would make predominant the Christian revolution."[34] He referred to the burning demands of freedom, justice, equality, brotherhood, and of the fierce or latent fires of racial tensions, economic slavery, religious persecution, and the plight of millions of refugees.

As he traveled throughout war-torn Europe after World War II, or visited primitive restless Africa with all its misery and injustice, or moved about among the teeming millions of India, Hong Kong, and the Philippines, or when he visited the vast interior of Brazil, Dr. Leber's heart was moved with compassion by what he saw and heard, and this gave a sense of urgency to the fulfillment of the Christian mission here and now, and to making the gospel relevant to human need, both spiritual and material.

Dr. Leber ended his days as he would have wished to do, had he been given the choice. While attending a meeting of the World Presbyterian Alliance in São Paulo, Brazil, in July, 1959, he passed away. There in that great city, where his voice had been heard a number of times over the years, the voices of representatives from churches in many countries around the world were raised in loving tribute to one who for them symbolized the new day and the advent of the ecumenical mission of the church.

The mantle of the General Secretary of the Commission on Ecu-

menical Mission and Relations fell on Dr. Leber's close associate over
the years, Dr. John Coventry Smith. Different in temperament and
gifts, but equal in his dedication to the ecumenical ideal, Dr. Smith
is the negotiator type, with a talent for quiet but effective persuasion.
During the crucial years of the 1950's, Dr. Smith was able to feel the
pulse of the churches in many lands across the world, and particularly
in representative gatherings of churchmen as they met to discuss their
plans and hopes for the future. While attending a long session at one
of these meetings, Dr. Smith would set down his impressions in precise and unmistakable language, with the main purpose of keeping his
colleagues in New York and in other areas informed of the thinking
of Christians in different countries. In addition to these gleanings and
impressions from church gatherings across the world, Dr. Smith related the work of the church, as it carries out its mission, to the
revolutionary social upheaval of our times, and sought to interpret
both in terms of the Biblical revelation. He sensed the interrelatedness
of what was happening in the field of science and technology, in
areas of racial tensions and social injustice, the swiftly moving cur-
rents of thought and change in Latin America, Africa, and Asia, as
well as the United States. It was all part of a whole within God's
purpose in history, and for Dr. Smith this was related to the task of
the Commission in its conception of ecumenical mission and ecumenical relations.

The coming of the ecumenical era brought new challenges and
problems in church-mission relations, in the best use of the Commission's funds and personnel, and Dr. Smith's experience as a missionary
for many years in Japan helped the newly formed Commission to reach
wise decisions in policy and strategy.

Representing the Board of Foreign Missions of the United Presbyterian Church of North America was its executive secretary, Dr. Donald Black. With his gifts as an administrator, Dr. Black took part in
the discussions and planning that led to the formation of the Commission on Ecumenical Mission and Relations, a process that required
a firsthand and detailed knowledge of all that was represented in the
Board of Foreign Missions, of which he was the chief executive, and
of the committees on ecumenical affairs and interchurch relations. Dr.
Black's ability to think through a problem and come up with an answer

was very valuable in this difficult process in which five bodies were merged into one.

For some time before the formation of the Commission in 1958, the two boards of foreign missions met simultaneously, Dr. Peter K. Emmons, President of The Board of Foreign Missions of the Presbyterian Church in the U.S.A., and Dr. Roy E. Grace, President of the Board of Foreign Missions of the United Presbyterian Church of North America, serving as cochairmen. The joint meeting served the purpose of allowing the Board members and staff of the two bodies to become mutually acquainted, and to know each other's fields.

This period of "courtship" was a time of happy fellowship, and the character and experience of the two chairmen contributed to this in no small degree. Both were pastors of large churches and had many years of experience in their respective boards of foreign missions, but also, both had a fine sense of humor, and this helped to smooth out any misunderstandings and difficulties.

In the formulation of plans for establishing the Commission, a process involving seemingly endless discussions of details of organization and one requiring imagination and creativity, three men were largely reponsible over a period of years. They were Dr. Charles T. Leber, whom we have already mentioned, Dr. Eugene Carson Blake, the Stated Clerk of the General Assembly, and Dr. Ralph Waldo Lloyd, chairman of the Permanent Commission on Interchurch Relations of the Presbyterian Church in the U.S.A.

If Dr. Mackay was the philosopher and Dr. Leber the prophet of the new day, Dr. Blake was the man who combined thought and action in such a way as to enable him to envisage the necessary structural adjustments in the denomination.[35]

"Foreign missions," it was agreed by all these leaders, belonged to an era that was coming to an end; a "new day" was dawning. Previously, these leaders had talked of unity and mission as being imperatives in the life of the Christian church. Now, they referred to unity *in* mission, and unity *for* mission. The implications of these new concepts were very great, and if the Presbyterian Church in the U.S.A. (which had not yet united with the United Presbyterian Church of North America) were to make a truly ecumenical witness in the world, then some kind of reorganization was essential. The old wineskin of structure could not contain the new wine of an entirely new concept. It was at this point that Dr. Blake was able to render a unique contribution, not only due to his position in the church and his background of experience in ecclesiastical affairs, but also because of his intuitive grasp of a situation. He sensed the dimensions of the present in order to speed the day of realization of new ideas and concepts. In the Presbyterian Church in the U.S.A., two bodies and an office were involved, the Board of Foreign Missions, the Permanent Commission on Interchurch Relations, and the Office of the Stated Clerk. Each of these had separate functions, and it appeared at first that they were not preparing to give them up. Fears were entertained by some that the Board of Foreign Missions would absorb Interchurch Relations. Others were afraid that Interchurch Relations would predominate and missionary zeal would diminish. Would the correspondence concerning interchurch relations continue to be carried on in the Office of the Stated Clerk? These were some of the questions which had to be answered, and there were others.

Dr. Leber's role as the prophet of the new day was widely recognized. He proclaimed the ecumenical dimensions of the mission of the church with passion and zeal across the United States and around the world. Not so well known is the role of Dr. Blake in the mid-1950's in the vital process of formulating plans, exploring with representatives of different groups divergent viewpoints on many matters, and attempting syntheses of these. Organizational charts and plans were often scratched on hotel stationery as meetings or consultations consumed many long hours.

Before 1954, informal discussions had taken place concerning the adjustments that would be necessary in a new day, and the General Council, the ad interim body of the General Assembly of the Presbyterian Church in the U.S.A., authorized the Board of Foreign Missions, the Permanent Commission on Interchurch Relations, and the Office of the Stated Clerk to explore possibilities of more adequate cooperation with churches overseas.

In the series of consultations and planning conferences prior to the formation of the Commission on Ecumenical Mission and Relations, the Rev. Dr. Ralph Waldo Lloyd represented the interests of the Permanent Commission on Interchurch Relations. Dr. Lloyd was chairman of this body, and of its predecessor, the Department of Church Cooperation and Union, from 1941 to the union of the churches in 1958. He was Moderator of the General Assembly of the Presbyterian Church in the U.S.A. in 1954-1955; he was North American Secretary of the World Presbyterian Alliance (from 1951 to 1959), and its president from 1959 to 1964. He served on the General Board of the National Council of Churches from 1950 to 1960, and on the Central Committee of the World Council of Churches from 1951 to 1961. During all these years he was President of Maryville College, a Presbyterian-related institution in Maryville, Tennessee. Thus, it can be said that Dr. Lloyd was well qualified to bring to the discussions on the formation of the Commission on Ecumenical Mission and Relations the necessary insight, knowledge, and experience on a variety of issues.

The origin of the Permanent Commission on Interchurch Relations of the Presbyterian Church in the U.S.A. goes back to 1903, the year in which the General Assembly authorized the Moderator to constitute "a Committee of Seven, four ministers and three elders . . . to consider the whole question of cooperation, confederation, and consolidation with other churches . . . and that they be instructed to enter into correspondence with any Churches of the Reformed family with whom, in the judgment of the Committee, such correspondence would be likely to promote closer relations."[36] This was the first time it appears that a church agency in the United States had ever been given such an assignment.

This body, which was appointed in 1903, was called the Special Committee on Church Cooperation and Union, and it served the church as such until 1923, when it became the Department of Church Cooperation and Union of the Office of the General Assembly. The Department was composed of twelve ministers and six ruling elders, elected by the General Assembly for a term of three years, the Moderator and the Stated Clerk being members ex officio, and it continued under this name and form until 1949, when the Permanent Commission on Interchurch Relations was created by the General Assembly to replace the former Department. It was provided that members could be elected by the General Assembly (in three classes of six each) and three would be members ex officio, the Moderator, the Stated Clerk, and the Secretary of the General Council.

During the period from 1903 to 1958, four distinguished church-men served as chairmen of this body, the Rev. Dr. William Henry Roberts (Stated Clerk of the General Assembly), from 1903 to 1920; President J. Ross Stevenson (Princeton Theological Seminary), from 1920 to 1939; the Rev. Dr. Paul C. Johnston (Pastor, Third Presbyterian Church, Rochester, New York), from 1939 to 1941; and President Ralph Waldo Lloyd (Maryville College, Tennessee), from 1941 to 1958. For more than three decades, until 1958, the Stated Clerk of the General Assembly served as Secretary (Dr. Lewis S. Mudge, Dr. William B. Pugh, Dr. Eugene Carson Blake).

The responsibilities of the Permanent Commission on Interchurch Relations included not only routine interchurch business and presentation to the General Assembly of fraternal delegates from other bodies, but also nomination of delegates and representatives to ecumenical and interchurch bodies such as the World Presbyterian Alliance, the World Council of Churches, the National Council of the Churches of Christ, and the American Bible Society, and delegates to ecumenical conferences; transmitting reports of ecumenical and interchurch bodies and conferences to the General Assembly; recommending policies and participation in interchurch and ecumenical programs at home and abroad; the handling of church cooperation and union approaches, conversations, and negotiations with other churches.

Obviously, this wide range of responsibilities had to be considered most carefully, and the proposal to transfer them to the Commission on Ecumenical Mission and Relations, then in process of formation, entailed new organizational relationships and alignments. It soon became apparent during the period of discussions that such a transfer meant that the new body would have to be radically different from a Board of Foreign Missions.

A similar set of organizational problems existed in the United Presbyterian Church of North America, although, in that denomination, organized development in this area had been less emphasized and more limited responsibilities had been divided between two bodies, the Permanent Committee on Inter-Church Relations and the Committee on Ecumenical Affairs.

The Minutes of the United Presbyterian General Assembly of 1910 refer to a "Committee on Closer Relations with the Presbyterian Church." In its report to the General Assembly, the Committee made it clear that "it was not authorized to consider the subject of organic union with the Presbyterian Church" and that the "agitation of the question in the United Presbyterian Church would do harm."[37] This General Assembly of 1910 proceeded to appoint a Permanent Committee on Church Relations to which would be referred "all questions of closer relations and co-operation with all evangelical Churches, and of union with such Churches as may seek union on satisfactory terms."[38] Members of the Committee included the officers of the General Assembly, the Corresponding Secretaries of Foreign Missions, Home Missions, Freedmen's Missions, Church Extension, Education, and a member of the Board of Publication and Sabbath Schools.

In 1929 the United Presbyterian General Assembly set up a Committee on Presbyterian Unity, and invited other bodies in the Presbyterian family to appoint similar committees to consider the possibility of one Presbyterian church. The Committee was dismissed by the General Assembly of 1934.

In 1939 the General Assembly authorized the appointment of a Permanent Committee on Church Relationships, the Committee to consist of five members. In 1943 the membership of this Committee was increased to seven, and it was instructed "(1) to keep in touch with movements toward closer relationship of all churches of Christ; (2) to keep in touch with movements toward closer relationship of churches of the Presbyterian order, especially the plan of reunion of the Presbyterian Church U.S.A. and the Presbyterian Church U.S."[39]

In 1955 the name of this Committee was changed to a Permanent Committee on Inter-Church Relations, and the number of members increased to nine. Over the years, two men served as chairman of this Committee, President Robert W. Gibson (Monmouth College, Illinois) for eight years, and the Rev. Dr. Theophilus M. Taylor

(Professor at Pittsburgh-Xenia Theological Seminary) for two years. Both of these men played an important role in the negotiations leading to the union of 1958.

The Committee on Ecumenical Affairs was first appointed by the General Assembly of the United Presbyterian Church of North America in 1951. As background for the appointment of this Committee, the Minutes of the General Assembly that year made reference to the "numerous libelous charges against the theological and moral integrity of the World Council, its officers, and its member Churches."[40] The General Assembly proceeded to appoint the Committee on Ecumenical Affairs, because of the increasing number of matters of ecumenical significance, the need for liaison with bodies such as the World Presbyterian Alliance and the World Council of Churches, and the desirability of creating a deeper consciousness of the work and concerns of the worldwide church of Jesus Christ. The Committee was composed of the General Assembly's representatives on the National Council of Churches, the World Presbyterian Alliance, the World Council of Churches, Church World Service, and the Committee on Church Relations. In all there were eleven members on the Committee.

The interests and responsibilities of these two bodies, the Permanent Committee on Inter-Church Relations and the Committee on Ecumenical Affairs, had to be coordinated, as did similar interests of the Presbyterian Church in the U.S.A., within the new structure, and all of this demanded real statesmanship.

In 1958 the General Assembly of The United Presbyterian Church in the U.S.A. set up a Committee on Church Union, with limited functions. In its report to the General Assembly of 1963, the Committee on Church Union recommended that it merge with the Commission on Ecumenical Mission and Relations. The Committee further suggested that the Division of Relations of the Commission set up a committee whose responsibility would be to cultivate other denominations in order to create a climate favorable to church union, and to make appropriate recommendations concerning the implementation of union negotiations. In 1963 the Committee on Church Union merged with the Commission on Ecumenical Mission and Relations, members of the 1964 and 1965 classes of the former becoming members of the latter.

The Meaning of the Name of the Commission

The name of the Commission contains four key words, "commission," "ecumenical," "mission," and "relations," and we shall comment on the significance of each of them.

"Commission." As discussions concerning the creation of a new body progressed, it soon became apparent that the term "board" was no longer adequate. As in the secular world, where control centers in a group of persons charged with making decisions affecting the operations of a concern, so it was, by analogy, in the missionary world. Boards were formed by ecclesiastical bodies in order to be responsible for, and to make the decisions concerning, the operations related to the missionary enterprise abroad. The term "commission" connotes a definite overall responsibility being given, or committed, to a group of persons by the church, but in no sense does it imply that they are to take decisions for the work formerly carried out by missions, or missionaries, now in the hands of autonomous churches overseas. "A 'Commission' is a body, a group of people, who are entrusted with something of very great importance. It becomes the function of a 'commission' to fulfill a trust faithfully and not simply to legislate or to carry out actions."[41]

"Ecumenical." The use of the word "foreign" in the name "Board of Foreign Missions" belongs to an era that has gone, an era usually referred to as the colonial period. In a dual sense, the word "foreign" can no longer be applied to Christian missions. In the first place, Christ is no longer "foreign" to the life and culture of nations around the world, but has largely become "indigenous," of the soil. In Christian art in Africa, for example, especially in wood carving, sculpture, and painting, Christ is not a white, Anglo-Saxon type, but rather an African, symbolizing the fact that Christ is already in the process of becoming "native" to the culture of the African people. In the second place, the word "foreign" connotes separation among the nations and fails to take into account the emergence of one world.

The statement made by the Board of Foreign Missions in 1955, from which we have already quoted, said:

> It may be argued that "ecumenical" is a strange word not now understood by the majority. One wonders how clearly the word "Presbyterian" was understood when chosen by our forefathers, or is fully comprehended by some Presbyterians today. There will be a great responsibility to interpret the meaning and significance of the ecumenical mission which will be not only an obligation but a productive educational opportunity. The progress made already in interpreting the ecumenical mission to clergy, laity and young people, both in the U.S.A. and overseas, has been exceedingly encouraging and has brought about definite advance in both interest and support.[42]

Shortly before his death, the German philosopher Hegel, having heard about Christian World Missions, is said to have exclaimed, "This is the most significant event of our time."[43] A hundred years later, William Temple, on the occasion of his consecration as Archbishop of Canterbury, referred to the emergence of the worldwide Christian community as the great new fact of our time. The task of evangelizing the world, that is, of proclaiming the Christian gospel to all men, is no longer the responsibility of the Western church alone, but of the Christian church, as it is found in every country.

Discussing the term "ecumenical" in 1953, Visser 't Hooft, the General Secretary of the World Council, pointed out that it "imposed itself and from the late twenties onward it became the widely accepted term to describe the new movement toward cooperation and unity of the Churches and of Christians generally."[44]

The Greek word *oikoumenē*, from which "ecumenical" is derived, was used by Herodotus as far back as the fifth century b.c. In the twentieth century as it is used by churchmen, its meaning is deeper and richer. For Herodotus, and also for Demosthenes, the connotation of the word was "the inhabited earth." The word "world" was an inclusive, vague term, whereas the *oikoumenē* was the part of the world that was inhabited. In time, the meaning changed to that of the Greek world or Hellenic civilization, and later, as the Roman Empire emerged, it was applied to the world that counted as far as Romans were concerned. However, as Visser 't Hooft points out, "while Oikoumene could be used and was often used to speak of the world in general, it was from now on most generally associated with the idea of the unified civilization which was growing up under the auspices of the Roman Empire."[45]

Much has already been written on the word "ecumenical" in an attempt to clarify its meaning and legitimate usage. In the modern era there was a time when it was not popular among church people and they were prone to avoid using it, probably because they were not quite sure of its connotation. More recently, the swing seems to have been in the opposite direction, many people using the word quite loosely and without evidence of much understanding of its meaning. "The word is still used for a great variety of events, things, and attitudes. Ecumenical tea parties which denominational women's groups organize for each other indicate that little more than restricted fellowship is sought with those who are of another denomination; ecumenical tourist offices offer trips to the Holy Land, using the word ecumenical as an indication of the willingness of the management to organize non-denominational trips under the guidance of a minister."[46] Some consider almost any aspect of interdenominational work as ecumenical in character.

The Central Committee of the World Council of Churches at its meeting in Rolle, Switzerland, in 1951, declared that "it is important to insist that this word [ecumenical], which comes from the Greek word for 'the whole inhabited earth,' is properly used to describe everything that relates to the whole task of the whole Church to bring the Gospel to the whole world."[47]

As far as the application of the word to the Christian church is concerned, it was not until the Conference on Church, Community and State held in Oxford, England, in 1937, that Dr. Mackay used the term "ecumenical" to describe the Christian church of our time. Taking the word in its secular meaning, he added the concept of the spiritual unity that is in Jesus Christ. What culture was as a principle of unity in the inhabited world, or *oikoumenē*, of the Greeks and the Romans, Christ, and his church became in "the whole inhabited earth" of our day.

In 1955, when the proposal to use the term "Ecumenical Mission" as part of a suggested new name of the Board was first being discussed, Dr. John Coventry Smith, then Associate General Secretary of The Board of Foreign Missions of the Presbyterian Church in the U.S.A., showed the new letterhead to Dr. John Baillie, noted theologian from Scotland, at a meeting in Argentina. After studying it for a few moments, Dr. Baillie said: "You are using the term 'ecumenical' in a new sense. We had thought that 'ecumenical' meant only those things which we all do together." Dr. Smith replied that the Board had not abandoned that meaning. Then Dr. Baillie added: "I see what you mean. You are engaged in the Presbyterian share of the world-wide mission of the world-wide church."

"Mission." The word "Mission," used in the singular in the name of the Commission, is replete with meaning. The term "missions" usually refers to the organizations of which missionaries are members in a given country. According to the *Manual* of The Board of Foreign Missions of the Presbyterian Church in the U.S.A. of 1952, "the Missions, with their well-defined responsibilities and functions, have been the administrative bodies which, under the general direction of the Board have carried on mission work in specified areas."[48] In Presbyterian work overseas, "missions," in the sense we have used the word, are rapidly disappearing, as churches mature and achieve autonomy. Dr. R. Pierce Beaver, in the introduction to his book, *From Missions to Mission,* says that "three-and-a-half centuries of pioneering by European and American foreign mission boards have come to an end. But the end of a period of trail blazing is not the end of the mission. The present moment marks the transition from a Western church operation, reaching out from a geographically defined Christendom to 'heathendom,' into a mission aimed at all the world from a base in a 'diffused Christendom' in a community of churches all around the world."[49]

When the two words "ecumenical" and "mission" were used together, something new came into the missionary enterprise. A new "togetherness" in the mission of the church around the world was seen as Christians from different nations were conscious of having the same calling to proclaim the gospel of their common Lord.

"Relations." The question is sometimes raised as to why the word "Relations" was added to the name of the Commission. It should be noted that, in the name, the word "Ecumenical" qualifies "Relations" as much as it does "Mission." In other words, the Commission has

the responsibility of furthering and giving meaning and relevance to ecumenical relations. Moreover, it must be remembered that "mission" and "relations" in the work of the Commission belong together. In 1958, it was believed that the time had come to put them together in one agency of the church. The boards of foreign missions had been responsible for mission—or missions—for many decades, while the committees on interchurch relations had taken care of relations with other bodies for nearly sixty years.

In ecumenical relations, the United Presbyterian Church, through the Commission, reaches out in meaningful ways to other Christian bodies in the United States and across the world. In giving the responsibility for "mission" and "relations" to the Commission, the denomination was pioneering in the missionary enterprise, and it thus symbolized in a dramatic way that unity and mission are inseparable. Unity is not for the sake of unity, but is *for* mission. Moreover, it becomes apparent that "the Commission, uniting *mission* and *relations*, broadens the areas of service, strengthens all emphases, makes more comprehensive and efficient the administrative operations and more inclusive and dynamic the program and strategy."[50]

One of the deeper meanings of the Commission is that The United Presbyterian Church in the U.S.A. is able more effectively to pursue its task of presenting the gospel of Jesus Christ and all its dynamic implications to a confused, needy, and suffering world. It opens up new opportunities and new dimensions of Christian service. The story of a Chinese Christian in Hong Kong illustrates how readily an Asian Christian grasped the significance of the ecumenical movement. Dr. John Coventry Smith tells of the incident that occurred after a conference of fourteen representatives of different denominations in six Asian countries in Hong Kong in July, 1954, a meeting which pointed the way to the formation of the East Asia Christian Conference a few years later. As Dr. Smith was leaving Hong Kong for Manila, a letter was received from a Chinese businessman in Hong Kong. He had heard of the plans discussed at the Hong Kong meeting to undergird personnel projects from one Asian country to another. For example, Japan was planning to provide theological professors needed in Indonesia and the Philippines. This Chinese businessman said he wanted to be the first to contribute to such a program and was enclosing his check, which was for the equivalent of $900 in U.S. money. Five hours later, when Dr. Smith arrived in Manila, word came that a report had just been received from a Christian hospital in Thailand, where they were short of nurses and wanted the church in the Philippines to select and send one. The hospital would be able to supply housing and salary, but had no funds for transportation. Thus, within a few hours, the first project was realized. A Christian nurse from the Philippines would be working in Thailand and partly supported by a Hong Kong businessman. Here we see the world church at its world mission.

The Ecumenical Era

As we have noted previously, the leaders of the United Presbyterian Church were convinced that the time had come when it should not only view its task but also seek to fulfill it in an ecumenical context. Because of the great changes that had taken place in the world, changes that were felt acutely after World War II, the old patterns of thought and practice no longer sufficed. An ecumenical era dawned upon the world, and the church, as part of the world, was in that ecumenical era, whether it wanted to be or not.

The phrase "ecumenical era" is attributed to the German philosopher Count Keyserling, who said that only such a phrase could be used to describe a world that had suddenly become one big neighborhood, largely through greatly accelerated means of communication, the instruments being the airplane and the radio. There appeared a new sensitivity among the different areas of the human family, any major happening in one having repercussions elsewhere. " 'The world is an ecumenical organism,' he [Keyserling] used to say, 'if you apply a major stimulus anywhere, it is felt everywhere.' An extreme sensitivity marks the world of our time. . . . All men belong for the first time to the *oikoumenē*, to the ecumenical order in a secular sense."[51] At a time when more than fifty nations were achieving political independence, a new interdependence was seen in the world, and nations could no longer live in splendid isolation. "Our confrontation with world crisis in Cuba, Germany, Taiwan, Korea, Vietnam, and countless other places, reminds us daily that we live in this world together, that if one nation is to be saved, then all of mankind has to be saved."[52]

The United Presbyterian Church believes that God is at work in history, and that he has a message for the world through his church. It is a message of reconciliation, a renewal of life through courage, hope, and faith, and a message that comes alive and dynamic as Christ reigns in men's hearts and dominates their relationships. "It was in him [Christ] that the full nature of God chose to live, and through him God planned to reconcile in his own person, as it were, everything on earth and everything in Heaven by virtue of the sacrifice on the cross."[53]

The United Presbyterian Church, furthermore, believes that the church must adapt itself to an ecumenical era if it is to be an instrument of God for the carrying out of his purpose. The United Presbyterian Church, through its Commission on Ecumenical Mission and Relations, is not alone in this conviction. Indeed, no church, as part of the body of Christ, can be truly ecumenical unless other parts of the body are ecumenical also. All churches are involved in this global task in a new unity in mission.

Chapter VII

THE FIRST SEVEN YEARS OF THE COMMISSION

The Nature of the Commission's Task

The first General Assembly of the newly organized United Presbyterian Church in the U.S.A. (1958) stated that: "The rise of indigenous churches, founded through missionary activity, has resulted in a new relationship among churches throughout the world. Recognizing this new day, the General Assemblies of both the Presbyterian Church in the United States of America and the United Presbyterian Church of North America accepted in principle the creation of the Commission on Ecumenical Mission and Relations."[1]

The tasks committed to the new Commission by the General Assembly of 1958 can be summarized as follows:

1. To further the ecumenical mission of the church, including interchurch service, the direction and oversight of such missions and institutions of the church outside the area of the United States of America (excluding the areas assigned to the Board of National Missions) in evangelism, Christian education, Christian social and welfare services, utilizing resources and the assistance of all boards and agencies of the General Assembly;

2. To carry on the program and interests of the church as they relate to other ecclesiastical bodies in the areas of (a) general cooperation, (b) interchurch, interconfessional, and ecumenical conversations and courtesies, recommending to the General Assembly official replies to ecumenical, interchurch, or ecclesiastical letters and messages;

3. To make recommendations to the General Assembly regarding fraternal delegates to and from other churches and ecclesiastical bodies;

4. To nominate to the General Assembly persons who are to represent the church on cooperative and interdenominational ecclesiastical bodies to which the church belongs.

The Boards of Foreign Missions of the two uniting churches had previously conducted missions in many parts of the world, and as we have seen, the two churches had commissions or committees on interchurch relations and on ecumenical affairs. These two broad areas of service and responsibility were now brought together in one organization, and the challenge was unprecedented in its scope and implications. How could the Commission on Ecumenical Mission and Relations adequately speak for, and act in the name of, the whole church? Obviously, a large and difficult task had been given to the Commission, especially when it is remembered that the situation across the world was changing rapidly.

The task was a new one, for the Commission was not just the boards of foreign missions with a new name. Both "mission" (as distinguished from "missions") and "relations" were new concepts in the life of the Christian church. In addition, these two were brought closely together for the first time in one organization.

So far as policy and program were concerned, a new element in the Commission's task was the challenge of exploring the full meaning of being related to autonomous, independent churches overseas. With this in mind, we shall attempt to depict the broad spectrum of ecumenical relations.

Ecumenical Relations

Until 1958, when the Commission on Ecumenical Mission and Relations was created, no mission agency, including the Boards of Foreign Missions of the two uniting churches, had ever engaged specifically in the task of establishing or widening ecumenical relations.

The work, therefore, that the Division of Relations undertook in 1958 could be described as a pioneer task on an uncharted course. From 1958 to 1965, Dr. Margaret Shannon, Associate General Secretary, served as chairman of the Commission's Division of Relations. With consummate skill, profound insight, and creative ability, Miss Shannon developed what might be termed a network of fraternal and ecumenical relationships around the world, as well as within the United States, so that it can be said that it is one of the Commission's major achievements during the first seven years. This does not mean that relations did not exist to any degree before 1958. It does mean, however, that the significance of these relations became more discernible when they were widened and deepened and as the Commission assumed a major responsibility for developing them.

When the Commission was created, the inclusion of "mission" and "relations" in its name meant that the policy of the new body would be shaped around these two concepts. In the former boards of foreign missions, there existed relations with other churches, including the younger churches, and with ecumenical bodies, but they were not given major emphasis. One reason for this was that ecumenical relations and interchurch relations were the recognized responsibility of committees appointed by the General Assemblies of the two churches for these purposes.

By putting "mission" and "relations" side by side, in one single organization, the General Assembly of 1958 gave recognition to an important fact, namely, that they belong together. The phrase "side by side," which we have just used, is not quite accurate or adequate, since in many instances "mission" and "relations" are almost coterminous. In other words, as we extend and enrich relations, we are pursuing the mission of the church, and, vice versa, when an organization or a church engages in "mission," it involves "relations." The terms "mission" and "relations" are avenues through which the United Presbyterian Church seeks to fulfill its obligation to spread the gospel of Christ, while at the same time it witnesses to the unity of the church and furthers that unity. This is why the terms are not mutually exclusive, but, on the contrary, are very intimately related. Therefore, as we consider the first seven years of the life of the Commission, we must not lose sight of the significance of the phrase "Ecumenical Mission *and* Relations."

Furthermore, the establishing of relations with churches and ecumenical organizations is not an end in itself. The aim is to further the mission of the church by developing new patterns of mission, undertaken together in a unity of purpose.

The range of ecumenical relationships is wide and comprehensive. In broad outline they involve other churches, ecumenical bodies, and judicatories, as well as other agencies of the United Presbyterian Church. The term "other churches," for our purpose here, includes the following:

1. Churches with which the Commission is related as members of the Council of Churches, with 214 full members and 8 associate members;[2] the World Presbyterian Alliance, which has 102 members;[3] and the National Council of Churches with 30 Protestant and Orthodox churches.

2. Churches with which the Commission joins in some phase of a program, for example, churches related to the American Bible Society or to the World Council of Christian Education.

3. Churches with which the United Presbyterian Church has been historically related in mission, and with which it has some understanding regarding continuing partnership as independent churches. This classification includes a number of churches mentioned above.

4. Churches to which the Commission makes grants-in-aid without its being involved in administering these.

5. Orthodox churches.

6. The Roman Catholic Church.

7. Churches sometimes referred to as the nonhistorical churches, such as the Pentecostal and conservative evangelical churches.

The most intensive and far-reaching relationships are those with other churches in the World Council of Churches, the World Presbyterian Alliance, and the National Council of Churches.

The Commission has the responsibility of presenting periodically to the General Assembly of the United Presbyterian Church nominations of: delegates and alternates to the World Council of Churches; delegates and alternates to the World Presbyterian Alliance; delegates to the North American Area Council of the World Presbyterian Alliance; delegates to the General Assembly of the National Council of Churches in the U.S.A.; and United Presbyterian representatives to official interdenominational conferences and consultations. This important assignment, formerly undertaken by three committees, involves a considerable volume of correspondence and committee work to ensure an adequate and balanced representation on all these bodies. Similarly, the Commission nominates representatives to the American Bible Society and the World Council of Christian Education.

All these bodies, or organizations, in which the United Presbyterian Church is represented carry on a large volume of diverse projects all over the world, and they are made possible by a vital and meaningful fellowship of Christian relationships at many levels.

The Commission also maintains relations directly with other denominations in the search for understanding and unity. Particularly is this true of other members of the family of Reformed churches.

Thus, the Division of Relations engages in a wide variety of activities and participates in many events of Christian significance. For example, it arranges almost every year for the visit of the Moderator of the General Assembly of the United Presbyterian Church to some area overseas, so that he can gain firsthand knowledge of conditions and opportunities there. Similarly, moderators or other church officers from overseas visit the General Assembly of The United Presbyterian Church in the U.S.A., and sometimes remain for extended tours around the country, with the purpose of getting to know the church. Soon after the Commission was formed in 1958, the Division of Relations arranged for delegates from the United States to attend the General Council of the World Presbyterian Alliance held in Brazil in 1959, the occasion being the hundredth anniversary of the founding of Presbyterian work in that country. Similarly, arrangements were made for visitors from the United States to be present at the celebrations of the centennial of Protestant work in Japan, and the four hundredth anniversary of the Reformed Church in France and Switzerland in 1960. These are only a few of the many events that occur from time to time across the world, providing opportunities for the enrichment of fellowship with sister churches and the strengthening of ties in a common task.

For administrative purposes, relations with churches overseas are divided functionally into work with youth, laymen overseas, women, and students. When the Division of Relations was established in 1958, there was only one full-time staff person, an associate secretary. During the first seven years of the Commission, six full-time staff persons were added, most of them from the former Boards of Foreign Missions, and these carry on regular correspondence with over one thousand persons in positions of leadership in the churches around the world. After a careful study, funds are allocated for scholarships for Christian young people wishing to study in the United States, for frontier interns, short-term personnel, and grants-in-aid for special projects.

New avenues of Christian witness and service have opened up for laymen as well as for youth and students from the United States as they travel abroad or go to live in a foreign country. Reference will be made in the next chapter to the way in which Christian laymen are participating in the mission of the church. The Commission, through its Division of Relations, has sought to increase the opportunities for such service by organizing seminars of youth, students, and laymen in business, government service, or other occupations, and by advising them concerning forms of service abroad. An example of how American laymen can be involved as Christians in different kinds of situations in a foreign country comes from Thailand.

In a weekend conference in Bangkok, Thailand, in 1964, attended by sixty-two laymen and church leaders from twelve countries (including the U.S.A.) the topic "The Christian Overseas" was discussed. In one session, with a panel composed of a Thai physician, an Australian industrialist, a German university professor, a Y.M.C.A. secretary, and a visitor from the National Council of the Churches of Christ in the U.S.A., the following were among the questions raised: (1) What are some of the daily problems of a Thai Christian? (2) Does a Christian businessman have to compromise in ethical principles? (3) What is the Christian concept of fair treatment of employees (domestic servants and industrial workers), including wages? (4) How can we as foreigners identify ourselves with the local church in its life and witness?[4] These questions indicate some of the ways in which Christian laymen from the United States can share in the life and witness of Christians in other countries.

Groups of Presbyterian laymen and of laywomen visit churches overseas, and in turn, similar groups from overseas come to the United States. Groups of women from several countries, including the United States, participate in study seminars, with the idea of deepening their understanding of the mission of the church.

Ecumenical relations have not been exclusively with traditional Protestant churches. Grants-in-aid have been made to some Orthodox churches, and studies have been undertaken with the purpose of deepening understanding of the Orthodox Church position. Similarly, friendly relations have been sought with leaders of the Roman Catholic Church, the Pentecostal churches, and the nonhistorical or conservative evangelical churches.

Relations with the Roman Catholic leaders are sometimes in the form of a dialogue, in an attempt to broaden mutual understanding of the Christian faith. Protestant and Catholic leaders are discovering that while serious doctrinal differences still persist, they also have much in common. In an introduction to his book *The Other Dialogue*, Monsignor Joseph Gremillion writes, "The very fact that we Christians are once again talking to each other does make Christ's message more 'hearable' to the rest of mankind."[5] Monsignor Gremillion believes that Pope John "sensitized the ears and hearts of the world by his dialogue with other Christians. So the two dialogues today are closely related."[6]

Another type of relationship in ecumenical mission is to be seen in Indonesia. Work in cooperation with the churches there began in 1950. At that time, Dr. Winburn T. Thomas, a Presbyterian missionary, assigned to the World Student Christian Federation, visiting the islands, was invited by the Rev. W. J. Rumambi, who was soon to become the first Secretary of the Indonesian Council of Churches, and by the Dutch Mission Consul, to assist the churches in developing relations with Western churches other than those of the Netherlands, Germany, and Switzerland, and with the American Methodists.

Out of these conversations grew a regular assignment in which Dr. Thomas became the Secretary of the Commission on Mission and the Commission on Inter-Church Aid of the Indonesian Council, with responsibilities for dealing with the English-speaking world.

The strategy was to persuade denominational mission boards to undergird the existing church bodies and emerging ecumenical and union institutions rather than to found daughter churches of their own. Thus, the resources of the Presbyterian Church in the U.S.A. were channeled primarily into ecumenical and union work, such as support of the Indonesian Council of Churches, the Djakarta Theological College, and the Indonesian Christian University.

Dr. Thomas left Indonesia in 1958, and was replaced by the Rev. Ernest L. Fogg, Presbyterian missionary in Thailand, in 1959. By 1965, the cooperative work developed to the point that through the office of the Indonesian Council of Churches, workers and support were coming from seven different countries and fourteen churches or councils of churches in English-speaking lands. Presbyterians have made a major contribution cooperatively through the Division of Overseas Ministries of the National Council of the Churches of Christ in the U.S.A.

The question of the relationship of the Commission to mission boards in the National Council of the Churches of Christ in the U.S.A. presents some unforeseen difficulties. In certain situations it is hard for a mission board executive of a sister denomination to think of the Commission as anything more than a board, with a few new responsibilities added to the old ones. Where the Commission is working alongside boards of foreign missions, or boards of world missions, in fellowship with a national church in certain countries, it is not surprising that the thinking of church leaders in those countries is not always clear concerning the difference between the Commission and the mission boards with which it is in fellowship or, for that matter, between the Commission and its predecessors, the Boards of Foreign Missions of the former Presbyterian Church in the U.S.A. and the former United Presbyterian Church of North America. To say that in a period of seven years the Commission has failed to solve some of the outstanding problems is to misunderstand the nature of the Commission's task. This cannot be conceived of as a set of problems that can be worked out once and for all; it is more of the nature of a continuum, a process involving relationships and new situations always being created.

Integration of Missions with National Churches

The new appreciation of what it meant to be related to churches overseas began to influence everything the Commission did. Traditionally the Boards of Foreign Missions had been related to missions in the various countries, but the emergence of strong independent churches around the world involved many changes in relationships, and consequently in mission policy.

In order to comprehend the variety of approaches and the fact that unity as well as mission has been an issue in some areas from the beginning, let us look now at several geographical areas.

The Philippines. To understand the unitive movement in the Philippines which came to full fruition in the period we are considering, it is essential to go back to the turn of the century. Work undertaken by an American mission board in areas occupied by American forces, after the Spanish-American War, had to be conducted under conditions somewhat different from those which obtained elsewhere. Cuba and the Philippine Islands were two such areas. Presbyterian work developed by the Board of National Missions was ecclesiastically related to the General Assembly of the Presbyterian Church in the U.S.A. The work in the Philippines under the Board of Foreign Missions was initiated along other lines. "Robert E. Speer inveighed against the concept of an indigenous self-governing church that allowed the incorporation of the young churches into the denominational structures in the Western nations."[7]

In the Philippines, Dr. James B. Rodgers, the first officially appointed missionary to the islands, sent by The Board of Foreign Missions of the Presbyterian Church in the U.S.A. in 1899, is credited with having been largely instrumental in fostering the spirit of unity from the beginning. In 1929, the United Evangelical Church of the Philippines was formed by the Presbyterian Church, the Congregational Church, the United Brethren Church, and the United Church of Manila. In 1943, the Evangelical Church in the Philippines was organized, with the participation of the United Evangelical Church of the Philippines, the Church of Christ (Disciples), the Iglesia Unida de Cristo, Iglesia Evangélica Nacional, some congregations of the Philippine Methodist Church,[8] and a number of local congregations.

The postwar restoration period dissolved what was done in wartime, but gave a new impetus to the unitive movement in the Philippines. At a Planning Conference held in 1946, it was agreed by the mission boards and the United Evangelical Church "that the United

Evangelical Church [should] take over the full responsibility for the entire work previously carried on by the missions, to take effect on or before October 1, 1947."[9] In 1948, a new and enlarged church emerged, under the name of the United Church of Christ in the Philippines, and it brought together the Evangelical Church, the Philippine Methodist Church, and the United Evangelical Church. The United Church of Christ in the Philippines has included the office of bishop in its form of government. The chairmen of the General Assembly, the highest ecclesiastical body, may be a minister or a layman, and along with the bishops who serve for four-year terms, he has oversight of the church. These bishops are ineligible for reelection after three terms. "The Bishop functions in the church much as does the Moderator of the Assembly in Presbyterian and other reformed churches."[10] Each bishop presides over the affairs of his own diocese during his term of office. Thus, in the Philippines, the process of unification of the churches and integration of the Presbyterian mission with the church took place more or less simultaneously.

During the first seven years of its existence, the Commission continued to maintain cordial relations with the United Church of Christ in the Philippines in a new sense of partnership in mission. The channel of communication is the Philippines Interboard Office which represents the mission agencies related to the United Church. The Interboard Committee now feels that the time has come for the establishment of a real church-to-church relationship with the cooperating churches. The continuance of an Interboard Office would mean the perpetuation of a feeling of separateness between the fraternal workers from the United States and the United Church of Christ in the Philippines. This church is a missionary church, and the Filipino missionaries it maintains overseas are committed to the care of the churches in the countries where they serve.

In 1963, an agreement was worked out between the Philippine Interboard Committee and the representatives of the United Church of Christ, whereby certain functions hitherto carried on by the Interboard Office would be transferred to the United Church. These functions include hospitality, public relations, and the transmittance of grants from cooperating boards in the United States for the church program. Pastoral counseling for missionaries and fraternal workers from the United States is the responsibility of church leaders and the field representative (of mission boards). The Interboard Office is now concerned almost exclusively with missionary maintenance, including the transfer of mission-owned properties. The tendency is for the United Church of Christ in the Philippines to assume most, if not all, of the functions of the Interboard Office.

Japan. There are certain similarities between the integration of church and mission in the Philippines and that in Japan, and yet the history of Christian unity and of cooperative efforts in Japan is unique in the annals of the missionary enterprise.

Protestant work began in Japan in 1859, but because of public law, the first Japanese Protestant church could not be established until 1872. When this was organized in Yokohama by Reformed and Presbyterian missionaries, they insisted that the church should not be constituted denominationally. The first article of its constitution read, "Our Church does not belong to any sect whatever." The organizers felt that in pagan lands the history of denominations could not be understood. Nevertheless, denominational differences did appear before long. In 1876, however, missionaries of the Reformed Church of America, the Presbyterian Church in the U.S.A., and the United Presbyterian Church of Scotland formed the Council of the Three Missions, with the purpose of setting up a single Reformed-Presbyterian denomination. The following year, the United Church of Christ in Japan came into being when missionaries of the three churches met with eight elders of local Japanese churches.[11] Several years later, missions of the Presbyterian Church U.S., the German Reformed Church, and the Cumberland Presbyterian Church joined the Council of Missions which cooperated with the United Church of Christ in Japan. Later, the word "United" was dropped from the title. In the early 1930's there were evidences that in the minds of missionaries, as well as of Japanese pastors and laymen, church union was only a matter of time. There are some who maintain that the formation of the United Church of Christ in Japan (Kyodan) in 1941 was precipitated by government pressure. It is true that the Religious Organizations Law of 1939 helped prepare the way for such a union, but a close reading of the history of the churches in Japan reveals a long-standing desire for union. As the *Japan Christian Quarterly* of January, 1959, puts it, "Helped along by the Religious Organizations Law of 1939, the various denominations purposed to enter into the union which had been in the minds and hearts of Japanese Christians ever since 1872."[12]

The Kyodan, which was organized on June 6, 1941, included thirty-four denominations. After the war was over, General MacArthur abolished the Religious Organizations Law, and the official pressure for union was removed. In the next few years, groups withdrew from the Kyodan and new missions established work in Japan. Members of the Kyodan represented about 65 percent of the total Protestant community in the country. In 1947, an Interboard Committee for Christian Work in Japan was organized, and this is the official channel for the following churches in North America: the United Church of Christ, The Methodist Church, the United Church of Canada, the Reformed Church in America, The United Presbyterian Church in the U.S.A., the Disciples of Christ, and the Evangelical United Brethren.

Thus, the process of integration of the Presbyterian mission with the Japanese Church was a gradual one. The fraternal workers work under the Kyodan in full partnership, and while the Kyodan is an autonomous body with Japanese leadership, there is expressed from time to time a desire to "de-Americanize the church." This is not to be interpreted as an anti-American sentiment, "rather they [the Japanese] are seeking the true 'worldification' . . . of their church; that is, wider and deeper relationships with the world-wide church, and thus a deepening, rather than a weakening, of ties with the North American churches."[13]

Thailand. The first Protestant missionary reached Thailand, which was then known as Siam, in 1828. Presbyterian missionaries arrived in 1840, and work on a permanent basis was begun in 1847. The Church of Christ was formed in 1934, and now includes Baptists and Disciples as well as Presbyterians. The mission had pioneered in many fields, but particularly in education and medical work. The integration of the Presbyterian mission and the Church of Christ in Thailand took place in Bangkok in August, 1957. With integration, the church assumed full responsibility for a number of outstanding institutions, with some support in finances and personnel coming as heretofore from the Commission in New York.

Korea. Presbyterian work began in Korea in 1884. The church, which was soon established, has grown in an extraordinary way, so that it is the largest indigenous Presbyterian church in Asia. In 1958, a decentralized pattern of integration of missions and church was agreed upon. In that year, the Commission, through its representatives, participated with the Korean Church in the formulation of a constitution that provided for the transfer of all administrative and work functions to a newly created Department of Cooperative Work in Korea. All requests for funds and personnel were to be channeled through this department. In addition, area departments were to be set up where mission stations had previously existed, and in these departments, missionaries and Korean churchmen would have equal participation. There were some delays in implementing this plan, and in 1964, it was superseded by the Mutual Agreement, which involved not only the Presbyterian Church in Korea and The United Presbyterian Church in the U.S.A. but also the Presbyterian Church U.S. and the Australian Presbyterian Church.

A new element in this agreement was that the churches of the three missions expressed their willingness to cooperate with the whole Presbyterian Church in Korea instead of on a unilateral basis, as previously. The new Department of Cooperative Work is responsible to the General Assembly in Korea, and it develops strategy and makes requests in the light of the overall program. Plans also develop at the area level where several presbyteries are involved, and Korean churchmen and missionaries participate equally in the formulation of plans. Requests for funds and personnel go from the Central Department of Cooperative Work to the three churches, two in the United States and one in Australia.

The process that took place can be described as a decentralized pattern of integration. The Korean Mission as an administrative organization went out of existence in 1959. The name of the mission was retained, but in reality it could best be described as a missionary fellowship that also shares with the Commission representative certain missionary maintenance functions.

Hong Kong. In Hong Kong the Commission participates in an Interboard Committee located in New York, which relates to the Church of Christ in China (Hong Kong Council), a united church body. The Hong Kong Council roughly coincides with a presbytery. It is strictly a Chinese body that, under the strong leadership of its General Secretary, carries out a very aggressive program of Christian education, social work, and also church building. There is an Interboard Missionary Maintenance Committee, and also a Presbyterian fraternal workers fellowship group, which has as its chief function a biweekly prayer meeting. The Commission also cooperates with a number of independent or semi-independent Christian institutions in Hong Kong, including Chung Chi College, the Christian Family Service Center, and several medical programs, such as the Junk Bay Medical Council, and the new Hong Kong Christian Hospital Committee. The channel of cooperation is through the United Board for Christian Higher Education, the Hong Kong Interboard Committee, and the Hong Kong Council of the Church of Christ in China.

India and Pakistan. Integration in India and Pakistan, involving the merging of mission organizations into the life of the church, has presented singularly difficult problems, mainly because the indigenization of the church and its growth into selfhood and maturity were conceived largely as a mere transfer of authority from Western missionary administrators to Indian and Pakistani Christians. In other words, the general structure of mission organizations remained essentially the same. Several church councils and synods were involved, and when integration took place, the tendency was for these to assume responsibilities which formerly belonged to the missions. This meant that, whereas previously missionary administrators were agents of the Commission on Ecumenical Mission and Relations, Indian and Pakistani executives of church councils and synods tended to assume this role. The same was true of other mission agencies.

United Presbyterian participation in mission work in India and Pakistan extends over a period of one hundred and thirty years, through the boards of the former Presbyterian Church in the U.S.A. and the former United Presbyterian Church of North America. In the first place the work of the former Presbyterian Church in the U.S.A. is now a part of the United Church of Northern India, which came into being in 1924, whereas the churches established by the United Presbyterian Church of North America resulted in the formation of the United Presbyterian Church of Pakistan, which came into existence in 1961. Only the Gurdaspur Church Council (related to the former United Presbyterian Church) was in India following partition and since then has become a member council of the United Church of Northern India.

A second complicating factor is the wide variety of mission board relationships that the United Church of Northern India has. The Commission of the United Presbyterian Church is related to four synods; the Church of Scotland Mission, to five synods; the United Church Board for World Ministries and the Canadian Presbyterian Church, each to two synods; the United Church of Canada, the London Missionary Society, the Welsh Mission, the Irish Presbyterian Church, the Moravian Church of England, the Presbyterian Church of New Zealand, and the Presbyterian Church of England, each to one synod. Needless to say, the viewpoints and policies of these agencies are not uniform, and this creates problems for the Indian and Pakistani churches. Furthermore, the United Church of Northern India with its synods and church councils extends over one thousand miles east and west, from the Punjab to Assam, and one thousand miles north and south, making it very difficult to achieve a sense of unity and for cooperative planning. In addition, there are unilateral relationships with church councils.

In view of these complicating factors, it is not surprising that the United Church of Northern India, with which the Commission is related, has experienced difficulty in achieving real independence and an autonomous church life. It has moved from dependence to interdependence, without having attained selfhood and independence, because the church has failed to discover the activities and the church structure essential to independence and responsible autonomy. It is significant to note, however, that autonomous church life was achieved in the areas where the former United Presbyterian Church of North America was active. This was due to its strong emphasis upon the policy of self-support for the pastoral ministry.

Over the decades, mission agencies had established schools, hospitals, and other institutions with a desire to meet the overwhelming needs of a teeming population. When integration took place, most of the institutions and a variety of special projects came under the administration of synods and church councils of the United Church of Northern India. Exceptions were made of certain large institutions that are administered by autonomous boards. Not only did funds from the United States continue to be needed, but they were used in the traditional manner. The tendency was for this administrative work to absorb the ablest church leaders, and as a result the parish ministry of the church suffered.

Church courts were largely composed of people who were dependent on funds for synods and institutions, and the gap between church leadership and the local church began to widen. Moreover, laymen were not challenged in sufficient numbers to Christian service and witness. The temptation has been to treat the church as an end in itself, and to become ingrown. Consultations in which Commission staff participated during 1963 and 1964 gave evidence of the growing conviction that the church must recapture its sense of mission, and to do this it must engage in a vital program of stewardship. Only in this way could the United Church of Northern India support its ministers and be an effective channel of Christian witness. Church growth and evangelism assume a new place of importance in the life of the church.

The Commission has been very much aware of the adjustments that are necessary in the use of funds and personnel in India and Pakistan. Initiative for the use of funds for the support of the church's ecclesiastical structure and the support of its ministry will rest with the Indian and Pakistani churches. The Commission, however, in consultation with the church in India and Pakistan will seek to express initiative in partnership projects of short-term duration with the churches.

Syria-Lebanon. The Syria-Lebanon Mission of the Presbyterian Church in the U.S.A. had been operative for more than a hundred and twenty-five years. For the last several decades of that period, the National Evangelical Synod had been independent of the Mission in structure, but dependent on the Mission for financial support and for missionary personnel. Large educational institutions, as well as medical work, were administered solely by the Mission. Mounting misunderstanding and tension over the abnormality of this situation stimulated earnest study and planning toward the achievement of a more appropriate working relationship.

Integration took place in Syria-Lebanon on April 15, 1959, and was marked by a special ceremony held in the Arab Evangelical Church in Beirut. There followed several years of major adjustment on the part of both the National Evangelical Synod and the Commission including the appointed fraternal workers in the area of the latter. It was a new relationship experience for all concerned, and uncertainty as well as anxiety was much in evidence.

Many fraternal workers were frustrated as the result of lessened participation in decision-making and also by frequent delays on the part of those carrying this responsibility. The National Evangelical Synod was frustrated as a result of unmet expectations concerning the immediate turning over to them of certain institutional properties. It was also almost overwhelmed by the volume of administrative detail it had assumed.

Perhaps the major mistakes made in the initial processes of integration were the assumption by the national church that it was the inheritor of the former "mission," and therefore should possess all of its assets, prerogatives, and structures, and the failure of the Commission on Ecumenical Mission and Relations to detect and correct this erroneous impression.

As a result of numerous consultations, climaxed in May, 1963, by a major consultation based upon *An Advisory Study*, to which more detailed reference will be made in Chapter VIII, the Synod and the Commission gradually came to a clearer understanding of the purpose and meaning of integration and of the working relationship best suited to the fulfillment of that purpose and meaning.

This understanding included (1) a clear definition of the meaning of partnership as applied to the missionary task; (2) emphasis upon the importance of careful delineation of area, of separate and shared responsibility on the part of both partners, as well as of any others who might be involved; (3) agreement upon priority in the use of contributed funds and personnel for those activities which are clearly a part of the growing edge of the church's life in the world; (4) definition of the role of each partner in an agreed-upon common endeavor; and (5) agreement as to the administrative structure and procedure by which the purposes of joint missionary activities may be realized.

Iran. For many years the Commission has been negotiating with the Evangelical Presbyterian Synod in Iran toward an agreement with regard to a more effective working relationship. Out of this process emerged the Agreement on Cooperation, which sets forth in detail the working relationship of Synod and Commission and the respective responsibilities of each. This Agreement became effective January 1, 1965. It might be described as "partial integration."

Under the provisions of this agreement, the former Iran Mission organization has been dissolved, and the Synod carries full administrative responsibilities for the life and program of the Evangelical Presbyterian Church in Iran and its related institutions, in accordance with the Synod constitution. Upon insistent recommendation of the Synod, administrative responsibility for medical work and certain Christian service programs founded by the former Iran Mission is vested in a Christian Service Board to which the Commission elects six missionaries, and the Synod elects four national churchmen. Missionaries working in the Synod program are under the Synod's supervision. Others are under the direction of the Christian Service Board. A missionary maintenance committee cares for the personal welfare concerns of all missionaries. After an experimental period of three years, this working relationship of Synod and Commission will be reviewed.

United Arab Republic (Egypt). While there has been no formal "integration" of mission and national church in the United Arab Republic, many of the aspects of "integration" have been achieved informally in the developing relationship between Synod and Mission. Former Mission schools are administered by the Board of Management for Evangelical Schools elected by the Synod. Literacy and rural extension programs are under the Coptic Evangelical Organization for Social Service, whose board is made up of people who are members of the Synod. Medical Work, Audio-Visual Services, and one or two other programs, though administered by the Mission Administrative Council, have the benefit of national churchmen participation in the meetings of the Mission Council. Missionary personnel requested to serve under the Synod are assigned to the Synod for oversight of their work. In all other matters, except strictly routine missionary maintenance questions, Synod and Mission are in full and frequent consultation. Thus, informally a very large measure of "integration" has indeed been achieved, and clearly this type of integration is the most suitable for the Egyptian situation at the present time.

Africa.   The Cameroun Presbyterian Church is the result of one of the earliest missionary efforts of the former Board of Foreign Missions of the Presbyterian Church in the U.S.A., when it established what came to be known as the West Africa Mission. As the church grew, presbyteries were formed and, later on, a synod. This body was a member of the General Assembly of the Presbyterian Church in the U.S.A. until 1957. On December 11, 1957, the Cameroun Presbyterian Church organized an independent General Assembly, and the West Africa Mission was dissolved.

In Africa, the development of nationalism and the establishment of twenty-eight independent nations since World War II have had a decided influence on the attitudes and feelings of church leaders. In the case of Cameroun, independence of the nation and of the Presbyterian Church was achieved more or less at the same time, and of the two, perhaps ecclesiastical independence has produced more difficulties. This is due to the fact that church-to-church relationships became operationally and psychologically unrealistic, because there is a wealthy and highly organized church on the one hand (The United Presbyterian Church in the U.S.A.), and on the other, a relatively weak, underdeveloped church that is beginning to achieve identity.

By contrast, the Commission on Ecumenical Mission and Relations has been able to establish relations and fruitful partnerships with churches in Kenya, Liberia, Nigeria, Gabon, Zambia, and Malawi. In these countries, the problems of identity, understanding, and mutuality in relationships were minimal, and there has been a genuine sharing in the life of the churches on the part of the Commission.

As time goes on, the church in the Cameroun, strengthened and matured by the weight of new responsibilities, will be able to broaden its perspectives by developing a fellowship in mission. The church has already established new vital relations with sister churches in the Cameroun, as well as with other churches in Africa and elsewhere. Related to this has been the establishment of new and mutually helpful relationships that are growing between the Presbyterian Church in the Cameroun and The United Presbyterian Church in the United States of America.

The Sudan. United Presbyterian activities in the Sudan are divided into two separate sections: North Sudan, and the province of the Upper Nile, formerly called South Sudan. In 1956, the Evangelical Church in the Upper Nile became autonomous and changed its name to the Church of Christ in the Upper Nile. In 1963, missionaries from the United Presbyterian Church and the Reformed Church in America were given an associate relationship to the church. In 1964, amid conditions of great unrest and turmoil in the Upper Nile, the missionaries were expelled from the country, and the property and equipment were transferred to the Church of Christ.

In North Sudan the church has been more closely associated with the Church in Egypt since work was established in 1900. In recent years political upheaval has created conditions of uncertainty among both church members and missionaries.

The Evangelical Church in the Sudan has assumed administrative responsibility for various aspects of the work formerly under the American Mission. In 1965, seventeen United Presbyterian missionaries continued to serve in educational and other forms of Christian witness by arrangement with boards constituted by the Presbytery.

Ethiopia. In Ethiopia the American Mission exists alongside the Bethel Evangelical Church, which comprises nineteen organized congregations. United Presbyterians and Reformed Church missionaries work together to strengthen the Christian witness of all the churches.

Apart from the capital of the country, Addis Ababa, conditions are still primitive, and the integration of church and mission has proved to be impracticable. However, studies are being undertaken to determine the best method of integration of the work of the mission into the life of the Christian community. In the meantime, the Bethel Evangelical Church is beginning to assume more responsibility for the spread of the gospel among primitive people in the outlying areas of Ethiopia. Reference is made later in this chapter to a new venture, especially in medical work, among these people.

Latin America. The missions were integrated with the Presbyterian Church of Colombia in 1959, the Evangelical Presbyterian

Church of Venezuela, and the Evangelical Presbyterian Church of Guatemala in 1962. The pattern of integration in Chile was somewhat different from that of the three churches just mentioned. In 1950, a Ten-Year Plan was adopted whereby transference of responsibilities would be made gradually to the Presbytery of Chile and the Evangelical Union, a property-holding body. This plan was revised in 1957, and it was agreed that, as their furloughs came due, missionaries would not return to Chile. This would allow the Presbytery to assume control of its work at a much earlier date than was at first anticipated. Since its formation, the Presbytery of Chile had been a member of the Synod of New York. In 1963, on the initiative of the Presbytery, this relationship terminated, and in the following year an independent synod was formed in Chile, and fraternal workers from Brazil and the United States are working under its direction.

The pattern of relationships in Brazil has been historically different from that of other Latin American countries. Presbyterian work was begun in Brazil in 1859, and the church has developed to such an extent that it represents one of the largest Protestant churches in Latin America. By virtue of the Brazil Plan of 1917, the missionaries relinquished their membership in presbyteries, and since then, the majority have worked in the interior of the country, in areas where there is usually no organized presbytery. In 1954, the Inter-Presbyterian Council was formed with representatives from the Presbyterian Church of Brazil, the Central Brazil Mission of the Presbyterian Church in the U.S.A., and the missions of the Presbyterian Church U.S. In 1962, the Central Brazil Mission took action whereby the evangelistic work under the mission was to be incorporated into the structures of the presbyteries of the Presbyterian Church of Brazil. Educational institutions, formerly under the mission, were to function under the Erasmo Braga Society, an organization of the church designed to coordinate Presbyterian educational work in Brazil. However, this plan has not been consummated, and, in the meantime, educational and medical institutions are under boards of directors on which are representatives of synods and presbyteries. Thus, in Brazil, integration has proceeded from the bottom up, rather than from the top down, as in other countries.

From Missions to Mission

Prior to the establishment of the Commission, the two boards had missions in foreign lands. We have already seen that according to the *Manual* of one of these boards, the term "missions" was defined as an organization of missionaries.[14] A later reference in the *Manual* shows that it also referred to geographical area as well, for purposes of specific designation and field administration.

The term "missions," therefore, was used in a dual sense. It referred to the group of missionaries in a particular country and it was also used in an administrative way. Thus it can be said that The Board of Foreign Missions of the Presbyterian Church in the U.S.A. had a mission in Brazil or in Korea, or that the Board of Foreign Missions of the United Presbyterian Church of North America had a mission in Egypt or in Pakistan. They were "foreign" missions because they conducted their work in a foreign land.

In most countries the mission met annually, but in one case, at least, it proved expensive to meet on an annual basis because of great distances and lack of transportation facilities. The standard practice was that each missionary presented a written report of his activities during the year, and then the group proceeded to wrestle for days, and nights, with the problems of budget and personnel requests for the coming year, or years. It was a time of fellowship and comradeship, and older missionaries had opportunities to get to know newly arrived colleagues. Together the missionaries renewed their faith through prayer and Bible study. The custom was, in most cases, to invite one or two leaders of the national church, generally the Moderator and the Stated Clerk of the General Assembly, to attend one or more of the sessions of the mission meeting. The writer remembers attending a mission meeting in a Latin American country when the Stated Clerk of the General Assembly was invited to the opening session. He was presented in generous terms to the group, and was asked to say a few words. He was happy that the missionaries were doing such fine work and hoped they would continue to do so. He knew little or nothing of the budget that was being prepared, or of the kind of missionary personnel that was being requested of the Board in

New York. The mission was an entity in itself, with its own life and peculiar responsibilities.

Outwardly, the mission in a given country had fraternal and friendly relations with the national church and its leaders, but they were not intimate. They were not the relationships of a family, but of two separate entities, whose tasks should have been similar but somehow were regarded as different. The lines of communication were with the Boards in New York, Philadelphia, or Nashville.

The churches in the United States were well adjusted to the idea of having missions in so many countries around the world. It was a traditional concept, shared with many other churches similarly engaged in the missionary enterprise, and it had preciseness and definition. In local churches, women's groups, with great earnestness and devotion, studied missions, which usually meant that they read about and discussed mission work in several countries of a given area or continent. The needs of the missions would be understood fairly well, and the appeal to raise funds to help meet them generally met with generous response. The missions performed their task well and faithfully; the nature of their work was communicated to the churches at home and these responded liberally year after year. The sacrifice, the devotion, the use of time and talent, both in the missions abroad and the churches at home, constitute glorious pages in the annals of the Kingdom. This was the traditional pattern for many decades, and the church of Jesus Christ owes much to it.

However, the day of "missions" has drawn to a close, and the day of the "mission" of the church has dawned. At the heart of the church is its mission, and for the younger churches to engage in mission, they must have a deep understanding of the nature of the Christian church and come to realize that where the church is, there the mission begins. Dr. Virgil A. Sly, speaking at the annual meeting of the Division of Foreign Missions of the National Council of Churches in 1958, said, "Our awareness of the transition from missions to mission involves the necessity of planting the concept of the church as mission deep into the heart and life of our churches."[15]

The transition from "missions" to "mission" also involves a change in attitude on the part of the church membership in the West. Supporters of the missionary enterprise have been accustomed to referring to "our missions," and often have made such statements as, "We have a mission in Thailand" or, "Our board has a mission in Egypt." "The message is God's message. It becomes our message whenever it possesses us, not when we possess it. The possessive note of Western denominational pride has no place in God's mission. We say with pride 'Our Mission'; we should say 'God's Mission.' "[16]

An important part of the Commission's task has been to secure an adjustment in perspective among church members in the United States. Accustomed to supporting "missions" with their gifts, their prayers, and their efforts, church people began to ask whether these would be needed any more. How could they "support missions" if the missions had gone out of existence? Thus, instead of the promotion of missions as in the past, the emphasis has changed to an interpretation of the church as a universal reality in which mission is seen as of its very essence.

The promotional office of a Board of Foreign Missions has become an Interpretation Office of the Commission on Ecumenical Mission and Relations. The relationship between missionaries or fraternal workers and congregations in the U.S.A. is now one of personal interest instead of direct financial support, and the personal interest of the congregation is extended to the national church in whose life and work the missionary or fraternal worker is engaged. Through this personal interest relationship the new concepts of the nature and mission of the church are interpreted, and a sense of involvement beyond financial support of the mission is developed.

All the missionaries of the United Presbyterian Church, whether at work in the U.S.A. or abroad, are supported out of a General Mission Budget which is raised by the denomination as a whole, and not in bits or pieces by individual missionaries, or by the unilateral efforts of boards and agencies.

As we have come to a new sense of the oneness of Christ's mission, so we have developed a unified interpretation of this one mission. In relationship to congregations in the United States, the separate boards and agencies now make their major thrust through a single Department of Interpretation and Stewardship of the denomination's General Council. Interpretation Secretaries of the Board of National Missions, of the Board of Christian Education, and of the Commission on Ecumenical Mission and Relations also serve on the staff of this Department which "promotes" and interprets the concerns of the entire church.

Another development from this new concept of mission and mission interpretation is the recognition by synods and presbyteries that the responsibility for interpretation ultimately rests with them. It has to do with nurturing church members and congregations in an understanding of the nature and mission of the church, and this is inescapable from the preaching and teaching responsibility to which all elders have been ordained.

The Commission assists the presbyteries and synods in the fulfillment of their task of mission interpretation by assigning fraternal workers on furloughs to the staffs of these judicatories. The fraternal workers are responsible to the synod or presbytery executives, and carry out duties of total denominational concerns. Their aim is to strengthen the judicatory's own program of General Mission Interpretation.

During the past seven years, the younger churches, which were formerly referred to as "our Presbyterian churches," have sought increasingly to become partners in the mission of the church. Fraternal workers have gone from one Asian country to another. The church in Japan has sent fraternal workers to more than one country; the United Church of Christ in the Philippines has sent nurses to serve in Iran, Ethiopia, and Lebanon; the Presbyterian Church of Brazil has sent fraternal workers to Portugal. Numerically, this group of fraternal workers from one country to another may not be large, because of the limitation of resources, but the essential concept of the church as mission is there. The East Asia Christian Conference constantly seeks to enlarge this commitment to the mission of the church among its members.

The change from missions to mission strengthens the unity of the Christian churches as they come to feel that they are a part of the vision of one world mission task. The distinction between the former geographically limited Christendom of the West and the non-Christian world has largely disappeared. After World War II, "people in Europe, Great Britain, and America were talking about their nations as a 'post-Christian society' in need of evangelization. Against that background the delegates at the Willingen Conference in 1952 caught a vision of one world mission of the one Church of Christ to the whole inhabited earth, with lines of witness running through every nation to all frontiers where Jesus Christ is not recognized as Lord. Since then, the term *mission* has come very widely to replace *missions*."[17] The Conference emphasized the relevance of unity to mission and the urgent need for the churches to exercise a new missionary initiative. The relation of unity to mission was brought out in the contention expressed at the Conference that the church should no longer speak of mission *and* unity, as if they were separable, but of mission *in* unity. From this it followed that the lack of unity among the churches was at least partly responsible for the weakening of the missionary drive or initiative.

The Search for Identity

We have attempted to trace the historical process from missions to mission, from the establishment of missions through the growth of younger churches with which in recent years the missions have integrated. In this process, the younger churches, now autonomous as far as their life and work are concerned, constantly seek identity and selfhood. Even when a church has arrived at a level of development whereby it becomes self-governing, self-supporting, and self-propagating, it may not necessarily have achieved identity. When some leaders of the United Church of Christ in Japan refer to the need to "de-Americanize" their church, they are seeking for identity or selfhood. They do not mean that this implies a process of becoming a Japanese church. The Kyodan is largely that now, but it is a United Church of Christ *in* Japan and not so much *of* Japan.

Achieving identity involves overcoming a sense of inferiority which characterizes many of the younger churches. A number of factors have helped to produce this inferiority complex. In the first place, most Christian communities in Asia, Africa, and Latin America are usually tiny minorities when compared with the total population. Christian leaders in the missionary enterprise have rejoiced in the fact that

Christian churches are to be found in practically every country in the world, but when that statement is made, there is a tendency to overlook the minority status of these communities. In addition to an inferiority in terms of numbers, Christians are often conscious of being regarded by their fellow countrymen as traitors to their cultural and religious heritage. A third factor is the effect of a long period of tutelage and dependence upon mission organizations in the West. Finally, Christians in many countries share the general feeling of inferiority of the people in less-developed countries by comparison with the West. It will take time to overcome these factors, and that is why achieving identity by younger churches is a slow process. One encouraging fact is the emergence of a number of well-qualified, able church leaders.

A calling, whether it be of an individual or a group such as a church, is always *for* something, that is, it is purposeful. In one of his epistles to the younger churches of his day, Peter wrote, "Ye are a chosen generation, . . . a peculiar people; that ye should show forth the praises of him who hath called you out of darkness into his marvelous light."[18] This means that a church is chosen, or called for a purpose, and that purpose is missionary, first in the nation in which it finds itself, and then beyond. As they were established in Japan, the Philippines, Chile, and so on, churches became worshiping communities, and before long they were active centers for evangelization.

On the road to achieving selfhood, the churches across the world are increasingly conscious that they are placed in the midst of a dynamic, revolutionary social situation, in a world that is fast being secularized.

Faced with a seemingly impossible task of witnessing to the dynamic power of the gospel in such a world, the younger churches are feeling the need for the warmth and strength that comes from being a part of a worldwide fellowship and a Christian movement.

The achieving of identity or selfhood and becoming integral parts of a whole church, independent and yet interdependent, having mission and purpose—these are the marks of maturing churches in Asia, Africa, and Latin America. In the search for unity and mission, relations between one church and another, or of one church with others, play an increasingly significant role in the one world of today.

Adjustments Arising Out of Integration

In view of what we have stated concerning the transition from missions to mission, it is only natural to assume that missions as understood in the past had to disappear or be merged into the life of the churches in the different countries. In some instances, this has turned out to be a rather painful process, both for the missionaries on the field and for the churches in the United States. With integration of the mission into the life of the national church, the status and relationships of the missionary had to be different, and this entailed considerable adjustment, both psychologically, and, to a certain extent, spiritually.

The Mohonk Consultation of 1956 recommended that step by step The Board of Foreign Missions of the Presbyterian Church in the U.S.A., the mission, and the church should plan to achieve the integration of church and mission, if possible, within a five-year period. There are now only a few missions remaining, and in one case at least, the national church has expressed a certain fear of integration and what it might mean, namely, that the missionaries would exert undue influence in the presbyteries of the church.

On the surface, integration of the mission into the national church would seem to be a relatively simple operation. Experience has shown that such is not the case. The main difficulties seem to be concerned with the question of the adjustment of relationships of the missionaries (now fraternal workers) and the national church, and also with the matter of institutions and property. One source of irritation is the fact that often the fraternal worker has funds for travel, whereas the national worker does not.

As a member of a mission, the missionary was given a definite assignment and his responsibilities were clearly outlined. As a fraternal worker, he is assigned by the national church. In some cases he was asked to continue in the duties and work he already had, and there was a minimum of difficulty and adjustment. In other cases the fraternal worker was assigned to work under a national leader, in a more subordinate role. This situation often demanded considerable adjustment and much Christian grace and humility. Formerly, in many cases, missionaries were chosen by their boards because of their qualities of leadership, and it was expected that they would be leaders of the younger churches. On the field they served as evangelists, teachers, or the trainers of national leaders. They were often called upon to formulate policy for a growing church, and to organize and supervise its institutions. In the meantime, national leaders have been prepared and they are ready to assume roles of responsibility and leadership. Most missionaries have known from the beginning of their careers that they were to "work themselves out of a job," and ultimately make way for national leaders. This is the natural order of things, but when the time arrives, it is still a rather painful process.

The new relationships in which the missionary finds himself can sometimes produce tensions and frustrations. In former days he had a fairly clear idea of who he was and what he was expected to do. Now he takes a new look at his missionary vocation, and with a troubled conscience and a feeling of uncertainty and ambiguity he asks himself what it means to be a missionary or a fraternal worker in a new day and within the context of the ecumenical mission of the church. In other words, the fraternal worker in many countries today is facing the problem of self-identification and the meaning of his vocation.

Dr. Thomas J. Liggett, with long experience as a missionary in Argentina, and more recently as the president of the Evangelical Seminary of Puerto Rico, in an address on "The Role of the Missionary in Latin America Today," asked if the missionary knows who he really is. To clarify the point, he refers to the situation in which the hero of Cervantes' classic Don Quijote de La Mancha finds himself. The reader will recall that Don Quijote puts on the armor of a medieval knight and goes forth to do battle for the cause of goodness and justice. "He soon finds himself fallen to the ground and unable, because of the weight of his armor, to get up. From this ridiculous position he has a short conversation with a woodsman in which he denies the identity attributed to him by the woodsman and affirms in the unforgettable words of Cervantes 'Yo sé quien soy' (I know who I am)."[19] These famous words in the Spanish language are a clue to the secret of the successful fulfillment of a man's vocation.

During the first seven years, the Commission has attempted to lead the United Presbyterian fraternal workers into a new understanding of who they are, and of what they are now called to. In recent years, annual conferences have been held with Commission members, staff members, furloughed fraternal workers and missionaries, with this purpose in mind. The situation, however, calls for continued efforts to help the fraternal worker understand his role within a national church in another country, caught up in all the challenges of a dynamic, revolutionary situation.

In one country, integration has not yet taken place because the national leaders fear that the government might take exception to the presence of Americans in the church and its institutions. How can a fraternal worker, a citizen of another country, become an integral part of a national church as a fellow worker with national colleagues, brothers in a family? This demands a great deal of the fraternal worker, since his cultural background, his foreignness, and his enjoyment of higher standards of living than his national colleagues have, have increased the difficulties and created tensions. In the Cameroun, integration of the mission into the national church took place not long after the country achieved its independence. Africans moved into government positions vacated by the departing French officials and they also moved into the houses formerly occupied by the French. It was perhaps natural for the African pastor now in a new position of authority in the church to follow the example of political counterparts by wishing to move into a missionary house.

Dr. D. T. Niles, General Secretary of the East Asia Christian Conference, expressed what may be a general feeling in Asia when he wrote, "The only thing we in the younger churches ask from our missionary brethren is that we be treated as adults."[20] On the other hand, Niles feels that it is very disconcerting to have missionaries who must be treated tenderly lest they get emotionally upset "or find the weather too trying, or get 'frustrated'—that blessed word which is now used to describe the mental condition in which a missionary is, either because his wife insists on a 'fridge' for the house, or because his national colleague does not have a sense of humor."[21] This may be a little rhetorical indulgence on the part of this distinguished Asian churchman, but it serves to illustrate the point we are trying to make that in the area of personal relationships are to be found many human situations, the solution of which requires patience, understanding, and mutual forbearance.

The matter of church properties created another series of problems. The national church usually expected that with integration all properties formerly held in the name of the mission, or by the Commission, would now pass into the hands of the national church. Legal difficulties presented themselves. In the first place, not all churches had legal standing before the government, and therefore could not hold property. Sometimes large properties were involved, land having been bought by the mission many years ago and having greatly appreciated in value. Not only good faith was required, but also specific guarantees that properties would be used for the purpose originally stated by donors in the United States. Unless their wishes were respected in this regard, there was always the possibility of a lawsuit, and this was a serious matter. Leaders of the national churches, especially pastors without legal training or experience in handling such matters, were at a distinct disadvantage. Furthermore, the ownership of property could be anything but an unmixed blessing, because it had to be kept in good repair, and this required additional funds. The Commission has been willing to help churches meet this problem, but there is obviously a limit to this also.

Educational and medical institutions represented another set of difficulties. These institutions have been an important and an integral part of the mission program of the Commission, and of the former Boards of Foreign Missions. In many cases, especially in the larger institutions, considerable funds and personnel are required to maintain them at a standard of efficiency increasingly demanded. The Commission has encouraged the formation of boards of trustees, or boards of directors, composed largely of competent laymen in the churches, to which institutions and property could be turned over. This is more difficult to do than in the United States, where the practice is a more common one. During the first seven years of the Commission, considerable progress has been made in this regard, although in some cases, the process was initiated under the former Boards of Foreign Missions, or the Women's General Missionary Society of the former United Presbyterian Church of North America.

There is no single pattern that can be applied to all countries, since situations vary considerably. The Presbyterian Church of Colombia at the time of integration already had boards of directors for the large educational institutions, but it was not prepared to assume responsibility for the properties, preferring to leave these in the hands of Christian Properties Corporation, a holding body of the Commission. In some cases, such as the Philippines and Japan, integration was with a united church rather than a Presbyterian one. In these two areas, the spirit of unity and cooperation was shared by both missionaries and national leaders for several decades before integration actually took place.

On New Geographical Frontiers

In this chapter we have mentioned some of the important developments that have taken place since the Commission on Ecumenical Mission and Relations was created in 1958, especially in the transition "from missions to mission." This process involved both "mission" and "relations" as they are conceived by the Commission.

While it is true that the greatest challenge facing the church today is on the frontiers of an increasingly technologically oriented world, there are still some geographical frontiers where the need for mission is most pressing. We shall refer to two of these, Nepal and Ethiopia.

Nepal. Situated high in the Himalayan Mountains, the Kingdom of Nepal, with a population of nine million people, in recent years began to emerge from medieval isolation, as it joined the family of nations on the road to progress. The opportunity and invitation to establish mission work came after two missionary doctors, one a Methodist and the other a Presbyterian, accompanied by a representative of the Chicago Museum of Natural History made several trips to Nepal in the early 1950's. His Majesty's government invited the missionaries to initiate regular missionary work in Kathmandu, the capital, and in Tansen. The missionaries concerned, and the mission boards they represented, felt that the invitation should be accepted, but that the work should be undertaken, not only by the two churches, the Methodist and the Presbyterian, but by a representative ecumenical group. The Protestant boards and societies in India, Japan, Australia, Great Britain, Europe, and North America met in 1953 and formed the United Mission to Nepal. The Commission on Ecumenical Mission and Relations and the India Council, representing the Presbyterian Churches in North India, participated in the Mission. Since 1953 other groups have joined, making a total of twenty-two, each member of the mission agreeing to provide both workers and funds. Nearly one hundred missionaries, and an even larger number of Nepalese, are engaged in a program that provides medical, educational, and agricultural services. Although no direct evangelistic work is undertaken, in compliance with the laws of the country, worshiping congregations have been established, four of which are in the city of Kathmandu. The Mission is filling a great human need with compassion and a Christian presence. A new geographical frontier has been claimed for the Christian movement on an ecumenical basis.

Ethiopia. In Ethiopia a similar opportunity to bring health to a neglected people presented itself in 1960 when His Imperial Majesty, Haile Selassie, approached the United Presbyterian Mission in Ethiopia with a request that a public-health and medical program be undertaken among several tribes in the Illubabur and Kaffa provinces. The project, which was initiated in 1962, involves establishing medical posts in strategic areas, using missionary personnel, doctors, and nurses in a government-built hospital. To date, two such cooperative ventures have begun at Gore and Mettu, with primary attention being given to meeting the serious health needs of the people, but with attempts being made to train Ethiopian personnel. The Ethiopian Government cooperates by providing tracts of land for hospital sites, funds for buildings, and maintenance. The work is of a pioneer nature among tribes never reached before.

In Ethiopia, alongside this development on a new geographical frontier, new forms of friendly relations have been established between Orthodox Christians and United Presbyterians. This fresh desire for cooperation was in evidence during the summer of 1965 in a project for students of the Orthodox Theological Seminary. Not all the activities that fall under the heading of "relations" are of the formal or structured kind, originating in the United States. Indeed, some of the more creative types of ecumenical relations occur on the local level.

Chapter VIII

DIMENSIONS AND CHALLENGES
OF THE TASK AHEAD

THIS book has attempted to trace the historical development of the
Commission on Ecumenical Mission and Relations and the involvement of The United Presbyterian Church in the U.S.A. in the ecumenical movement. We have seen how the Presbyterian Church was
established, the way in which it became a missionary church, and how
boards of foreign missions were formed and women's work begun.
Today, United Presbyterians, indeed, have a heritage of which they
can be justly proud, and it must be recognized that churches, like
many other organizations, build on the foundations that were laid
in the past.

However, important as all this is, it does not constitute the main
purpose of this book. Just as the church is not an end in itself, so it
is with the Commission on Ecumenical Mission and Relations. Therefore, the historical approach has been made with the purpose of trac-
ing developments in order to provide a basis for interpretation.

The United Presbyterian Church believes it has a calling in today's
world, and the Commission on Ecumenical Mission and Relations
shares that calling. An ecumenical missionary task has been committed
to it, and the Commission seeks to fulfill this task amid all the complexities of the modern world, and in a new pattern of relationships.
The Commission is ever seeking to understand the nature of a revolutionary, changing world, and to discern the best way to use whatever
resources God puts into its hands. It does so in the new dimensions
of an ecumenical fellowship, or movement, which means that the
United Presbyterian Church is aware of the way in which churches
long separated are now discovering one another, and in a new sense

of unity are joining together in the fulfillment of a common mission to the world under the guidance of the Holy Spirit. These considerations lay behind the decision to undertake what has come to be known as *An Advisory Study*.

An Advisory Study

An Advisory Study is a document produced by a committee of fifteen persons, carefully chosen by the Commission on Ecumenical Mission and Relations, less than two years after this body was created. The idea of having such a study grew out of the conditions and world events that led to the formation of the Commission in 1958. However, it largely came to fruition in the heart and mind of Dr. Charles T. Leber, General Secretary of the Commission at that time. In expressing this view in its report, the committee referred to "the Christ-dedicated vision of Dr. Charles T. Leber."[1]

Under Dr. Leber's leadership the Commission felt that a special study needed to be made of the nature of the church's mission in a revolutionary era, and how it could best carry out that mission. Merely to decide to do more of what the church was already doing by the relatively simple method of increasing funds and personnel was felt to be quite inadequate. If a quantitative approach to the missionary task was to be made, then the creation of the Commission would have been unnecessary. The broad question that the Commission faced, and that prompted the calling together of an Advisory Study Committee was, "How can the Church witness effectively to Jesus Christ in the contemporary situation?"

The Commission decided not to appoint a committee composed only of some of its own members or of the staff. It was convinced that if The United Presbyterian Church in the U.S.A. was to find answers to some of the fundamental questions relating to ecumenical mission and relations, the insights and value judgments of people representing different cultures and backgrounds were essential. The fifteen members of the committee were drawn from Brazil, Cuba, Egypt, France, India, Iran, Korea, Lebanon, Nigeria, Switzerland, Taiwan, and the United States. Three were Commission members, two were United Presbyterian missionaries. Among the group were ministers, laymen, laywomen, educators, student workers, a doctor, a sociologist, and a specialist in audio-visual work. Of the fifteen, ten were laymen, five were ministers.

The Committee divided its work broadly into observation and study, over a period of nearly two years. In groups of two or three, members of the Committee visited many of the younger churches in Asia, Africa, the Middle East, and Latin America. However, the Committee was not charged with the responsibility of submitting specific recommendations concerning this area or that, one reason for this being that the Commission was no longer in a position to make decisions by itself, that is, without reference to the younger churches themselves, and in consultation with other denominational agencies and ecumenical bodies. The main purpose was to gain a new perspective on the total task of the church. It should be noted that the Committee had available to it, as background, numerous books, brochures, reports, and other documents dealing with missionology and the Biblical basis of mission.

An Advisory Study, which is the name given to the Committee's report, consisted of two main parts. The first part dealt with the Biblical concept of mission; and the second, the task before each church as well as before the churches together. The title of Part One, "Captives in Christ's Triumphal Possession," is rich in content and suggestive in character. Amid the turmoil of a revolutionary world, and the trends toward nihilism and secularism of today, the Christian church can speak with an accent of triumph and serenity, for "the God who meets us in Christ has pronounced once for all a clear and decisive 'Yes' for the world."[2] To a world sunk in despair and fear, the church proclaims that God is a living God, who acts in history and through history.

Using Biblical images and concepts, the report describes the Christian church as the "Firstfruits of the New Humanity in and for the World."[3] The church itself is not the new humanity, but its firstfruits, the purpose being to make visible what a new and redeemed order of life in Christ would be like. In this context the church sees itself "as a pledge of the new harvest, God's promise of a new humanity. The Church, therefore, itself becomes a part of the Good News it proclaims."[4] *An Advisory Study* puts great emphasis on this Biblical concept of the Christian church as the firstfruits and a divine pledge of the full harvest to come. In any given nation, the firstfruits are a tangible evidence of the fact that God is at work there.

A second Biblical image that *An Advisory Study* stresses is that of the *oikos*. Following the crucifixion of Jesus, it will be recalled, a handful of his disciples met behind locked doors, and he appeared to them as the risen Lord, saying, "Peace be unto you." The house where they met was an *oikos*, a place or environment where men had an experience of the risen Christ, an experience that transformed them from a fear-stricken, disillusioned group of plain men into a group with a mission. "With the word of peace pronounced by the risen Lord, the *oikos* with its locked doors becomes a true household once again, a home filled with joy, a community with its inner cohesion and harmony restored."[5] In addition to the words of peace, Jesus said to his disciples, "As *my* Father hath sent me, even so send I you."[6] In the instances we have cited, and as recorded in John's Gospel, the house was an *oikos*, and it was set within a larger *oikos*, the city, which was within still larger ones, the nation and the world.

In the dynamic society in which the church now finds itself, "traditional *oikoi* in which men lived for centuries are now shaken up. Old structures are breaking down and new ones are taking their place."[7] Momentous decisions must be taken, and new forms of service and witness discovered, so that the church may not only renew its own life but also make a dynamic impact on the world with the life-giving power of the Christian gospel, and be a channel of redemption and reconciliation in a world alienated from God and sundered by hatred and strife.

The gospel was to be proclaimed unto the uttermost parts of the world. In the early Christian era, that world was circumscribed by the bounds of Greek and Roman civilizations. Today the world has become larger, not only geographically but also sociologically and functionally. "God is leading the church today on the road of radical renewal for faithful participation in his redemptive work. Our disobedience can result only in our becoming irrelevant and marginal to the life of man today."[8]

When the Commission appointed the Advisory Study Committee in 1960, it was conscious of the task that had been committed to it by the

United Presbyterian Church. With this in mind, the Commission set up the Advisory Study Committee in an unprecedented way. Many committees, commissions, and deputations had been named in former years, and they had presented reports out of which emerged new lines of strategy, modifications in program, and creative forms of service. These were consultations not only with missionaries on the field but also with the church leaders in different countries. In a sense they had participated in whatever decisions were taken by the Boards (Presbyterian Church in the U.S.A. and the United Presbyterian Church of North America). The responsibility, however, belonged to those bodies, and they had the authority to formulate decisions and carry them out.

The Commission saw itself in a different role. As we have pointed out, it urgently desired to have the best thinking of a representative, international group, concerning the nature of today's world, and some authentic word on what "the Spirit was saying to the churches" in the mid-twentieth century. The Commission acted with deliberateness and purpose in naming the kind of committee that was appointed, and in the way in which this was done. When the report was printed, the cover carried this phrase, "A Working Paper for Study—Not to Be Interpreted as the Policy of the Commission." The Commission has never approved or disapproved the report. The Committee was given full freedom to write the kind of report it wished to make, and the Introductory Statement made it quite clear that, given the nature of the contemporary world situation and the place which the so-called younger churches occupy in the worldwide Christian church, the Commission did not wish to act unilaterally. Furthermore, it stated that "the Commission is aware that it requires for its evidence the insights of other church bodies which share in world-wide mission."[9]

In the intervening years since the report appeared, it has been read, digested, discussed, praised, and criticized. Some have criticized this document, but none could ignore its prophetic voice, or fail to recognize its deep insights. Three situation conferences were set up in Asia, and consultations were held in Latin America, the Middle East, and Africa. Within these areas, groups of fraternal workers and church groups, largely interdenominational in character, have studied the document. In addition, *An Advisory Study* has been widely read and discussed by a number of sister denominations, and the effect it has had on their thinking is difficult to assess. It is safe to say that even outside the Presbyterian family, this prophetic document has raised old issues in a new way, and has stimulated creative thinking.

An Advisory Study did not set out to furnish answers to all the problems the churches face today. Its purpose, rather, was to provoke discussion and thinking, which is basic to the whole study, and represents a departure from the old way of doing things. The Advisory Study Committee was saying in effect: "Here is our own thinking, and such insights as we have on some of the major issues before the church today. Let the churches use it as a basis for their own deliberations and study, in the hope that they will come to a new understanding of what God wants us to do." This approach was psychologically sound, for it is one thing to have a set of propositions, or lines of action, presented to a group, but for that group to go through the process of formulating its own lines of thought and action is creative and meaningful.

The breadth of An Advisory Study is revealed in the word that came from a United Presbyterian synod executive in the United States: "Many of the observations which are made in this study concerning the younger churches could be stated just as validly concerning the church in our own land."[10] Another church executive in the United States felt that An Advisory Study was the most exciting document he had read in a long time, and expressed the view that it should serve to revitalize the missionary program of the church in the United States.

From 1960 to April, 1966, approximately 15,600 English copies of An Advisory Study were distributed, and it was also circulated in twelve other languages. Besides being studied and discussed at situation conferences and consultations in Asia, Africa, and Latin America, An Advisory Study has been used as a basis for discussion by ecumenical bodies such as the World Council of Churches, the National Council of Churches, the East Asia Christian Conference, the All Africa Conference of Churches, and in consultations of various denominational bodies. An Advisory Study has indeed engaged the attention and provoked fresh thinking among many groups of Christians around the world. For the Commission itself the Study set in motion a continuing examination of the basic assumptions underlying its policies and programs, and created a new awareness of the changes that have to be made in order to make the mission of the church relevant to a world social revolution.

Partnership in Mission

The authentic word that came out of the International Missionary Conference held at Whitby, Canada, in 1947 was "partnership in obedience," and in 1952 the Willingen Conference chose as its theme "The Missionary Obligation of the Church."

However, it was *An Advisory Study* that emphasized the essential kind of relationship which must exist between an older and a younger church, between the United Presbyterian Church and a church in India, Africa, or Latin America, before there can be a genuine partnership in mission. *An Advisory Study* recognized that a younger church must achieve authentic selfhood before this can take place, and that relationships between older and younger churches go through three stages: dependence, independence, and interdependence.[11] In order to facilitate these changes in relationships and to allow an authentic selfhood to develop among churches in the mission field, the Commission has had to disentangle itself from the inner life of these churches, so that they might be independent, and free to engage in mission as churches in their own right. Partnership in mission, therefore, did not automatically come into existence as a consequence of a recognition of the principle of "partnership in obedience," or even in fulfillment of the missionary obligation of the church. "Partnership in obedience can always become partnership in disobedience in the face of our missionary calling."[12]

The fulfillment of the missionary obligation of The United Presbyterian Church in the U.S.A. is committed to the Commission on Ecumenical Mission and Relations. In Japan, the United Church of Christ has followed a similar pattern by naming its own Commission on Ecumenical Mission and Relations.

Other churches around the world are in various stages of achieving selfhood and independence and are seeking to engage in mission on the basis of true partnership. "All over the world we Christians are learning more and more that as the company of the people of Jesus Christ we are called to share in His mission to the people around us."[13]

It must be admitted that, in actual practice, partnership in mission on a bilateral basis, involving the Commission and a younger church, is very difficult to achieve because of differences in size and strength. The desire to work out a correct relationship tends to focus undue attention on the relation of one to the other, whereas the chief purpose of partnership in mission is the mission itself. *An Advisory Study* emphasized some of these difficulties and recommended "a multilateral approach to mission within a wider context than that of a single church, country, or confession."[14]

A sense of missionary obligation is inherent in the nature of the church, and this applies to the local church and to the total church or denomination to which it belongs. It also means that mission is not an exclusive possession of the West. The churches of the West must engage in partnership with other churches across the world, either directly or through ecumenical bodies.

We have seen how in the case of the Presbyterian churches in the United States, in the early days, the sense of missionary obligation began as a concern among individuals, and that this concern found expression in an active participation in missionary societies, beginning in the early part of the nineteenth century. We have noted that in the 1830's the conviction prevailed that the Presbyterian Church in the U.S.A. should have its own board of foreign missions. This meant that the concern of individuals became the concern of the whole church, at least in theory. In practice today, however, it means that in some Protestant churches, members are taught that it is their duty and obligation to "support missions." It is quite possible to do this without having a clear idea of the mission of the church. For many, church and mission have been two separate entities, "missions" often being peripheral in the thinking of all but a devoted group of people who have caught the meaning of the church and its centrality in the Christian faith and have kept missionary interest alive. Support of missions as something marginal or optional in the United Presbyterian Church is quite different from the essentiality of the missionary obligation of the church.

The Commission on Ecumenical Mission and Relations has stated that "partnership in Mission presupposes two or more autonomous church bodies which voluntarily limit their own independent action in missionary outreach in order to insure a mutually satisfactory and a more highly productive interdependence in missionary endeavor."[15] The statement makes it clear that such a relationship can exist only where there is mature respect, affection, and confidence.

Joint Action for Mission

Another dimension of the church's task is summed up in the phrase "Joint Action for Mission." Since the Third Assembly of the World Council of Churches held at New Delhi in 1961, increasing attention has been given to steps beyond partnership in mission, which, as we have seen, involves relationships in mission, between mission agencies of the older churches and the younger churches, on a bilateral basis. Some progress has been made toward the goal of "one church" and "one mission," since the days when comity arrangements were made by missions in a given area. Comity was the word used to describe the process of agreeing on separate geographic areas of work, so that missions would avoid duplication of effort and overlapping. A kind of territorial integrity was assured to each mission, and the plan served its purpose. However, the time came when missions and churches, particularly the latter, were impelled toward closer cooperation. National councils of churches developed and there was joint planning in evangelism, audio-visual work, rural missions, and so on. Partnership in mission expressed the idea of growing relationships between older and younger churches. Projects and tasks requiring pooling of resources and joint planning were undertaken.

The next step beyond this is what has come to be known as "Joint Action for Mission," which means that the missionary thrust can be made through multilateral channels without regard to denominational labels. In a given area, churches and the missionary agencies, with which they have been related, can join together in facing the challenge of a total missionary task in that area. It does not mean necessarily the pooling of resources or their redistribution. The emphasis rather is on meeting the challenges of new frontiers and in the essential oneness of Christ's mission, regardless of denomination or nationality.

This plan goes beyond cooperation, and involves the breaking away of some traditional relationships, sectional interests, patterns, and practices. In 1963, the East Asia Christian Conference convened Situation Conferences in Madras, Tokyo, and Singapore. These were attended by Asian church leaders and by representatives from mission agencies in the West and from the World Council of Churches. In their search for leading questions concerning the nature and demands of their Christian calling, special consideration was given to Joint Action for Mission. At Singapore the report to the churches and councils in Asia said: "We believe God's mission in our varied circumstances is challenging us to think out new ways of obedience. Even before we have solved the problem of Faith and Order and our separation as Churches, there is a vast area where we are free to think, pray, plan, and act together. Only as we use this freedom can we enlarge the area of our common life. We have been concerned to face up to this in terms of Joint Action for Mission."[16]

The following principles for Joint Action for Mission were agreed upon at the Situation Conferences held in Asia in 1963:

1. Real sharing and complete frankness about successes and failures, and about resources—physical, financial, and in persons.
2. Agreement about priorities, which will certainly involve hard decisions and conflicts of power.
3. The putting of resources of manpower and money from any one country and from outside it at the disposal of a denomination or united body made responsible for a piece of work with no expectation of denominational dividend or return.
4. The trusting of each other in our separate denominations to do the particular tasks allotted to us—without this trust, joint action is impossible.[17]

The initiative for undertaking such action must rest with the churches on the field rather than with any of the churches of the West. This will necessitate an evaluation of resources of manpower and funds in a given area and a study of the most urgent and visible projects for this kind of operation. Priorities of funds and personnel as between one area and another will also need to be established. A common plan may be agreed upon, where a particular denomination will be asked to act for the total group. In other cases, several denominations may supply staff for a particular project, or there may be agreement to erect one building that can be used by several denominations, rather than each one putting up a separate building.

The nature of the work or projects to be undertaken in this way will be largely determined by the pressures arising out of the social revolution of our time—new housing developments, urbanization, growing industrialization, vast student bodies largely unreached by the Christian message, rural reconstruction—all on the new frontiers, which the traditional church activity does not normally reach.

At its Assembly in Bangkok, Thailand, in February-March, 1964, the East Asia Christian Conference discussed Joint Action for Mission. It recognized the Biblical basis of this as being that "the people of God everywhere are one body, put in one world with a mission to proclaim one Gospel."[18] The Asian church leaders also stated frankly that "something much more costly than a new set of administrative arrangements for the deployment of resources"[19] was demanded. With the leading of the Holy Spirit, churches will have to exercise greater frankness and honesty in their relations with one another, and manifest a greater readiness than hitherto to subordinate the power, prestige, and resources of their own particular group, in a larger commitment to God's service in the world. The Asian leaders further recognized that Joint Action for Mission would be impossible without the cooperation of many mission boards and church agencies outside Asia.

On March 16-17, 1964, the Commission on Ecumenical Mission and Relations took the following action:[20]

> The Commission VOTED to inform the churches in Asia with which it is closely related in mission that when they are ready to participate in Joint Action for Mission Conferences in national or smaller geographical areas, the Commission is ready to participate also and to face constructively the implications of our being part of God's people in one place.

The Commission would encourage the synods and church councils to which it has been historically related to enter into joint action with other church bodies in strategic locations, irrespective of whether the project is located in an area where the church has been traditionally at work.

The Commission endorses the steps suggested in the report of the Madras Situation Conference:

1. Church groups, in the whole country, region or district, would review together the total task and the total resources and would seek to reach a common mind as to which projects should be carried out jointly, and which separately.

2. Projects which different church groups have consented to undertake jointly or as part of a common strategy should be given priority in any allocation of funds and personnel. It is understood that Joint Action for Mission will be concerned with central missionary tasks and not with merely peripheral matters.

3. If it is decided by everybody in consultation that a certain project will best be done denominationally, Joint Action for Mission implies that other church groups would still support the project without seeking denominational advantages.

4. Where projects are of such size as to require new financial resources, representatives of Christian agencies whose assistance is being sought should be brought into consultation. It is important that churches seeking such aid should reveal all sources of aid open to them for any project.

5. It is understood that where resources of personnel and funds from outside the area are involved, provision should be made for the full participation of related mission agencies in planning and decision.

The Ecumenical Approach to Theological Education and Christian Education

For a number of years, concern had been expressed by mission boards and church leaders about the great need to raise the level of ministerial or theological training among the churches in Asia, Africa, and Latin America. No single mission board, either in the United

States or Europe, could feel satisfied with the progress made in recent decades.

At the International Missionary Council meeting in Ghana in January, 1958, the decision was taken by the Assembly to establish the Theological Education Fund. The overall purpose of this new ecumenical venture was "for the advancement of theological education in Africa, Asia, and Latin America in accordance with a five-year plan."

Funds were immediately available for an initial grant from John D. Rockefeller, Jr., and special funds from eight American mission boards, including the Commission on Ecumenical Mission and Relations. Supplementary grants were made by societies in Australia, Canada, and Scotland. As a result of its successful work and in view of the continuing needs, it was decided to continue the fund beyond the first five years. The new program launched in 1965 has received funds from nearly one hundred donors on every continent. "Seldom has an ecumenical project evoked such wide commitment."[21]

It is one thing for a single denomination to command the resources in personnel and funds for the vast and complicated needs of theological education across the world. However, when a number of denominations in different lands combine their resources, it is not difficult to visualize the advantages in making an ecumenical approach to the problem. During the first five years a little over $4,250,000 was expended in major grants to seminaries overseas for textbook programs, libraries, and special projects, the main thrust being to help provide better standards of scholarship in ministerial training. Extensive and careful studies were made by the staff of the Theological Education Fund, utilizing the services of experts in different fields, and the selective method was largely used in order to ensure long-range and lasting benefits.

The achievements of the Theological Education Fund during the first seven years of its operations have been due largely to the fact that it was a joint effort. The denominational emphasis has been subordinated to the ecumenical character and direction of the undertaking for the broad interests of the Kingdom.

The experience of the Theological Education Fund has been influential in stimulating interest for a similar operation in the field of Christian literature. The Christian Literature Fund has been organized to serve another great need felt by all churches and mission agencies.

Patterns of Service for Ecumenical Personnel

We have seen how the younger churches across the world have emerged as more or less independent bodies, and that in most countries where The United Presbyterian Church in the U.S.A. has been engaged in the traditional type of mission work, missions as entities have been dissolved, and missionary personnel from the United States became fraternal workers under the church of that country, whether it was a Presbyterian or a United Church.

An important question arises as to the place and the role of fraternal workers or ecumenical personnel. The fact that fraternal workers appointed by the Commission go from one church, the United Presbyterian Church, to another church, in India, or Colombia, or elsewhere, is of significance. As we have already pointed out, this changes the pattern of relationships. In former times, it was the mission on the field that largely determined not only the number but also the kind of missionaries that were sent out. In actual practice, it was the functional type of missionary (evangelist, teacher, doctor, and so on) that was sent by the mission, whereas the number who went out each year was subject to budget consideration. In some cases, the church on the field was consulted about the types of missionaries to be requested each year.

When integration of missions with churches on the field took place, the appropriate organization of the church, in consultation with the fraternal workers' committee, determined the types and number of missionaries to go to a particular country each year.

Among church people in the United States, there is the possibility of a misunderstanding concerning the new relationship of the fraternal worker, or indeed whether he is needed at all, in view of the fact that independent churches have assumed more and more responsibility for the work. To reach such a conclusion is to misread the situation in the world today, and in any given country. The churches with which the Commission is related around the world are facing overwhelming opportunities and challenges, with very limited resources in personnel and funds. Moreover, the rapid social changes taking place in industrial, urban, and rural communities, and the great need for reaching the growing student bodies create openings for workers with special training and skills. It is not surprising, therefore, that Dr. John Coventry Smith, the General Secretary of the Commission, told an audience that the need for the Commission to work with these churches was greater than ever, and that every year requests for additional missionaries were coming from these new churches. As a matter of fact, since integration took place, the requests for personnel reaching the Commission from churches overseas have been far greater than available funds would allow, even if all the personnel could be found.

In recent years the continuing need for fraternal workers from the United States has been reiterated time after time not only by individual churches but also by churches meeting together in consultation. The Synod of North India and the Synod of Punjab, meeting together in November, 1963, said: "The presence of fraternal workers sent by churches of other lands is deeply significant for the work and witness of the church in India. They are needed for particular positions in schools, hospitals, and Church Councils; for special projects of the church; for the initiation of experimental types of work; as a witness to the unity and world-wide fellowship of the Christian community."[22]

In the consultation, the view was expressed that when fraternal workers for India are selected, the primary emphasis should not be on the type of positions they might fill, important as that consideration is; rather, "the greatest need is for fraternal workers with a compelling missionary intention, committed to Christian service, possessing creative and imaginative qualities, and sensitive to human relationships in cultures other than their own."[23]

In the development of an indigenous church from the state of dependence to that of selfhood there may be instances where missionary personnel from the United States should be radically reduced in number or withdrawn entirely from a particular country. This actually happened in the case of a South American country. Where the church has achieved selfhood and self-support, the American missionary is usually welcomed and appreciated as a kind of symbol of the ecumenical church. Indonesia is one example of this, and possibly two factors account for it. In the first place, the Protestant community numbers about five million, and in the second place, before independence, Indonesia was a colony of the Netherlands. In other countries, in varying degrees, the fraternal worker from the United States and the church have to solve the problems of adjustment in a new relationship on a basis of mutual trust and confidence.

We have used the term "fraternal worker" to designate a person who goes from one church to another to assist the latter in its task, and when the term was first used, it served to dramatize the new church-to-church relationship. The term "foreign missionary" had connotations or associations of colonialism and paternalism, as well as of outmoded mission structures. However, there is a tendency in some circles to restore the term "missionary," since it is expressive of the missionary intention.

Over the years, an increasing proportion of Presbyterian missionaries were unordained, that is, they were teachers, doctors, nurses, audio-visual experts, agriculturists, and so on. The challenge of the contemporary social revolution, the nature of the problems faced by the churches in their communities, will give a new urgency to the need for missionaries with competence in the fields of sociology, economics, urbanization, and community development.

Personnel for new forms of witness could well be ecumenical, in the sense that, while coming out of different denominational and national backgrounds, they are able to witness to the ecumenical church and the total mission of the church. It is essential to remember that such projects as are contemplated under plans for Joint Action for Mission must be in relation to the church, and thus an expression of the mission of the church. While the church is God's instrument for the communication of the gospel, yet it must never become an end in itself, never just an institution.

The churches in Asia, Africa, the Middle East, and Latin America are at a point where they must move out to the frontiers of social, economic, and industrial life, or else become totally irrelevant. This task provides one of the new dimensions of ecumenical personnel, and it is important to remember that the term "ecumenical personnel" is not confined to citizens of the United States.

The younger churches are engaging more and more in mission, sometimes among the remote tribes, or other unreached groups in their own country, sometimes by sending missionaries or fraternal workers to some other country. In 1961, a survey was made of all these missionaries by the Missionary Research Library in New York.[24] The East Asia Christian Conference alone estimated in 1961 that its member churches maintained about two hundred missionaries to other countries. The United Church of Christ in Japan in 1961, for example, had missionaries in Okinawa, Formosa, India, Thailand, Canada, and South America (Brazil and Bolivia). The United Church of Christ in the Philippines maintained workers in Thailand, Indonesia, Hawaii, Iran, Ethiopia, the United States, Turkey, Italy, and Greece, in addition to those workers among mountain tribes in their own country.

The Asian churches are taking seriously the recommendations of the East Asia Christian Conference, formulated at its meetings in Kuala Lumpur and Madras, concerning plans for a total Christian witness in their areas. At its meeting in Bangkok, Thailand, in February, 1964, the East Asia Christian Conference raised four questions: "What tasks of mission are we now doing and with what success? What new challenges face us and what new tasks should be taken in hand? What resources of men and money are available to us? . . . How should we together redeploy these resources in the way best calculated to fulfill the tasks God has given us in this area?"[25]

The Commission on Ecumenical Mission and Relations has not confined its appointments of personnel to citizens of the United States. From time to time it has appointed Italians, Dutch, French, and Latin Americans, but has always followed the rule of never sending such nationals as missionaries to the land of their birth. The Commission has been guided by two ideals in the past, and will continue to be in the future. They are: "(1) The desirability of internationalizing personnel at work in any given area so as to demonstrate the universality of the Gospel and of the Church; (2) the importance to the life of the Church in every place of stimulating its engagement in mission, not only within its own nation, but to the ends of the earth."[26]

Another dimension of the task in the future, as far as ecumenical personnel are concerned, are the Christian laymen who leave their own country to reside in another as businessmen, industrialists, educators, technical assistants, or diplomatic personnel under governments. The number of such laymen who have gone overseas since World War II has grown to considerable proportions. Without some orientation and preparation, few Christian laymen are equipped to make a positive witness in another country and in a different culture and environment. The Commission, along with mission boards in the United States, is giving increasing attention to this potential form of Christian witness and has gone so far as to call such Christian laymen "paramissionaries." The Introduction to the Report of the Willingen Conference (1952) referred to such laymen as "unofficial missionaries,"[27] and in its section on "Missionary Vocation and Training," said, "We believe that God is calling the Church to express its mission not only through foreign missionaries sent by the boards, but also through an increasing flow of Christian laymen and women who go out across the world in business, industry, and government and who do so with a deep conviction that God calls to them to witness for Him in all of life."[28] Likewise, the presence of students from Asia, Africa, the Middle East, and Latin America presents many opportunities for Christian witness on a nonprofessional basis.

A new venture in study and service was initiated as a result of discussions at the 18th Quadrennial Student Conference on the Christian World Mission, held at Athens, Ohio, in December, 1959. The Conference, attended by thirty-five hundred students from ninety-two countries, focused its attention on crucial or strategic areas where the church's witness seemed to be the weakest. Traditionally, the frontiers of the missionary enterprise were geographic; rapid social change in a revolutionary world has brought into prominence the sociological frontiers of life.

The Frontier Internship Program was approved by the Commission on Ecumenical Mission and Relations in March, 1960, to be administered by the Commission's Office of Student World Relations under the leadership of Miss Margaret Flory and in cooperation with the National Student Christian Federation. The program consisted of enlisting mature and dedicated students to serve on a subsistence salary for two years in a frontier situation in a country abroad. A frontier intern is a person with a deep sense of Christian mission who is free to experiment in a creative way in Christian presence and ministry, under the guidance of a local counselor, but not working within the structure of the church as such. The diversity of programs undertaken calls for initiative, creativity, sensitivity, and deep concern. No set pattern of work or activity is laid down by the Commission, the initiative being left to the individual. One student with degrees in mechanical engineering and philosophy from Yale University spent two years in Kenya, Africa. He learned enough Swahili to be able to engage in conversation and teach Bible in government and Roman Catholic schools. He wrote: "The Body of Christ is one, and we are living in the single Spirit of Christ, but what does this mean when one comes up against an African living in a grass hut? How is fellowship possible when one's subsistence salary is higher than the wages of most of the African workers, and when one has brought with one many possessions, like books and clothing."[29]

Following the Ohio Student Conference, a list of frontiers was drawn up by the Commission, and in 1966 was revised as follows:

Racial Tensions

Developing Nationalism

Economic Development and Industrialization

Ideologies and Resurgent Religions

Emergent International Community

Urbanization

Revolution in Rural Life

Uprooted and Estranged Peoples

University World

Since 1961, when the program was initiated, four groups of frontier interns have served abroad. A total of forty-two interns served in twenty-one countries; thirty-one were United Presbyterians, the other eleven representing five different denominations. Ten interns were assigned to Frontier Study and Service Projects of the World Student Christian Federation. The largest group during the years 1961-1965 served on the university world frontier, thus highlighting the significance of students in today's world.

The greatest challenge to the Christian church today is on the frontiers, reference being made to the nongeographical frontiers. The church of today is weighed down by the heavy baggage of institutions and organized programs. In the Western world, Christians have often celebrated the ideas, facts, and doctrines of the church, and have more or less imprisoned Christ within the walls of the church. Jesus' parable of the Last Judgment makes it clear, however, that the ultimate test will not be whether we always worshiped correctly or faithfully, or whether we were diligent in running the institutions of the church. Rather, it will be whether or not we fed the hungry, clothed the naked, visited the sick and those in prison, all symbols of acute human need.

Christ dwells on the frontiers of life, whether they be political, social, or industrial. "He dwells where the danger is greatest, where the struggle is fiercest, where the need of advance is most crucial, where new ideas of life must be won for His Kingdom."[30]

In other words, the church must be a "pilgrim" church, traveling light. This comes as a real challenge to churches in the West, as well as in the East. The church in the West is thoroughly institutionalized and highly organized; the new churches in Asia, Africa, and Latin America are on the way to becoming so. What the pattern of the "pilgrim" church will be no one can tell, but the challenge remains.

In the statement read to the General Assembly at the time the Commission on Ecumenical Mission and Relations came into being in 1958, there is the following paragraph:

> To radiate the light of God and mediate the love of God, the Church must be a pilgrim Church. God summons us to pilgrimage, to life on the missionary road. We must journey not only along desert paths and jungle trails, but in the teeming alleys of our cities. God commands us to be missionaries not only in the community where we live, not alone in the national environment of our home church, but to the ends of the earth. The Church's place is the frontier.[31]

A new dimension of the missionary task of The United Presbyterian Church in the U.S.A. has emerged with the enlargement of the area of cooperation and coordination between the Commission on Ecumenical Mission and Relations and the Board of National Missions and the Board of Christian Education.

Plans have been made to effect joint consultation and action in the following areas: Urban-Industrial Ministries, Community Organization and Development, Church Location and Development, Church Architecture, and Ecumenical Action Projects.

In 1965, the Joint Office of Leadership Development and the Joint Office for Urban and Industrial Ministries were established jointly by the Board of National Missions and the Commission on Ecumenical Mission and Relations.

Since the major challenge to the church today is on the frontier of the world's socioeconomic life, urbanization and industrialization in all countries, including the United States, create new situations and problems for the churches in all lands.

The two agencies now face these common problems and an attempt is being made to develop a strategy for an urban industrial ministry, encouraging and stimulating responsible field bodies toward the development of plans and programs suited particularly to the environment. At the heart of the implementation of programs and policies is the development of adequate, trained leadership. To discover the best ways of training such leadership will be the joint task of the two agencies. Efforts in the area or urban industrial communities are coordinated with those of Joint Action for Mission and of the Division of World Mission and Evangelism of the World Council of Churches.

The Christian Presence

Whether we call the person who goes from the United Presbyterian Church to serve under a church in another country a fraternal worker or a missionary is not of paramount importance. What is important is the role of such a person within the total context of the mission of the church. We have seen how he is involved in patterns of service in the framework of partnership in mission and Joint Action for Mission. What he *is* may be just as significant as what he *does*. He goes out as one who is sent by the United Presbyterian Church to a sister church. However, at the same time, he is a visible expression of the ecumenical church, for what takes him to India or to Africa, or anywhere else, is not the fact that he is an American, or even that he is a teacher, a doctor, or an evangelist, but a Christian. His strength is the strength of weakness, of being a follower of Jesus Christ, rather than a citizen of a powerful country with air power, marines, and money. It is not worldly power which unites men, but love.

As the General Secretary of the World Student Christian Federation put it: "The church has lost, or is beginning to lose, the worldly power which it wielded for centuries. What does remain is the true power known as love—love for one's neighbor, which makes it possible really to be with others. In such a new world, the church can lay no claim to a superior understanding and technical explanation of the world; rather, it learns to listen, to be present."[32]

During the India-Pakistan conflict in September, 1965, it was reported from a particular area in India that whereas all other Americans had left, United Presbyterian fraternal workers, about sixty in number, remained. In some places, American government personnel were ordered by the American Embassy to evacuate, but the missionaries were "advised" to leave. They remained. Without being unfair to American personnel sent by the United States Government, it can be stated that the reason for their being in India (or Pakistan) was different from the reason why the fraternal workers were there. In time of crisis and danger, the fraternal workers felt impelled to stay. They were not immune from the threatening dangers of those days; they could not count on any protection from the United States Government, but their weakness became their strength. In a very real sense, the fraternal worker identified himself with the people among whom he lived.

In an address that he gave at the Whitby International Missionary Conference in 1947, Dr. John A. Mackay said that those who are engaged in the missionary task are the "'people of the Presence.' The greatest thing we can do is not to formulate principles or to make pronouncements, but to make manifest a Presence; to allow Jesus Christ to speak and act through us."[33]

It may be that the place and importance of proclaiming and of speaking has been exaggerated in the past. Missionaries and fraternal workers have to learn to listen as well. Jesus' use of the terms "salt" and "leaven" seems to indicate that the vocation of the Christian is "being" as much as, or even more, than talking. The term "presence" does not mean simply being in a given place, or an anonymous presence; it does mean getting involved in the structure of society, and being very much a part of life at the level of understanding or of conflict. "When we say 'presence,' we say that we have to get into the midst of things even when they frighten us,"[34] and being present in a given situation may provide the occasion for a fearless witness to Christ in ways that are unpredictable.

Similarly, with the fraternal worker sent out by the United Presbyterian Church, his presence in India, Indonesia, Iran, or any other country means that he is there as a member of the body of Christ, willing to identify himself with people, and that the fact of his presence transcends all barriers of race, nationality, and culture.

New forms of missionary "presence" are emerging on the frontiers of modern industrial and urban communities. Wherever the fraternal worker is involved in service to refugees, in groups seeking international understanding or solutions to deep social problems, or in house churches in new communities, it is his presence which counts, the fact that he is caught up in the search for truth and brotherhood in human fellowship.

The Mission of the Church

What, then, is the mission of the church? Is the mission of the church, in today's revolutionary world, and in an ecumenical era, different from what it was when the Presbyterian churches, to which we have made reference, began to be conscious of their missionary obligation in the early nineteenth century?

Essentially, the mission of the church is the same today as it was last century, and yet it has to be pursued in a vastly different way and in a new context. Our understanding of the mission of the church, and its dimensions, is much broader and deeper than before, although all the implications are not yet fully apparent. It is seen within an inescapable ecumenical framework, and in terms of a New Testament eschatology which lends increased urgency to the total mission of the church. The dimensions of the church's task are ecumenical and eschatological.

Blauw affirms that the missionary commission to proclaim and actualize a Kingdom which knows no geographical boundaries "is from the very beginning an ecumenical commission, a commission which concerns the whole inhabited world. Thus the criterion is simply: that one must have *heard* of Christ in order to be able to believe in Him."[35] However, it is also true that missions of the eighteenth, nineteenth, and early twentieth centuries were a necessary prelude to the emergence of the worldwide Christian community of the contemporary world. The *oikoumenē* of today, using the word in a Christian sense, is a much more complex one than that of the early Christian era. The call to mission, in the context in which the gospel now has to be proclaimed, demands new ways of approaching people who have never heard of Christ, and also the use of forms, expressions, and methods that are relevant on the frontiers of today's increasingly technological world.

Certain presuppositions are inherent in the Christian understanding of the church's purpose.

1. God acts within history. This is evident in the Old Testament, where one of the central events was the deliverance of the Hebrews from Egypt, an event that provided a focus for their perception of reality. "As such, it symbolized the deliverance of man out of a sacral-political order and into history and social change."[36] In the coming of Christ into the world, God acted supremely in history, and this event in time and place, that is, in history, marks the beginning of the Christian era. A new period in world history dawned with the coming of Christ, for he is the end of a world and the beginning of a new one.

While it is true that the mission of the church is both conditioned by and affected by the unfolding of world history, the proclamation of the Kingdom and of Christ's dominion over the world is not dependent upon world history. Rather, world history, in a very real way, is dependent upon that proclamation.

2. "It is only in Christ that human history can have a meaning."[37] The amazing increase in man's knowledge of the universe and his phenomenal ability to control the forces of nature in recent times have not brought happiness to mankind. On the contrary, the more man advances scientifically and technologically, the more ominous the possibility of his own destruction seems to be. At a time when man can boast of having probed many of the secrets of the universe, and reached up into the heavens, there never was a period of greater

anxiety, confusion, and foreboding concerning the future. The basic presupposition, then, is that while much material progress has been made over the centuries, and man has become more sophisticated and better educated, all this is no substitute for his becoming a new creature in Christ, for there is no other way in which his progress as a true human being can be made.

A spiritual renewal alone can enable man to overcome his innate self-centeredness, greed, and pride, all of which are the basis of his alienation from other men and from God. "Therefore if any man be in Christ," says Paul, "he is a new creature: old things are passed away; behold, all things are become new."[38] The phrase "in Christ," used 169 times in Paul's writings, is the key to his thinking. The experience of being "born again" or becoming "a new creature in Christ" is not intended to be merely for personal satisfaction and enjoyment. It opens up a new way of life, for it involves reconciliation with God and with men, and ushers in a new order. The new relationship is seen in a Christian fellowship which is now worldwide, and in a new spiritual unity toward which the ecumenical movement strives. The only way to reconciliation, peace, and harmony among the nations is the Christian way.

3. Jesus inaugurated a new era in human history, and it was revolutionary in character. He began his ministry by announcing this new era in these words:

> The Spirit of the Lord is upon me,
> because he has anointed me to preach good news to the poor.
> He has sent me to proclaim release to the captives
> and recovering of sight to the blind,
> to set at liberty those who are oppressed,
> to proclaim the acceptable year of the Lord.[39]

Jesus ushered in the Kingdom, and yet he taught his disciples to pray, "Thy kingdom come." This is what produces in the Christian and in the church itself what Bishop Newbigin calls the inescapable tension between "having" and "hoping."

4. The world, not the church, is the object of God's concern. It is a fundamental tenet of the Christian faith that God was in Christ reconciling the world, not the church as such, to himself. It is a world that is alienated from God, divided against itself and without real

meaning. This is the world Christ came into and for which he died.

5. The Christian church, to be true to itself and its purpose, cannot be considered an end in itself. The church is a major instrument of God's concern for the world, a concept reiterated throughout this book, for we have considered The United Presbyterian Church in the U.S.A., as well as its sister churches overseas, as instruments in God's hands, for the working out of his purposes. The essential nature of the Christian church is that of a community called out of the world to be sent forth into the world. As we have noted in Chapter I, The United Presbyterian Church in the U.S.A. views the ends of the church as the proclamation of the gospel for the salvation of men, the nurture and spiritual fellowship of Christians, maintaining divine worship, preserving the truth, promoting social righteousness, and exhibiting the Kingdom to the world.

6. Although the program of the church involves diverse institutional forms, these are only means to an end. The church is not primarily an institution. It is a people; the Bible calls it "the people of God." If we regard the church as a people composed of those called according to God's purpose, then we can see the institutions of the church in their proper perspective, namely, as enabling God's people to participate more fully in his work in the world. Institutions are judged in the light of their usefulness and instrumentality, especially in their relation to a flexibility in the carrying out of the mission of the church, now considered essential in a day of new sociological frontiers.

7. While the Christian church is the instrument for the proclamation of the Kingdom, it is also the firstfruits, that is, a demonstration of what the new humanity is to be. These thoughts are expressed in the Constitution of the United Presbyterian Church as follows: "The great ends of the Church are the proclamation of the gospel for the salvation of men . . . and the exhibition of the Kingdom of Heaven to the world."[40]

8. According to New Testament eschatology, we are living "between the ages," that is, between the last days of the present evil age and the coming age of promise, an age already manifest in the firstfruits of the Kingdom. It is an age that is characterized by judgment and crisis. Moreover, it is a time of inescapable tension between the

"having" and the "hoping," between the "already" and the "not yet," for the coming of the Kingdom is both a fulfillment and a promise. "And he [Jesus] said unto them [his disciples], it is not for you to know the times or the seasons, which the Father hath put in his own power."[41]

9. The church is the body of Christ. As such the church can be true to its own nature only when it carries out Christ's mission of love in the world. This Biblical figure of the body of Christ also presupposes a wholeness, without which the witness of the church is seriously impaired.

These are not only the presuppositions, but they also largely determine the nature of the church's mission to the world. In broad terms, the church's mission is to continue the work that Jesus himself began, the proclamation of the Kingdom as the good news, a witnessing to the ends of the earth that Jesus Christ is Lord, and a ministry of reconciliation. The church is called, as Jesus was, to a threefold ministry, summed up in the language of theology in the three Greek words *kērygma, diakonia,* and *koinōnia.* Kerygma is the proclamation of the message of good news, that is, the gospel; diakonia is service to others in the name of Christ and reconciliation of men alienated from one another; koinonia is the fellowship, the living of a common life together, with worship as a means of inner nourishment and also as a living witness to the world of a spiritual reality.

These are our main presuppositions in a consideration of the mission of the church. The word "mission" comes from the Latin word *missio,* which means "to send." Jesus told his disciples that he had been sent by the Father for the redemption of mankind and to establish the Kingdom, the rule of God in men's hearts and lives. In one of his prayers, Jesus said, "As thou hast sent me into the world, even so have I also sent them into the world."[42] "There is no other Church than the Church *sent* into the world."[43]

The nature of the contemporary world with all its changing emphases and new challenges has obliged the church not only to reappraise its own being and nature but also to reexamine its threefold mission of kerygma, diakonia, and koinonia. Clergy and laity alike are coming to realize the inescapable relationship of the individual and the social aspects of the gospel in this threefold mission of the church. Berdyaev put it cogently when he said that "the greatest religious and moral truth to which man must grow, is that we cannot be saved individually. My salvation presupposes the salvation of others also, the salvation of my neighbour, it presupposes universal salvation, the salvation of the whole world, the transfiguration of the world. . . . The period of the end is not only a period of destruction, but also a period of divine-human creativeness, a new life and a new world."[44]

Perhaps the most challenging aspect of the church's mission to the world today is the form of the church's approach to the world. In the past there was the element of triumph, of conquest of the world, but now, by contrast, the church is rediscovering the "servant image" in the life and work of Jesus himself. He came to serve rather than to conquer. What does this say to the church which is the body of Christ? The theme of the Eighteenth General Assembly of the World Presbyterian Alliance, held in São Paulo, Brazil, July, 1959, was "The Servant Lord and His Servant People." While the theme was not new, this conference of Presbyterian leaders from all over the world rediscovered it in relation to the church today, and they gave contemporary expression to what Dr. Mackay calls "the essentially instrumental, missionary character of the Church which is native to the Reformed tradition."[45]

In the Gospel of John we read that Jesus came as the servant of the Lord who made himself the servant of men. Paul begins his epistle to the Romans with the words, "Paul, a servant of Jesus Christ," and the term "servant" appears many times in the New Testament. The report of the São Paulo Assembly pointed out that whereas the churches of the Reformed tradition have a rich heritage in church order, confession, liturgy, and practice, these must be subordinate to Christ as the Servant Lord and to the demands of the gospel. "Ultimately, the Church can only claim to be the Church, in so far as she is rendering the service of Christ to the world. This merits a new emphasis in ecumenical conversation."[46] This means that the status of the church is not important, but its ministry of love or diakonia is "a service of those called and commissioned to spend and to be spent, that God may be brought to men, and men to God."[47] In other words, the church fails in its mission when it becomes an end in itself, for to be the church it must serve the world in a redemptive way.

At São Paulo, a prophetic word was also uttered by a delegate from Ceylon. Speaking on the topic "Called for Suffering," he said: "We belong to the ecumenical age. Yet the ecumenical Church is a cheap and sentimental slogan unless it means that today, too, we realize that the togetherness of Christian people brings pain and suffering. When one suffers, Paul reminds us, all suffer."[48]

The Conference on The Healing Ministry in the Mission of the Church, held at Tübingen, Germany, in May, 1964, under the sponsorship of the Commission on World Mission of the Lutheran World Federation and the Division of World Mission and Evangelism of the World Council of Churches, emphasized a wider concept of the healing ministry than Christian medical work. Salvation means healing, health, and making whole; and the whole of man—body, mind, and spirit—is involved. "There is a parish in England," said James C. McGilvray, United Presbyterian delegate to the Tübingen consultation, "where the small congregation has become a therapeutic community—visiting the sick, counseling with those on the threshold of a broken marriage, making evident their deep and loving concern for all in need—and these are ordinary members of the church, not clergy nor specialists employed for this task."[49]

This book began with the story of how a church was established, and it proceeded to show the manner in which individuals in that church caught the vision of spreading the Christian message to others. The time came when the Presbyterian Church in the U.S.A. and its sister church, the United Presbyterian Church of North America, established Boards of Foreign Missions to serve as agents of the church in carrying the gospel to the ends of the earth.

In the providence of God, and under the guidance of the Holy Spirit, these two churches came together in 1958, and one of the first acts of the newly formed body was to create the Commission on Ecumenical Mission and Relations. The United Presbyterian Church in the U.S.A. committed to this body the task of acting for, and in the name of, the whole church, in carrying out its mission overseas.

Together with other agencies of the denomination's General Assembly, especially the Board of National Missions and the Board of Christian Education, the Commission is engaged in an ecumenical witness on behalf of the United Presbyterian Church. It was this task which led the ministers and laymen attending the General Assembly of 1962 to affirm that:

> The Commission on Ecumenical Mission and Relations represents many historical streams: mission, faith and order, life and work. God's direction of history has changed the world in which the Church is called to serve, has shaped the Church, has brought the United Presbyterian Church to the moment when participation in mission and unity have cast a whole new framework for action.[50]

What does this mean for The United Presbyterian Church in the U.S.A.? The United Presbyterian Church is emerging from the period when the mission of the church was the interest of only some of the members, and merely a peripheral concern for the majority. Increasingly, laymen and clergy alike are coming to understand the mission of the church in a new perspective, that of history. Since Christ is the clue to history, the mission of the church is to make him known to the ends of the earth, and in all aspects of human life.

Laymen and ministers have come to see that the church is involved in a missionary task that is central to its being and basic to its calling—a task that is to be accomplished on six continents, that is, on the church's own doorstep, and to the ends of the earth. Furthermore, United Presbyterian clergy and laymen are increasingly realizing that God is calling his church to an earnest striving for the wholeness of the worldwide Christian church, with the intent that the whole gospel may be taken to the whole world by the whole church, that is, by a church which will, by the grace of God, have healed its divisions. For United Presbyterians to grasp the meaning and to follow the implications of this vision will bring newness of life and purpose, and a fresh sense of direction, vitality, and power to their church as a part of the body of Christ. The church will find its life only by losing itself in serving the world. This is part of its ecumenical witness.

Appendixes

1. IN UNITY—FOR MISSION
   A message to all congregations from the Uniting General Assembly
   of The United Presbyterian Church in the U.S.A., 1958

2. COMMISSION ON ECUMENICAL MISSION AND RELATIONS
   An Interpretation, *by John A. Mackay*

3. COMMISSION ON ECUMENICAL MISSION AND RELATIONS
   A series of articles published in 1958, giving the meaning of the Commission:

I.	THE CONTINUING DYNAMIC IN MISSION	*Charles T. Leber*
II.	RELATIONS AND MISSIONS BELONG TOGETHER	*Ralph Waldo Lloyd*
III.	HOW THE COMMISSION WORKS	*Donald Black*
IV.	AMERICA, TOO, IS IN THE WORLD	*Hermann N. Morse*
V.	SOME PERSONAL OBSERVATIONS	*Eugene Carson Blake*

4. IMPORTANT DATES IN PRESBYTERIAN HISTORY

5. DATES WHEN PRESBYTERIAN MISSION WORK BEGAN

6. IMPORTANT DATES IN ECUMENICAL HISTORY

7. DATES OF MISSIONS AND NATIONAL CHURCHES

8. ECUMENICAL TREE

9. GENEALOGY OF PRESBYTERIAN CHURCHES IN THE NEW WORLD

1. IN UNITY—FOR MISSION

A message to all congregations from the Uniting General Assembly of The United Presbyterian Church in the U.S.A., adopted by the General Assembly of The United Presbyterian Church in the U.S.A., May 30, 1958. *

I. The Church Is God's Servant

By the gracious providence of Almighty God, we who formerly were two Churches of the same tradition are no longer two but one. We give heartfelt thanks to God for those who have prayed and labored for this day, many of whom, having died, saw its fulfillment only from afar. We are strengthened by the contemplation of our heritage, but God forbid that reflection upon it should engender false pride or create complacency. It is all too easy for the Church to become a venerated but sterile institution in the society in which it exists. Neither the Church itself nor any of its achievements, whether its structure or its doctrine, its unity or its work, can ever be mere ends in themselves; all are but means to serve the ongoing purpose and redemptive love of God.

We look forward, in faith, to the unfolding of God's purpose for our new Church. As The United Presbyterian Church in the United States of America, the largest in the world-wide Presbyterian family, we must understand our Reformed tradition and relate it to our day.

The Church is truly the Church when it serves God, when God's sons and daughters joyously become their Father's servants. God gave a mission to his people: "You are my servant, Israel, in whom I will be glorified . . . I will give you as a light to the nations, that my salvation may reach to the end of the earth." The Christian Church is the new Israel, God's new servant, the fellowship of those for whom Jesus Christ is Lord. The Church exists to glorify God, to make Him manifest to men, to reflect the splendor of His nature, and to serve His eternal purpose in Jesus Christ, who is the sole Head of the Church.

To the Church united in this purpose, the Holy Spirit gives power. Unity

---

* *Minutes of the General Assembly of The United Presbyterian Church in the U.S.A.,* 1958, Part I, *Journal,* pp. 155-160. Dr. John A. Mackay noted that "the approval of this document constituted the first action taken by the General Assembly of the new United Church."

is Christian unity when all the members of the Body of Christ are one in their obedience to Him. As Christians we are fellow workers with God. Let us, therefore, in comradeship with one another, be heralds of God's glory and so fulfill the Church's mission for our time.

II. It Is the Church's Mission to Radiate the Light of God

The Church is called to radiate the light of God in every society and in every age. In this day when Christian ideas are widely rejected or distorted, the Church is called to point our generation to the fountain of Truth and Goodness, to God Himself as He is revealed through Holy Scripture in Jesus Christ the Word made flesh. In the light of Jesus Christ, and only in that light, does man's thought become luminous and relevant.

Our Lord Jesus Christ lays upon us an inescapable obligation to "discern this time," to examine the life of man in the light of God. Like our ancestors, we must zealously search for truth, truth about God and the world, truth about man and his destiny, truth about the Church and its responsibility toward the nation and toward mankind.

In our day, revolutionary unrest is rampant. Nations are tragically divided. This is a time of judgment. Mankind journeys through dread. The world is in the darkness of nuclear despair, but Christians need not lose their calm. We believe God. He reigns. He is sovereign over men and nations, over all the forces of nature and of history. God and His righteousness, not the falsehood and villainy of men, shall have the final word.

We must discern the Word of God in the Bible. God's wrath falls upon nations whose rulers willfully and openly deny Him, but He may use them to execute His purpose and chastise His own people. Against Israel, He used the imperial power of Assyria as the rod of His anger and the staff of His fury. He may in our time use Communist or other godless powers to chastise privileged, nominally Christian nations who forget God and ignore their indebtedness to Him. Our nation, favored by God, stands in the same jeopardy as ancient Israel. Are we subtly yet surely dethroning God in our national life? Are we patronizing God and ceasing to serve Him? Are we trying to fit the Almighty into our own little schemes, instead of fitting ourselves into His great plan for the world?

A nation, as well as an individual, can lose its soul. We Americans are in danger of rejecting the heritage which made us what we are. With penitence let us confess that as a people we are becoming less interested in righteousness than in national security and international superiority. Relations between us and other peoples are no longer primarily determined by moral principles or by considerations of human need. The ancient words *justice* and *righteousness*, emptied of their true content, are used as weapons in international politics. Self-interest is becoming the great absolute. Even baptizing *self-interest* with the adjective *enlightened* does not make it Christian.

Our fathers' concept of *freedom* is also being debased. For them, freedom flowed from obedience to God. We must be deeply disturbed by the contemporary myth of the *free world*. This nation counts among its allies some nations which are in no sense free. By our actions we proclaim to the world that lands where human freedom is utterly dead can qualify for membership in the *free world* simply by supplying military bases or strategic commodities. This kind of international hypocrisy should be abhorrent to Christians, and in its presence the Church dare not keep silent. In the effort to achieve a posture of power, our nation must not ignore the suppression of God-given human rights in any land. We call, therefore, for a reappraisal of the current concepts of *freedom* and the *free world*.

Today, as always, "the fear of the Lord is the beginning of wisdom." Wisdom stems from a spiritual relationship between God and man which, in turn, transforms relations among men. Wisdom's supreme expression is a ministry of reconciliation, the bringing of estranged and alienated people to God through the Gospel. Thus a human society becomes possible in which the reality of brotherhood prevails between nation and nation, between class and class, between race and race.

Wisdom teaches that in the pursuit of human understanding there can be no substitute for personal encounter. Estranged people must meet one another; they must talk with one another and strive to understand one another. They must probe the causes of their alienation. They must overcome enmity and distrust by the sharing of goods, knowledge, and human resources for the welfare of mankind. When men who profess the Christian religion make no adequate provision for a face-to-face encounter with their enemies, they betray the religion which they profess. Yet in human tensions today, nations continue to talk at one another and about one another, instead of talking with one another. This is one of our greatest perils. When men talk solely in declamatory tones, they only add clamor to disorder.

Neither is there any substitute for forgiveness. Civilization at its best stands in need of divine forgiveness. While some nations are greater sinners than others, there is no righteous nation upon earth. We as a people should, therefore, be ready to admit our faults to other nations as a prelude to seeking a basis of understanding. Contrition for our own sins will do more to create an atmosphere conducive to peace than press releases denouncing the sins of others.

Two things we must remember. First, all persons and peoples are loved by God and live under His sovereign governance. Second, the command "Love your enemies" is our Lord's command. We must explore the implications of this command for international relations. Statesmen may be completely sincere, perfectly well intentioned, eminently patriotic, but if their policies have no place for the command to love one's enemies, the consequences of those policies will be disastrous.

Another tragic error is the deification of scientific knowledge. The theologian and the scientist agree that man and the universe are to be understood as fully and as accurately as possible, but the irrational cry for intensified education in technological science arises from man's failure to understand man. To put our faith in science, not as a partner in the search for truth but as a fabricator of weapons, is to worship the graven image of technology. The glorification of technology can make men, even churchmen, skilled barbarians; it cannot produce spiritually creative men and women. Technology, enshrined, creates both physical power and spiritual terror. It can only accelerate the race toward disaster.

Scientists dedicated to the search for truth are needed. But the greater need is for enlightened men and women, including scientists, educated in human relations and the social sciences, in the arts of understanding, and communicating with, peoples of all nations and cultures. With God's help such men and women can do much to terminate this present peril.

To accept the inevitability of increasing hostility between Communism and the West reveals our loss of faith in God and in the power of truth and goodness, as well as our ignorance of the sobering lessons of history. We need, instead, to ask some serious questions. What gave birth to Communism? What are the things that make its progress possible and its peril real in many parts of the world? Communism can be met in a positive way only by the promotion of truth and the practice of goodness. People will not be convinced that we are interested in them for their own sakes, unless, indeed, we are. Selfish ends do not foster friendship among men or nations, nor can friendship be faked or purchased.

It is imperative that the voice of history echoing the wisdom of the Christian ages be heard. A false and baneful doctrine is being persistently proclaimed, namely, that in the present world situation there are only two alternatives, either victory over the new Communistic powers, or the annihilation of the traditional democracies. There was a time when Christians and Moslems fervently held that one group or the other had to be totally vanquished by force. But eventually they learned to live in the same world. At a later period in history, Protestants and Roman Catholics thought that one side or the other had to be wiped out. But the time came when they, too, learned to co-exist as they do today. In neither situation, however, does coexistence imply the compromise of Christian convictions and the abatement of evangelistic zeal. Persuasion rather than force is the true means of conversion. So, also, while still striving for the freedom of all men, we today must co-exist with Communist nations. In this nuclear age, the only alternative to coexistence is coextinction.

III.   It Is the Church's Mission to Mediate the Love of God

The supreme mission of the Church is redemptive in character. We are loyal to the Church's redemptive mission when we proclaim to all men the Gospel of Christ and when we love all men with the affection of Christ.

Christian truth is personal truth. It centers in a Person, Jesus Christ. It expresses itself in the lives of persons who become Christ's followers, whose lives bear His likeness, and who live under His leadership in church and society. The Lordship of Christ in the Church and in the world begins in individual persons.

The Lordship of Christ illuminates the contemporary concern: "What is the purpose and meaning of life?" This question is identical with our historic question: "What is the chief end of man?" The answer we learned in our childhood has even more relevance today: "Man's chief end is to glorify God, and to enjoy Him for ever."

Man is truly man when in his personality he displays the character of God, when in his behavior he serves the purpose of God, and when in his life he enjoys communion with God. True human freedom is born when a man becomes God's captive. Saints in the Biblical sense are God's men and women. They are sons and daughters of God who, with joyous abandon and a sense of privilege, make themselves His loyal and devoted servants. The Church exists to bring such men and women into being and to mobilize them for Christ's missionary service.

For the first time in history there exists a world Christian community. This community is, in great part, the result of Christian missionary effort. In every land today there are groups of Christians who gather together to worship God in the name of Jesus Christ. In the comradeship of Churches that are the fruit of a century's missionary devotion, and in cooperation with older Churches, in this and other lands, we are pledged to mediate the love of God, by word and deed, to the uttermost bounds of human habitation.

IV.   The Church's Mission Is on the Frontier

To radiate the light of God and mediate the love of God, the Church must be a pilgrim Church. God summons us to pilgrimage, to life on the missionary road. We must journey not only along desert paths and jungle trails, but in the teeming alleys of our cities. God commands us to be missionaries not only in the community where we live, not alone in the national environment of our home church, but to the ends of the earth. The Church's place is the frontier. But for the Church in the discharge of its God-given mission, the frontier is more than a location. It is wherever any sector of thought or life has to be occupied in the name of Jesus Christ.

Only as church members become Christ's missionaries in their several vocations, in government and diplomacy, in industry and commerce, in the home and in the classroom, in the clinic and on the farm, will men perceive that Christ is *the* Way, *the* Truth, and *the* Life.

The world is no better than it is primarily because we Christians are no better than we are, and for the same reason the Church is no better than it is. We have not abandoned ourselves to God's will. We have not assumed a full measure of responsibility for the world in which we must continue to live. We are haunted by our Lord's own question, "What do ye more than others?" Our Lord calls the Church to unqualified obedience. The measure of our obedience is the measure of our power. Let the Church demonstrate by the consistency of its life the validity of its claims.

This we call upon our churches to do. Every congregation should be a reflection of the holy, catholic Church. "There is neither Jew nor Greek, there is neither slave nor free, there is neither male nor female; for you are all one in Christ Jesus." In Christ racial, cultural, social, economic, and sex distinctions become meaningless and are erased. As the Church is commissioned to make disciples of all nations, so each congregation is called upon to evangelize, and to welcome into its membership, all the unchurched people of its community without regard to their racial, economic, or cultural background and condition. To fail at this point is to deny the efficacy of the Atonement in our own lives and to betray the very Gospel we seek to proclaim.

Christ has called us friends. "You are my friends," he said, "if you do what I command you." Abraham, the Biblical example of a friend of God, showed his friendship by his obedience. At God's command, he embarked on an adventure into the unknown. Let us today dedicate ourselves as a Church to a new Abrahamic adventure. Let us be so constrained by the love of Christ that we shall show our love for Him by becoming channels of His love to others.

Let us, therefore, implore our Father in Heaven for a fresh outpouring of His Spirit upon us. We pray that this union will mark the beginning of that spiritual awakening which our Church, and all the Churches, and the whole human family, so sorely need in this hour.

Jesus promised his followers that he would be with them in holy companionship to the end of the road, to the close of the age. As we gird ourselves for our pilgrimage, our courage is in His pledge. And, as we journey, our strength is in the imperishable hope that the kingdoms of this world shall become the Kingdom of our Lord and of his Christ.

The grace of our Lord Jesus Christ be with us all.

THEOPHILUS M. TAYLOR, *Moderator*
EUGENE CARSON BLAKE, *Stated Clerk*

2. COMMISSION ON ECUMENICAL MISSION AND RELATIONS OF THE UNITED PRESBYTERIAN CHURCH IN THE U.S.A.— AN INTERPRETATION

by John A. Mackay

It is usual in human life and thought when something new emerges, or something old is set in a new perspective, that an appropriate name be found to describe it. Never in history have so many new words been minted as in our time. The reason is obvious. Never before have so many new things been discovered or promoted as today. Each new thing needs its own name, both for identification's sake and in order that what it signifies may be interpreted.

A very striking example in history of a new name that had to strive for its existence is the term "sociology." Before August Comte, sociology had been studied as a branch of philosophy. The historical record brings to our attention that the famous French sociologist, the first of his kind, had to fight hard before the new term was accepted, a term which is now so familiar.

The merger of two Boards of Foreign Missions and three agencies dealing with Ecumenical Relations is not only appropriate but the proposed name "The Commission on Ecumenical Mission and Relations" can be luminous and dynamic.*

Here are four terms: "Commission," "Mission," "Ecumenical," "Relations."

Commission

"Commission" is derived from the word "commit"—"to entrust oneself to." A "commission" is a body, a group of people, who are entrusted with something of very great importance. It becomes the function of a "com-

* Proposed for merger into this Commission: from the Presbyterian Church in the U.S.A., the Board of Foreign Missions and Permanent Commission on Interchurch Relations; from the United Presbyterian Church of North America, the Board of Foreign Missions, Permanent Committee on Inter-Church Relations, Committee on Ecumenical Affairs.

mission" to fulfill a trust faithfully and not simply to legislate or to carry out actions. The moment we use the term "commission" in the context of the Christian Church, we think of the whole fellowship of the Church out of which certain men and women are selected in order to be entrusted with something of very great importance. In this instance they are put in trust with the Gospel. It becomes their responsibility to give a world-wide expression to the Evangel, to carry the Good News to the ends of the earth.

Mission

But the question is asked, with what is this church "commission" entrusted? It becomes the body whose responsibility it is to see that the essential mission of the Church is fulfilled. This carries us to the term "mission" as associated with the Church. It is not too much to say that *mission* is of the very essence of the Church, and that no Church, whether congregation, denomination, or world body, is true to its inmost nature when it does not fulfill its mission. The moment you think in terms of "mission," the most fitting image that comes to you is the image of a servant. This is the figure or image which the Church needs most at the present time if it is to be saved from becoming an end in itself, or even to be satisfied with good relations and tensionless unity. It is the mission of the Church to serve God in such a way that it shall in "the form of a servant" become the instrument or medium whereby God unveils His splendor, that is, His true nature, and carries forward His redemptive purpose in the world. The Church as God's servant is most like God when it reminds people of God and when it fulfills the purpose of God.

It is at this point that Christ and the Gospel come in, for God unveiled His splendor in one who was not ashamed to take the "form of a servant," one in whom the splendor of Deity became manifest in servant form. Our Lord Christ said that He lived to "glorify" God on earth, that is, to make manifest the divine glory, God's true character, and to carry forward His purpose. The Christian Church is true to its nature and fulfills its mission when it unveils the splendor and fulfills the purpose of God. Concretely, that is done when the Church commits itself to Jesus Christ in faith and in trust, allowing Christ to grip it in such a way that it is caught up into participation with Him in "the form of a servant" to make God's purpose in Christ known to the whole world.

The Church is truly the Church when it fulfills its mission. That is what the Church is for—to unveil the splendor of God everywhere, to carry forward the purpose of God to all the world. This means that the mission of the Church must be "ecumenical."

Ecumenical

"Ecumenical" means "that which has to do with the whole world, with the inhabited globe." It is an interesting fact that both *oikoumene*, "the inhabited earth," and *ecumenical* never did have a purely geographical or mathematical connotation. In the Greek world the *oikoumene* was the world conquered by the phalanxes of Alexander and evangelized or influenced by Greek culture.

The Romans spoke about the *oikoumene* as the world conquered by the Roman legions and brought under the control of Roman law, "the whole world that should be taxed," according to the famous decree of Caesar Augustus (Luke 2:1). That for the Romans was *oikoumene*.

In more recent time *ecumenical* was used by Count Keyserling, the German philosopher, to denote the world not as a mere geographical entity, but as a vast and diversified sphere united by technology into one. Herman Keyserling began to speak of the "ecumenical era." "The world is an ecumenical organism," he used to say. "If you apply a major stimulus anywhere, it is felt everywhere." An extreme sensitivity marks the world of our time. Economics and politics and all the rest have become inter-related due to the advance of modern technology. All men belong for the first time to the *oikoumene*, to the ecumenical order in a secular sense. In a Christian sense that which is ecumenical is that part of mankind, of the human race, who have accepted the Gospel, who have been brought into the family of God and are members of the household of faith. These con-stitute that world-wide community of faith, the ecumenical community, or the ecumenical Church, which today is a reality for the first time in human history. This is the important point. A truly ecumenical community exists today in the form of a Christian community which is world-wide. A Chris-tian *oikoumene* is real for the first time in history. It is as real as the *oikoumene* of the Greeks and Romans, and the technological *oikoumene*, first described in Keyserling, which is today so potent a reality.

Let us advance a step further. The term "ecumenical" has in its Chris-tian context two meanings. One meaning denotes the Christian missionary thrust with the Gospel into the uttermost recesses of human habitation. The other meaning denotes the pursuit of unity on the part of the Christian forces that occupy the *oikoumene*. The primary meaning of "ecumenical" is missionary and dynamic. It is the movement in the name of Christ, in the companionship of Christ, and in the power of the Holy Spirit, to make known God's revelation in Christ to the ends of the earth. This denotes a dynamic movement from wherever Christ is, into all the inhabited earth in fulfillment of the mission of the Church.

This is what "ecumenics" means as a new science. Another view of "ecumenics" and "ecumenical" stresses merely the study of the differences among Christian denominations and confessions with a view to the achieve-ment of unity among them. But for what? Neither community nor unity on any level can be an end in itself. If it be Christian, it must be com-munity or unity for mission.

In this new name—Commission on Ecumenical Mission and Relations—

we possess an instrument to enable us to undertake the task of interpretation with regard to many basic and ultimate Christian themes. We stand for a movement into the *oikoumene*. We desire to gather older and younger Churches together in order to fulfill the Church's mission, and to take Christ's Saviourhood and Lordship seriously. This means an everlasting movement, from wherever Christ is, along the road towards the frontier; for the Church must ever be a pilgrim Church, the Church of the great frontiers. The moment the vision of the frontier disappears we are through; we shall lose our significance and betray the cause.

Relations

We come, finally to the meaning of *relations*. We speak about "Ecumenical Mission *and Relations*."

To this Commission have been committed all the questions of church relations with Churches beyond the seas, as well as with sister Churches at home. We want to have good relations with those Churches, not merely to remove tension, but that they and we together may move into the *oikoumene*, beginning right where we are. We want relations between the Churches, between all the members of the Body of Christ, to be what they should be. All Churches together must take the "form of a servant," as did Jesus Christ Himself, in order that they may fulfill the redemptive will of Him who is Head of His Body the Church.

In addition, the Commission will study relations with culture, and with the contemporary situation in general. Studies are being instituted on trends in contemporary culture in order that the Church in the fulfillment of its mission may be aware of such trends and recognize the challenge which they present.

So, too, there will be studies and action in relation to the State and society, and to the new Confessional Movement. There will be included the problem represented by the Roman Catholic Church. In the course of time studies will be set up within the Commission whereby colleges, universities, seminaries, and everybody who has something to offer, may be given an opportunity to provide insight and guidance to help the Church, through the Commission, to fulfill its ecumenical mission and develop its ecumenical relations, even to the ends of the earth.

3. ARTICLES ON THE COMMISSION ON ECUMENICAL MISSION AND RELATIONS OF THE UNITED PRESBYTERIAN CHURCH IN THE U.S.A.

In a series of articles published by Monday Morning, *a magazine for United Presbyterian pastors, leaders of the two Churches that merged to form The United Presbyterian Church in the U.S.A. analyzed the meaning and work of the newly created Commission on Ecumenical Mission and Relations.* *

I THE CONTINUING DYNAMIC IN MISSION

by Charles T. Leber

The question is being asked: "Will the Commission on Ecumenical Mission and Relations continue the historic emphasis upon 'foreign missions'?" The answer is an unqualified affirmative.

Over the centuries "foreign missions" has been the ever-growing expression of the fulfillment of the Great Commission "Go ye into all the world and preach the Gospel." The Great Commission has been and continues to be the fundamental purpose and the most powerful motivation of the Christian Church. Until recent times, the Churches of the West have been almost entirely the base from which foreigners arrived in foreign lands organizing "foreign missions," having as their major objective the building of the Church. This was right, good and challenging, and great results are to be seen, as well as the invisible results in the souls of men which no one but God can evaluate.

---

* As a guide to understanding the way in which the work of the five agencies brought together in the Commission on Ecumenical Mission and Relations continues, and the nature of the task it faces, the *Monday Morning* articles were reprinted in a pamphlet, in virtually the same form in which they first appeared. Rev. Frank H. Heinze, editor of *Monday Morning*, graciously consented to the reprinting of the articles in this form. (New York, July 1, 1958.)

As one result of the dynamic of foreign missions, the Church has been built in every land save two—Tibet and Outer Mongolia. These younger Churches vary in size and strength. In the large majority of lands, the Church, though small, has become sufficiently adequate for the American missionary organization to be dissolved, and its life and work merged into that of the Church. This we call integration, the transferring of the leadership and direction of mission to the Church of the land, with the missionaries becoming fraternal workers as an integral part of the indigenous Church's fellowship and program.

When the younger Churches are not as yet sufficiently adequate to accept the responsibilities in integration, the Missions continue. Where Missions continue as missionary organizations, missionaries continue. Only when the Mission is merged into the Church do the missionaries become fraternal workers, but the fraternal workers always carry on the purpose, tradition, qualification, and dedication of the missionaries.

The *relationships* among the Churches of the world, in developing unity, cannot be separated as they have been in the past from the *mission* of the Churches and be effective. One will dry up without the other. This split personality saps the vitality of the Church in its presentation of the Gospel.

This has been the chief handicap which the Christian movement has faced over the past decades, particularly in the organizational separation of the World Council of Churches and the International Missionary Council, even though they have been "associated" with each other. Before the large number of "younger Churches" came into existence, and when they were not strong enough to take their place as "partners in obedience," there may have been some justification for the two world organizations. In this connection it is good news to note that, by 1960, sufficient progress may have been made by a persistent group of believers in integration so that by then the World Council of Churches and the International Missionary Council will unite.

The Commission on Ecumenical Mission and Relations of The United Presbyterian Church in the United States of America developed out of concern with this archaic dualism, and as the result of six years of studied effort to meet the challenge presented by the growth of the "younger Churches" and to meet the increasing demand of all the Churches that they deal with each other in unity *and* mission, and not in unity *or* mission. The Presbyterian U.S.A. and the United Presbyterian groups concerned agreed that the time had come for definitive action.

The Commission on Ecumenical Mission and Relations not only conserves the values of the historic foreign missionary movement, but enlarges and enhances them by wider scope and larger participation. The Commission, uniting *mission* and *relations*, broadens the areas of service, strengthens all emphases, makes more comprehensive and efficient the administrative operations and more inclusive and dynamic the program and strategy.

Ecumenical is the word to define this development. Ecumenical comes from the two Greek words which mean *global* and *household*. The Head of the household is Christ. The household is the family of Christ in all its relations. Wherever Christ is, there is the base of mission. The entire global Christian family in all its relationships is involved in mission under the Lordship of Christ from whatever land as the base, uniting Christians of all lands in going *into* the world *together*.

It is because of the devoted and enduring commitment over the centuries of Christian missionaries, their colleagues and supporters, that this "New Day" has come. No longer is the Christian mission that of a few in foreign lands. No longer can interchurch relations be but an ecclesiastical concern.

But let us be sure to remember that the genius of ecumenical mission and relations is neither framework nor strategy, it is personnel: church men, women, and youth; missionaries, fraternal workers. In the development of ecumenical mission and relations, many more are needed and will be needed. Well-trained, highly qualified persons, humbly recommitting themselves daily before the Cross of Christ, by the power of His resurrection and in the companionship of the Holy Spirit, alone are able to share the fellowship of His sufferings as most certainly is required in our time. They alone are adequate for a Christian place in the encounter and sufficient to present to the uncommitted the Way of Redemption. They alone are able to provide the dynamic. For ecumenical mission and relations is essentially a matter of consecration, the unceasing dedication of all of us, of every one of us, to Jesus Christ in our time.

II RELATIONS AND MISSION BELONG TOGETHER

by Ralph Waldo Lloyd

Mission must always be at the heart of The United Presbyterian Church in the United States of America. It is everlastingly true that "mission is of the very essence of the Church." And this is the mission: to make God in Christ known, obeyed, and glorified in all areas of life and among all peoples.

Mission is the responsibility of the General Assembly, of every judicatory, of every congregation, of every board and agency. Nothing in the program of the Church is more important. To the historic Boards of Foreign Missions of the two branches of the Presbyterian Church which have united and now to the Commission on Ecumenical Mission and Relations, special responsibilities for world-wide (ecumenical) mission have been and will be committed. Likewise in other aspects, to the Board of National Missions, to the Board of Christian Education, to the General Council, and to every other arm of the Church, there is assigned responsibility for mission.

Although the missionary task for which Christians were commissioned by our Lord is but well begun in the world, yet under the power of the Holy Spirit there have been born in many lands indigenous, self-governing Churches. Thus is created a whole new range of interchurch relationships which cannot be administered effectively apart from the program of mission.

Interchurch relations have had high priority in both of the united Churches. Both were charter members of the World Presbyterian Alliance in 1875, of the Federal Council of Churches in 1908, of the World Council of Churches in 1948, of the National Council of Churches in 1950.

It is interesting and instructive to note that ours was the first American Church to set up a specific agency with responsibility for interchurch re-

274

lations. Prior to 1903, the Minutes of our General Assembly reported participation in the World Presbyterian Alliance, and made occasional mention of conversations regarding Church union. But there were no references to interchurch or ecumenical affairs as we know them today. In 1903 the General Assembly appointed a "Special Committee on Church Cooperation and Union," with a membership of seven which in 1906 was enlarged to twenty-one. In 1923 this Special Committee was changed to "The Department of Church Cooperation and Union of the Office of the General Assembly." Twenty-six years later, in 1949, it became "The Permanent Commission on Interchurch Relations."

Thus for fifty-five years, under three different names and in three different forms, the Permanent Commission was an established agency of the General Assembly of the former Presbyterian Church in the U.S.A. charged with handling general and specific matters of interchurch and ecumenical relations. The former U.S.A. Church and the former United Presbyterian Church, although its corresponding committees were younger and somewhat less established, have been for a half century and more leaders in interchurch cooperative enterprises, as they have been for a full century and more in the missionary enterprise.

The writer believes that "relations" must be increasingly a major concern of our Church. He is convinced that it was wise to maintain, under conditions of the past, separate agencies for mission and relations; else he would not have been willing to serve as Chairman of the Permanent Commission these past seventeen years. But "new occasions teach new duties" (as well as new names) and to him it seems clear that, although our structure and program have been distinguished by their progressiveness and relative effectiveness, the "new day" and the new Church need a combination of efforts toward mission and unity such as are incorporated in the newly established Commission on Ecumenical Mission and Relations.

There has been a growing realization that ecumenical relations and mission belong together in administrative structure and program, as well as in philosophy, pronouncements and strategy. This realization took form in action when in 1957 the two General Assemblies adopted sets of recommendations which in substance and in part read as follows:

> The Permanent Commission on Interchurch Relations [and the United Presbyterian Committees on Inter-Church Relations and Ecumenical Affairs], therefore, joins with the Board of Foreign Missions [and the Board of Foreign Missions of the United Presbyterian Church] in recommending that the 169th General Assembly approve the following proposal and adopt its recommendations. . . .
>
> It is understood that if the plan of union between the United Presbyterian Church and the Presbyterian Church in the United States

of America is approved, the recommendation of the Permanent Commission on Interchurch Relations is that said proposal be commended by the 169th General Assembly to the Committee on Consolidations provided for in the Plan of Union. The proposal is that:

1. The General Assembly direct the Stated Clerk of the [united] General Assembly, the [united] Board of Foreign Missions, and the Permanent Commission on Interchurch Relations [and two U.P. Committees] to initiate jointly such procedures as will make it possible to establish a commission subject to the supervision of the [united] General Assembly, to be known as THE COMMISSION ON ECUMENICAL MISSION AND RELATIONS.

2. This Commission . . . shall replace and succeed the present Permanent Commission on Interchurch Relations [and the two U.P. Committees] and the present [two] Board[s] of Foreign Missions.

Since the union of the two Churches was approved, also in 1957, the Special Committee on Consolidations, made up of twenty representatives from each Church, considered and approved the proposal for recommendation to the united General Assembly.

All of these actions testify to the growing realization that ecumenical relations and mission belong together.

Half a century confirms this realization. One of our most distinguished Church leaders pointed out recently that "the whole course of what we call the ecumenical movement has taken place within fifty years. My own generation has seen it all." He was using here the strong Greek word for household or the inhabited earth, with its comprehensive and meaningful new usage to describe the world-wide family of those who have accepted the Christian Gospel. Thus, the ecumenical movement has two aspects, not one: extension of the Gospel and the Church around the world, and unity of the Church around the world. As one result of the missionary enterprise of the past century, we can for the first time in history call the Christian Church truly world wide. In country after country of Asia, Africa, and Latin America, where Presbyterian and United Presbyterian "missions" were established, there are now autonomous Churches living and working in the midst of overwhelmingly non-Christian populations. With these our Church should maintain relations after the manner of its relations with the older Churches, while at the same time it continues to provide cooperation, personnel, and support for their independent life and work.

More than once in the Central Committee and other units of the World Council of Churches, this writer has heard wise voices warn against the shallowness and sterility of the efforts for unity apart from the dynamic of mission. On the other hand, one sees evidence on every side that where cooperation and unity are wanting, the mission of the Church is limited and weakened. It is a profoundly significant fact of the present day that the World Council of Churches, the most extensive expression of ecumenical relations, and the International Missionary Council, the most extensive expression of cooperation in ecumenical mission, are, in spite of many practical problems, moving toward merger. Why? Because relations and mission belong together.

III HOW THE COMMISSION WORKS

by Donald Black

A new organization necessarily keeps flexible during its formative years. The Commission on Ecumenical Mission and Relations was established by the 170th General Assembly in May, 1958. Since the Commission itself must develop the various facets of its structure, only a basic organizational plan is here outlined and described.

An organization exists to perform a task, and the nature of that task to a great degree shapes the organization. The Commission on Ecumenical Mission and Relations is charged with supervising the new United Presbyterian Church's responsibilities in ecumenical mission (those responsibilities formerly carried by the two Boards of Foreign Missions) and with maintaining the relationships of this new Church with other ecclesiastical bodies and organizations (the duties formerly carried by the Permanent Commission on Interchurch Relations—U.S.A., Permanent Committee on Inter-Church Relations—U.P., and Committee on Ecumenical Affairs—U.P.). The Church is drawing into one great effort its calling to mission and unity.

The Commission on Ecumenical Mission and Relations is composed of sixty-six members. Initially these have been drawn from the five bodies listed above, and the General Assembly will elect annually twenty-two members for a term of three years. Two major committees supervise the entire field—the Commission's Committee on Ecumenical Mission and the Commission's Committee on Ecumenical Relations. Committee structure gives proper consideration to a multitude of items, but the entire task is still the responsibility of the whole group. This does not put missions and relations under one roof, but rather blends two great areas of the Church's life into one common thrust. The Church is expressing unity in mission.

The Commission's Committee on Ecumenical Mission maintains the

278

broad reaches of world evangelism and service. Blending this arm of the Church with the movement toward Christian unity increases its opportunities for service.

Within the Committee on Ecumenical Relations falls a specialized task, for to the Commission is committed the responsibility for contacts and negotiations looking toward Church union.

The Commission will elect three members to the General Assembly's Committee on Church Union, thus providing liaison between the Commission and this Committee.

The Commission has two other committees with special responsibility. A separate committee on interpretation carries interpretive responsibility for the Commission's entire task, both that of mission and relations. This plan opens broad areas of opportunity in making the concept of ecumenical mission and relations known both to the Church and the world.

An Executive Committee on Policy and Methods draws together the officers, committee chairmen and other elected representatives for special supervision and coordination.

The Commission's staff administers its broad tasks. Five major administrative officers—a General Secretary, an Associate General Secretary for Ecumenical Mission, an Associate General Secretary for Ecumenical Relations, an Associate General Secretary for Administration, and a Treasurer—coordinate the Staff Council, composed of all executives. A Staff Division of Ecumenical Mission, with its Associate General Secretary as chairman, and a Staff Division of Ecumenical Relations, with its Associate General Secretary in charge, supervise the major thrust of mission and relations. Within each division are separate departments for specialized functions—for example, the Department of Personnel in the Division of Ecumenical Mission, or a Department on Laity in the Division of Ecumenical Relations. Two separate departments directly related to the central administration are the Department of Ecumenical Interpretation and the Treasury. Once again, the staff's division into departments with special responsibilities is only a means of carrying on what must of necessity always be a united effort as the Church moves forward in mission and relations.

The United Presbyterian Church cannot remain static in either mission or relations. Here is an organization with a creative thrust into the world. In mission it reaches forth to the world that knows not Christ; in relations it extends the hand of Christian fellowship to other parts of Christ's Body. The years ahead hold many creative opportunities for increasing the impact of a new United Presbyterian Church as it proclaims the Gospel.

IV AMERICA, TOO, IS IN THE WORLD

by Hermann N. Morse

Some people use the phrase "ecumenical mission" as though it applied to all the world except our own country. Similarly, in certain churches Boards of Foreign Missions have been renamed Boards of World Missions, with no change of basic concept. Used in such a context, where what is meant is obviously not the entire world but the world outside of the United States, Canada, Alaska, the West Indies, the Canal Zone and the Hawaiian Islands, "world mission(s)" and "national missions" become mutually exclusive concepts. The implied distinction is understandable, even inevitable, for administrative purposes, where the world is divided into two spheres of influence. Obviously, the "missionary" relation of our Church to other Churches in other lands involves both obligations and objectives quite different from those involved in the missionary program within our own Church in our own land.

In the Commission on Ecumenical Mission and Relations of our new Church, there is a sense, of course, in which this distinction is continued. The program of National Missions is not subsumed under the phrase "ecumenical mission" in the title of the new Commission. That phrase, considered as defining the administrative responsibility of an agency, is limited geographically and functionally. Nothing but confusion could result from failing to recognize this fact. There is, however, another sense, a larger and deeper sense, in which the concept of "ecumenical mission" does not and cannot exclude America, since America, too, is in the world.

There is an analogy here from the political realm. The colonialism that for four centuries was the dominant influence in the relation of the strong nations to the weak is now a chapter of history. It could not survive into the modern age when social and cultural as well as political and economic influences flow freely in every direction around the world. No one today is

280

to be excluded from the aspirations that used to be thought the exclusive right of the most favored peoples. This introduces a new dimension of mutuality into the relations among nations.

Today, our well-intentioned national efforts to be helpful to the disadvantaged of the world are often frustrated by characteristics of our own national life that seem to belie our protestations of concern. It is a commonplace to say that we can export only what we have. It is equally commonplace to say that the most important thing we have to export is what we are. It is futile to resent the fact that proffered gifts will often seem less important than what the recipients conceive to be the spirit expressed in them.

The relation of this to the Church's mission is obvious. We can't have two missions, one for ourselves and one for others. The mission of the Church is one, ecumenical in the deepest sense. Many years ago we had a slogan in Home Missions—"to make America Christian for the friendly service of the world." Probably its full significance has never been realized, but it needs to be. It used to be said that one lynching could undo the work of a hundred missionaries. Everyone knows the propaganda uses made today of the more unlovely aspects of our national life, and that what people think we are speaks more persuasively to them than our words or gifts.

Naturally, this is not a problem for "ecumenical mission" alone. It is a problem on the doorstep of every congregation in its ministry to its own parish. It is a problem of our collective ministry to the needy and unreached of our own population. The Church can speak no persuasive word to any from whom it withholds fellowship. It can perform no healing ministry that does not have its origin in understanding and love. The mission enterprise, whether at home or abroad, can express only what is in the heart of the Church and comes to fruition in the life of the Church.

What this means is simply that, however we define our administrative distinctions, we are all a part of the ecumenical mission of the Church. What we are, what finds expression in the life of every congregation, what we do for the establishment of the Kingdom and the extension of the Gospel—in our own lives, in our local parishes, across the nation and across the world—all of this is a part of ecumenical mission. If we fail anywhere, it weakens the whole. If God gives us victory anywhere, it strengthens the whole. The Church is one. The Christian mission is one. The world is one. And we are all a part of it.

V SOME PERSONAL OBSERVATIONS

by Eugene Carson Blake

The new Commission on Ecumenical Mission and Relations had its first meeting in New York on June 16, 1958. By design it was a brief meeting—taking only those actions necessary to cover emergencies for the summer and to prepare for the permanent organizing and launching of the Commission next September.

As I sat in the room at 156 Fifth Avenue, I asked myself what were we doing there. Here through so many years the far-flung operations of the Board of Foreign Missions had been conceived, controlled and guided. The names of old leaders, the great men of the past, ran through my mind: Robert Speer, Cleland McAfee, Arthur J. Brown. These were the men who had led our Church into one of the largest and most effective foreign missions operations in the 2,000 years of Christian history.

But as I sat, I began to think of another group of men of our Church, William H. Roberts and Lewis Seymour Mudge, J. Ross Stevenson and Williams Adams Brown. These men were the leaders of our Church in the creation and fostering of the World Council of Churches and the other councils with their increasing network of relationships that have been binding us in love, service and fellowship with other Churches at home and throughout the world.

I mention these two groups of names to emphasize that it is a merger that we have witnessed. If I had known the United Presbyterian Church of North America well enough to select the corresponding great names of their past fifty years in these two areas of Christian concern, I would have named them too.

My reason for making this emphasis is a very simple one. The only people with whom I have talked who were really against or reluctant about the new Commission have revealed in further conversation that they didn't understand in its depths what was proposed.

The most common objection has been: Why give to the Board of Foreign Missions the handling of all these relationships both at home and abroad?

Put in this way there is no answer. Unless this merger is a real one, modifying the Boards of Foreign Missions' other programs until they are really unrecognizable, modifying our habits and programs of interchurch and ecumenical relations and building them up to the new level required by the ecumenical movement, unless this happens and a new entity— really new—happens, we have made a grave mistake.

But I am sure we haven't. We shall have problems and difficulties and differences. For two reasons these will not dominate: (1) Everyone concerned believes in the validity of the idea of the Commission and wants it to succeed. (2) The world task before us is so challenging and so new and so full of possibilities, that to do our task well, there must be a new creativity such as we have not known before.

I believe that the leaders of the past applaud as The United Presbyterian Church in the U.S.A. boldly girds itself for its worldwide leadership in a new day. Nobody knows the future. May Jesus Christ give us the joy of serving in it boldly.

4. IMPORTANT DATES
IN PRESBYTERIAN HISTORY*

1562   French Huguenots (Presbyterian) arrived in Florida.

1611   First Puritan Presbyterians settled in Jamestown, Va. Alexander Whitaker organized a church with four elders, and formed a congregational presbytery at Henrico and Bermuda Hundred.

1620   First Puritan Presbyterian settlers reached New England.

1643   First Presbyterian church established in New Amsterdam (New York City).

1680   Scotch-Irish immigration in the New World began.

1683   Rev. Francis Makemie, chief founder of organized Presbyterianism in America, arrived in Maryland.

1706   First presbytery organized in Philadelphia through the efforts of Rev. Francis Makemie.

1717   General Synod, with four presbyteries (Philadelphia, New Castle, Long Island, and Snow Hill), organized in Philadelphia, Pa. Only the first three were actually erected.

1741   Rev. Azariah Horton appointed by Board of Correspondents in New York as first Presbyterian missionary in America. Mr. Horton, a member of the Presbytery of New York, went to labor among the Indians of Long Island.

1742   First Associate Presbyterian church (Seceders) established at Londonderry, Pa.

1743   First Reformed Presbyterian church (Covenanters) established at Middle Octorara, Pa.

1753   Associate Presbytery of Pennsylvania organized by Rev. Alexander Gellatly and Rev. Andrew Arnot, two ministers originally of Associate Presbytery of Scotland.

* For dates when Presbyterian mission work began, see Appendix 5.

1758   Synod of Philadelphia and Synod of New York merged to form Synod of New York and Philadelphia.

1774   First Reformed Presbytery in America constituted in Paxtang, Pa.

1782   Associate Reformed Church formed by union of Reformed Presbyterian Church (1743) with Associate Presbyterian Church (1742). This was the first church union in North America. Small groups of both churches reestablished themselves after the Union, the continuing Associate Church being most vigorous.

1788   General Synod, meeting in Philadelphia, adopted Constitution of Presbyterian Church in the U.S.A.

1789   First General Assembly of Presbyterian Church in the U.S.A. met in Philadelphia.

1794   Service Theological Seminary founded in Service Creek, Beaver County, thirty miles west of Pittsburgh, Pa., with Rev. John Anderson, resident professor. This is the oldest antecedent of Pittsburgh Theological Seminary.

1796   The New York Missionary Society formed. This was the first voluntary interdenominational missionary organization in the New World. Presbyterians participated.

1801   Plan of Union began cooperative work between Congregational and Presbyterian churches in western New York and old North West. Plan was abrogated by the Presbyterians in 1837.

1802   Standing Committee on Missions established by Presbyterian Church in the U.S.A. Later this Committee became known, at different times, as Board of Missions, Domestic Missions and Home Missions, and finally, Board of National Missions.

1802   Synod of Pittsburgh organized itself as The Western Missionary Society.

1810   American Board of Commissioners for Foreign Missions organized in Boston, with Presbyterians and Congregationalists cooperating. For many years after this date, Presbyterian missionaries went out under this Board.

1810   Presbytery of Cumberland separated from Presbyterian Church, leading to establishment of Cumberland Presbyterian Church.

1812   Princeton Theological Seminary organized.

1817   United Foreign Missionary Society formed, Congregationalists, Presbyterians, Dutch Reformed, and Associate Reformed Presbyterians cooperating.

1818   First Presbyterian Women's Society formed in Derry, Pa.

1831   The Western Foreign Missionary Society established by Synod of

Pittsburgh. This Society was the forerunner of The Board of Foreign Missions of the Presbyterian Church in the U.S.A.

1837 Board of Foreign Missions established by Old School General Assembly of the Presbyterian Church in the U.S.A. (absorbing The Western Foreign Missionary Society). New School General Assembly continued to cooperate with American Board of Commissioners for Foreign Missions and American Home Missionary Society until 1861.

1837 Old School Assembly and New School Assembly separated and carried on parallel activities for thirty-two years.

1840 Missions Library created by The Board of Foreign Missions of the Presbyterian Church in the U.S.A.

1852 Presbyterian Historical Society formed.

1858 United Presbyterian Church of North America formed by union of Associate (Presbyterian) Synod (1742) and General Synod of Associate Reformed Church (1782).

1861 Old School Presbyteries in the South separated from Old School General Assembly of Presbyterian Church in the U.S.A. and formed The Presbyterian Church in the Confederate States of America, whose name was changed in 1865 to Presbyterian Church in the U.S.

1870 Reunion of Old School and New School General Assemblies in Pittsburgh to form one church.

1870 Woman's Foreign Missionary Society of Presbyterian Church in the U.S.A. organized in Philadelphia.

1875 Presbyterian Church in the U.S.A. and United Presbyterian Church of North America became charter members of "The Alliance of the Reformed Churches Throughout the World Holding the Presbyterian System" ("System" changed to "Order" in 1954), which is now officially called also The World Presbyterian Alliance and The World Alliance of Reformed Churches; organized in London.

1883 Women's General Missionary Society (United Presbyterian) formed (Board of Directors appointed in 1886).

1903 Special Committee on Church Cooperation and Union appointed by General Assembly of the Presbyterian Church in the U.S.A.

1906 Cumberland Presbyterian Church reunited with Presbyterian Church in the U.S.A. A section of the church continued as Cumberland Presbyterian Church.

1908 Presbyterian Church in the U.S.A. and United Presbyterian Church of North America cooperated with other churches in the formation of Federal Council of Churches of Christ in America.

1910   General Assembly of United Presbyterian Church of North America set up a Permanent Committee on Church Relations.

1920   Unification of women's boards and societies of Presbyterian Church in the U.S.A. and formation of Women's Board.

1920   Welsh Calvinistic Methodist Church merged with Presbyterian Church in the U.S.A.

1923   Reorganization of boards and agencies of General Assembly of Presbyterian Church in the U.S.A., Women's Board merging with Board of Foreign Missions.

1923   The Special Committee on Church Cooperation and Union became the Department of Church Cooperation and Union of the Office of the General Assembly.

1924   United Mission in Iraq formed, with participation of Presbyterian Board of Foreign Missions.

1930   Women first admitted to eldership in Presbyterian Church in the U.S.A.

1939   General Assembly of United Presbyterian Church of North America appointed a Permanent Committee on Church Relationships.

1941   The Kyodan (United Church of Christ in Japan) organized, with thirty-four denominations, including the Presbyterian.

1942   National Council of Presbyterian Women founded.

1945   The Board of Foreign Missions of the Presbyterian Church in the U.S.A. united with three other mission boards to form United Andean Indian Mission with work in Ecuador, South America.

1946   Restoration Fund of $23,000,000 raised for rehabilitation and reconstruction of churches in Europe.

1946   Committee on Presbyterian Cooperation in Portugal formed (Presbyterian U.S.A., Presbyterian U.S., Presbyterian Church of Brazil). Committee was dissolved in 1964.

1947   Interboard Committee for Christian Work in Japan organized.

1947   The Board of Foreign Missions of the Presbyterian Church in the U.S.A. established an audio-visual office.

1948   RAVEMCCO (Radio, Visual Education and Mass Communications Office) established by the Foreign Missions Conference of North America and lodged administratively in Presbyterian Audio-Visual Office (continuing this arrangement for some years).

1948   United Church of Christ in the Philippines established.

1948   Presbyterian Church in the U.S.A. and United Presbyterian Church of North America became charter members of World Council of Churches, formed in Amsterdam.

1949 Permanent Commission on Interchurch Relations replaced Department of Church Cooperation and Union in Presbyterian Church in the U.S.A. (1902 and 1923).

1950 Presbyterian Church in the U.S.A. and United Presbyterian Church of North America became charter members of National Council of the Churches of Christ, formed in Cleveland, Ohio.

1951 General Assembly of United Presbyterian Church of North America appointed Committee on Ecumenical Affairs.

1952 Committee on Cooperation in the Upper Nile formed.

1953 United Mission to Nepal formed with participation of The Board of Foreign Missions of the Presbyterian Church in the U.S.A.

1955 Study Fellowship established by The Board of Foreign Missions of the Presbyterian Church in the U.S.A. to prepare missionaries for the "New Day."

1955 Permanent Committee on Inter-Church Relations (U.P.N.A.) replaced Permanent Committee on Church Relationships.

1955 Presbyterian Commission on Cooperation in Latin America (CCPAL) organized at Conference in Campinas, Brazil. (In 1965 the name was changed to Association of Presbyterian and Reformed Churches in Latin America.)

1956 Mohonk Consultation called by The Board of Foreign Missions of the Presbyterian Church in the U.S.A., with representatives from Presbyterian churches overseas.

1956 Women first admitted to the ordained ministry in Presbyterian Church in the U.S.A.

1956 Women's General Missionary Society united with Board of Foreign Missions of United Presbyterian Church of North America.

1957 Integration of Presbyterian Mission in Thailand with Church of Christ in Thailand.

1957 Integration of West Africa Mission with Cameroun Presbyterian Church.

1958 The United Presbyterian Church in the United States of America formed in Pittsburgh, Pa., by the merging of Presbyterian Church in the U.S.A. and United Presbyterian Church of North America.

1958 Creation of Commission on Ecumenical Mission and Relations by General Assembly of The United Presbyterian Church in the U.S.A.

1959 Ecumenical Training Center (formerly Study Fellowship) established at Stony Point, N.Y., by Commission on Ecumenical Mission and Relations of The United Presbyterian Church in the U.S.A.

1959 Korea Mission integrated with Presbyterian Church in Korea.

1959 Syria-Lebanon Mission integrated with National Evangelical Synod.

1959   Presbyterian mission in Colombia integrated with Presbyterian Church of Colombia.

1959   Interboard Committee for Christian Work in Philippines established.

1961   Missionary Orientation Center, Stony Point, N.Y., established by purchase of land and buildings of Ecumenical Training Center from Commission on Ecumenical Mission and Relations of The United Presbyterian Church in the U.S.A., the Commission being one of the co-purchasers and sponsors of the new center.

1961   Interboard Committee for Christian Work in Hong Kong established.

1962   Presbyterian mission in Venezuela integrated with Evangelical Presbyterian Church of Venezuela.

1962   Presbyterian mission in Guatemala integrated with Evangelical Presbyterian Church of Guatemala.

1966   Dr. Eugene Carson Blake, Stated Clerk of General Assembly of The United Presbyterian Church in the U.S.A., elected General Secretary of World Council of Churches.

5. DATES WHEN PRESBYTERIAN MISSION WORK BEGAN

I. Presbyterian Church in the U.S.A.

1823   Syria Mission begun by missionaries of American Board of Commissioners for Foreign Missions, with which Presbyterians cooperated. Work in Syria transferred to Presbyterian Board of Foreign Missions in 1870.

1834   Punjab Mission begun at Ludhiana.

1835   Iran Mission begun by American Board of Commissioners for Foreign Missions in which Presbyterians cooperated. Work transferred to Presbyterian Board in 1870.

1836   North India Mission begun at Allahabad.

1840   Thailand Mission.

1844   East China Mission. (In 1951, The Board of Foreign Missions of the Presbyterian Church in the U.S.A. dissolved the China Missions and the China Council, and established work in Hong Kong.)

1849   Lahore Mission.

1850   Spanish Guinea (part of West Africa Mission); later called Río Muni.

1856   Colombia Mission.

1859   Japan Mission.

1859   Central Brazil Mission.

1870   Western India Mission begun at Kolhapur.

1872   Mexico Mission.

1873   Chile Mission.

1879   West Africa Mission (Cameroun).

1882   Guatemala Mission.

1884   Korea Mission.

1897   Venezuela Mission.

1899   Philippine Mission.

1924   United Mission in Mesopotamia; later called United Mission in Iraq (work shared with other mission boards).

1945   United Andean Indian Mission (Ecuador); work shared with three other mission boards.

1951   The Board of Foreign Missions of the Presbyterian Church in the U.S.A. began work in cooperation with the Council of Churches in Indonesia.

1952   The Board of Foreign Missions of the Presbyterian Church in the U.S.A. began work in cooperation with the Presbyterian Church of Formosa.

1953   United Mission to Nepal; work shared with other boards and agencies.

II. United Presbyterian Church of North America

1854   American Mission in Egypt.

1855   American Mission in India (Sialkot Mission). Most of this area became part of Pakistan with the partition of 1947.

1900   American Mission in Sudan (Synod of the Nile). The Presbytery divided in 1948; then each part became an independent church on the following dates:
    Church of Christ in the Upper Nile—1955.
    Evangelical Church of the Sudan—1963.

1920   American Mission in Ethiopia.

1948   American Mission in South Sudan (Upper Nile Province) separated from North Sudan to form independent mission.

6. IMPORTANT DATES IN ECUMENICAL HISTORY

1900   Ecumenical Missionary Conference, New York.

1908   Federal Council of the Churches of Christ in America organized.

1910   World Missionary Conference, Edinburgh, Scotland.

1914   World Alliance for International Friendship Through the Churches, Constance, Germany.

1921   International Missionary Council organized.

1925   First World Conference on Life and Work, Stockholm, Sweden.

1927   First World Conference on Faith and Order, Lausanne, Switzerland.

1928   International Missionary Conference at Jerusalem.

1937   Second World Conference on Life and Work, Oxford, England.

1937   Second World Conference on Faith and Order, Edinburgh, Scotland.

1938   International Missionary Conference, Tambaram (Madras), India.

1939   Provisional Committee of World Council of Churches formed at Utrecht.

1939   First World Conference of Christian Youth, Amsterdam, Holland.

1947   Enlarged meeting of International Missionary Council and of the Committee of the Council, Whitby, Canada.

1947   Second World Conference of Christian Youth, Oslo, Norway.

1948   First Assembly of World Council of Churches, Amsterdam, Holland.

1950   National Council of the Churches of Christ in the U.S.A. formed.

1952   Enlarged Meeting of the International Missionary Council and of the Committee of the Council, Willingen, Germany.

1952   Third World Conference of Christian Youth, Travancore, India.

1952   Third Conference on Faith and Order, Lund, Sweden.

1954   Second Assembly of the World Council of Churches, Evanston, Illinois.

1957   East Asia Christian Conference organized at Prapat, Indonesia.

1957   Ghana Assembly of the International Missionary Council.

1961   Third Assembly of the World Council of Churches, New Delhi, India. (At this Assembly the International Missionary Council merged with the World Council of Churches.)

1963   All Africa Conference of Churches organized at Kampala, Uganda.

1963   Fourth Conference on Faith and Order, Montreal, Canada.

1964   Conference of European Churches organized.

1964   Near East Christian Council became the Near East Council of Churches.

7. DATES OF MISSIONS AND NATIONAL CHURCHES

Country	Date Mission Work Began[a]	Presb. Board	Name of Indigenous Church or Council of Churches	Date of Integration
BRAZIL	1859	Presb. U.S.A.	Presbyterian Church of Brazil	1957
CAMEROUN	1879	Presb. U.S.A.	Cameroun Presbyterian Church	1964
CHILE	1873	Presb. U.S.A.	Presbyterian Church in Chile	1959
COLOMBIA	1856	Presb. U.S.A.	Presbyterian Church of Colombia	
ECUADOR	1945	Presb. U.S.A.	United Evangelical Church of Ecuador (formerly United Andean Indian Mission)	1965
EGYPT (U.A.R.)	1854	U.P.N.A.[b]	Coptic Evangelical Church in the Nile Valley	
ETHIOPIA	1920	U.P.N.A.	Bethel Evangelical Church	
GUATEMALA	1882	Presb. U.S.A.	Evangelical Presbyterian Church of Guatemala	1962
HONG KONG	1844[c]	Presb. U.S.A.	Church of Christ in China (Hong Kong Council)	
INDIA			United Church of Northern India/Pakistan begun in 1924:	
Western India	1870	Presb. U.S.A.	Kolhapur Church Council	1957
North India	1836	Presb. U.S.A.	North India Synod	1957
Punjab	1834	Presb. U.S.A.	Punjab Synod	1957
INDONESIA	1951[d]	Presb. U.S.A.	Council of Churches in Indonesia	
IRAN	1835	Presb. U.S.A.	Evangelical Presbyterian Church of Iran	1965
IRAQ[e]	1924	Presb. U.S.A.	Arab Evangelical Church	
JAPAN	1859	Presb. U.S.A.	United Church of Christ in Japan	1941
KOREA	1884	Presb. U.S.A.	Presbyterian Church in Korea	1959
MEXICO	1872	Presb. U.S.A.	National Presbyterian Church of Mexico	

NEPAL	1953	Presb. U.S.A.	United Mission to Nepal	
PAKISTAN				
East (Sialkot)	1855	U.P.N.A.	United Presbyterian Church of Pakistan	
West (Lahore)	1849	Presb. U.S.A.	United Church of Northern India/Pakistan: Lahore Church Council	1924
PHILIPPINES	1899	Presb. U.S.A.	United Church of Christ in the Philippines	1947
REPUBLIC OF THE SUDAN				
Sudan^f	1900	U.P.N.A.	Evangelica' Church of the Sudan	
Upper Nile		U.P.N.A.	Church of Christ in the Upper Nile	
RIO MUNI	1850	Presb. U.S.A.	Evangelical Presbyterian Church in Río Muni	
(Spanish Guinea)				
SYRIA and LEBANON	1823	Presb. U.S.A.	National Evangelical Synod of Syria and Lebanon	1959
TAIWAN (Formosa)	1952g	Presb. U.S.A.	Presbyterian Church of Formosa	
THAILAND	1840	Presb. U.S.A.	Church of Christ in Thailand	1957
VENEZUELA	1897	Presb. U.S.A.	Evangelical Presbyterian Church of Venezuela	1962

NOTES:

a. Information taken from Appendix 6, "Dates When Presbyterian Mission Work Began."

b. U.P.N.A.—United Presbyterian Church of North America.

c. HONG KONG—In 1951, The Board of Foreign Missions of the Presbyterian Church in the U.S.A. dissolved the China Missions and the China Council, and established work in Hong Kong.

d. INDONESIA—The Presbyterian Church in the U.S.A. sent fraternal workers to work in cooperation with the Council of Churches.

e. IRAQ—The United Presbyterian Church in the U.S.A. participates with other mission boards in the United Mission in Iraq, a union project.

f. SUDAN—Begun in 1900 as a mission, the church was then established as part of the Synod of the Nile of the United Presbyterian Church of North America. The presbytery divided in 1948; then each became an independent church on dates as follows: Church of Christ in the Upper Nile—1955; Evangelical Church of the Sudan—1963.

g. TAIWAN—The Presbyterian Church in the U.S.A. sent fraternal workers to work with the Presbyterian Church of Formosa.

8. ECUMENICAL TREE

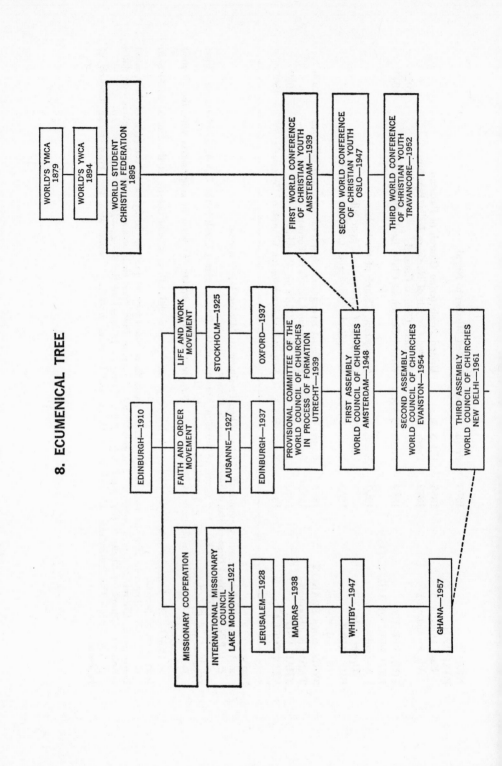

WORLD'S YMCA 1879

WORLD'S YWCA 1894

WORLD STUDENT CHRISTIAN FEDERATION 1895

FIRST WORLD CONFERENCE OF CHRISTIAN YOUTH AMSTERDAM—1939

SECOND WORLD CONFERENCE OF CHRISTIAN YOUTH OSLO—1947

THIRD WORLD CONFERENCE OF CHRISTIAN YOUTH TRAVANCORE—1952

EDINBURGH—1910

LIFE AND WORK MOVEMENT

STOCKHOLM—1925

OXFORD—1937

FAITH AND ORDER MOVEMENT

LAUSANNE—1927

EDINBURGH—1937

PROVISIONAL COMMITTEE OF THE WORLD COUNCIL OF CHURCHES IN PROCESS OF FORMATION UTRECHT—1939

FIRST ASSEMBLY WORLD COUNCIL OF CHURCHES AMSTERDAM—1948

SECOND ASSEMBLY WORLD COUNCIL OF CHURCHES EVANSTON—1954

THIRD ASSEMBLY WORLD COUNCIL OF CHURCHES NEW DELHI—1961

MISSIONARY COOPERATION

INTERNATIONAL MISSIONARY COUNCIL LAKE MOHONK—1921

JERUSALEM—1928

MADRAS—1938

WHITBY—1947

GHANA—1957

BIBLIOGRAPHY

A bibliography for a volume such as this could be quite extensive. It has therefore been necessary to limit it within the following: (I) Books and Pamphlets, (II) Periodicals, (III) Reports, and (IV) Significant Papers, a series published by the Commission on Ecumenical Mission and Relations. The author has drawn freely from General Assembly *Minutes* (of the Presbyterian Church in the U.S.A., the United Presbyterian Church of North America, and The United Presbyterian Church in the U.S.A.), from reports of boards of foreign missions, of the National Council of Churches, and of the World Council of Churches, as well as from field reports and mimeographed documents.

I. Books and Pamphlets

Bacon, Leonard Woolsey, *A History of American Christianity* (American Church History Series, Vol. XIII). Charles Scribner's Sons, 1900.

Bates, M. Searle, and Pauck, Wilhelm (eds.), *The Prospects of Christianity Throughout the World.* Charles Scribner's Sons, 1964.

Beard, Charles A. and Mary R., *A Basic History of the United States.* The New Home Library, 1944.

Beaver, R. Pierce, *Ecumenical Beginnings in Protestant World Mission: A History of Comity.* Thomas Nelson & Sons, 1962.

———— *From Missions to Mission.* Association Press, 1964.

Berdyaev, Nicolas, in Will Herberg (ed.), *Four Existentialist Theologians.* Doubleday & Company, Inc., 1958.

Blauw, Johannes, *The Missionary Nature of the Church: A Survey of the Biblical Theology of Mission.* McGraw-Hill Book Co., Inc., 1962.

Bridston, Keith R., and Wagoner, Walter D. (eds.), *Unity in Mid-Career: An Ecumenical Critique.* The Macmillan Company, 1963.

Brown, Arthur Judson, *One Hundred Years.* Fleming H. Revell Company, 1936.

———— *Unity and Missions.* Fleming H. Revell Company, 1915.

Butterfield, Herbert, *Christianity and History.* Charles Scribner's Sons, 1949, 1950.

Carman, Harry J., and Syrett, Harold C., *A History of the American People* (Vol. I, to 1865). Alfred A. Knopf, Inc., 1952.

Centenary Memorial of the Planting and Growth of Presbyterianism in Western Pennsylvania and Parts Adjacent. Pittsburgh: Benjamin Singerly, 1876.

A Century for Christ in India and Pakistan: 1855–1955. Published by the United Presbyterian Church of Pakistan, 1955.

Child, D. L., *The History of the Condition of Women in Various Ages and Nations,* Vol. II. Boston: John Allen & Co., 1835.

Christy, Wayne H., *The United Presbyterian Church and Church Union.* Doctoral thesis presented to the University of Pittsburgh, 1947.

Come, Arnold B., *Agents of Reconciliation.* The Westminster Press, 1960.

The Constitution of The United Presbyterian Church in the United States of America (in bound volume, *The Presbyterian Constitution and Digest*). The Office of the General Assembly of The United Presbyterian Church in the U.S.A., 1963.

Conversations with Roman Catholics on the Nature of the Church and on Ecumenism. Resources for Ecumenical Encounter, No. 1 (prepared by Margarethe B. J. Brown). Commission on Ecumenical Mission and Relations, 1965.

Cox, Harvey, *The Secular City.* The Macmillan Company, 1965.

Davies, A. Mervyn, *Presbyterian Heritage.* John Knox Press, 1965.

Davis, J. Merle, *New Buildings on Old Foundations: A Handbook on Stabilizing the Younger Churches in Their Environment* (Studies in the World Mission of Christianity, No. V). International Missionary Council, 1945.

Douglass, H. Paul, *Church Unity Movements in the United States.* Institute of Social and Religious Research, 1934.

Drury, Clifford Merrill, *Presbyterian Panorama.* Board of Christian Education, Presbyterian Church in the United States of America, 1952.

Eastman, A. Theodore, *Christian Responsibility in One World.* The Seabury Press, Inc., 1965.

Elder, Earl E., *Vindicating a Vision.* Board of Foreign Missions of the United Presbyterian Church of North America, 1958.

Elsbree, Oliver Wendell, *The Rise of the Missionary Spirit in America, 1790–1815.* The Williamsport Printing and Binding Company, 1928.

The Encyclopedia of Missions, 2d ed. Edited under the auspices of the Bureau of Missions by Rev. Henry Otis Dwight, Rev. H. Allen Tupper, Jr., and Rev. Edwin Munsell Bliss. Funk & Wagnalls Company, 1904.

Encyclopedia of the Presbyterian Church in the United States of America, ed. by Alfred Nevin. Presbyterian Encyclopedia Publishing Co., 1884.

Fisher, Galen M., *John R. Mott: Architect of Co-operation and Unity.* Association Press, 1953.

Forman, Charles W., *A Faith for the Nations* (Layman's Theological Library). The Wesminster Press, 1957.

Fulton, Evlyn Wehling, *A History of the Women's General Missionary So-*

ciety of the United Presbyterian Church of North America. A thesis submitted to the Faculty of the Pittsburgh-Xenia Theological Seminary in Partial Fulfillment of the Requirements for the Degree of Master of Religious Education, May, 1949.

Geyer, Alan F., *Piety and Politics: American Protestantism in the World Arena.* John Knox Press, 1963.

Gillett, E. H., *History of the Presbyterian Church in the United States of America,* rev. ed. The Board of Publication and Sabbath School Work, 1864.

Gordon, Andrew, *Our India Mission.* Published by Andrew Gordon; Philadelphia: 1886.

Green, Ashbel, *Presbyterian Missions: A Historical Sketch or Compendious View of Domestic and Foreign Missions of the Presbyterian Church in the United States of America.* Philadelphia: William S. Martien, 1838.

———— *Presbyterian Missions.* Appendices by J. C. Lowrie. Anson D. F. Randolph & Company, Inc., 1893.

Gremillion, Joseph Berton, *The Other Dialogue.* Doubleday & Company, Inc., 1965.

Hanzsche, William Thomson, *Our Presbyterian Church: Its History, Organization, and Program: A Study Unit of Thirteen Lessons.* Presbyterian Board of Christian Education, 1933.

Hart, Isabel (ed.), *Historical Sketches of Women's Missionary Societies in America and England.* Published privately by Mrs. L. H. Daggett; Boston: 1879.

Historical Sketches of the Missions Under the Care of the Board of Foreign Missions of the Presbyterian Church. Published by the Woman's Foreign Missionary Society of the Presbyterian Church, 1886.

Hodge, Charles, *The Constitutional History of the Presbyterian Church in the U.S.A. Part II—1741 to 1788.* Philadelphia: William S. Martien, 1840.

Hogg, W. Richey, *Ecumenical Foundations: A History of the International Missionary Council and Its Nineteenth-Century Background.* Harper & Brothers, 1952.

———— *New Day Dawning.* World Horizons, Inc., 1957.

———— *One World, One Mission.* Friendship Press, 1960.

Howard, William D., Missionary Address, in *History of the Origin of the Board of Foreign Missions.* New York: Mission House, 1872.

Iglehart, Charles W., *A Century of Protestant Christianity in Japan.* Charles E. Tuttle Company, 1959.

Imbris, William M., *The Church of Christ in Japan* (A Course of Lectures). The Westminster Press, 1906.

Jamison, Wallace N., *The United Presbyterian Story: A Centennial Study (1858–1958).* The Geneva Press, 1958.

The Jerusalem Meeting of the International Missionary Council, March 24–

April 8, 1928 (Vol. III, "The Relation Between the Younger and the Older Churches"). International Missionary Council, 1928.

Johnson, R. Park, *Middle East Pilgrimage*. Friendship Press, 1958.

Jurji, Edward J. (ed.), *The Ecumenical Era in Church and Society: A Symposium in Honor of John A. Mackay*. The Macmillan Company, 1959.

Kraemer, Hendrik, *Religion and the Christian Faith*. London: Lutterworth Press, 1956.

Latourette, Kenneth Scott, *Christianity in a Revolutionary Age: A History of Christianity in the Nineteenth and Twentieth Centuries* (Vol. III, "The Nineteenth Century Outside Europe"). Harper & Row, Publishers, Inc., 1961.

Leber, Charles T., *The Church Must Win! The Place, Power and Promise of the Christian Church in the Conflict of Our Time*. Fleming H. Revell Company, 1944.

Liggett, Thomas J., *The Role of the Missionary in Latin America Today*. The Committee on Cooperation in Latin America, Division of Foreign Missions, National Council of the Churches of Christ in the U.S.A., 1963.

Loetscher, Lefferts A., *A Brief History of the Presbyterians*. The Westminster Press, 1958.

López, Alfonso, *La Estirpe Calvinista de Nuestras Instituciones*. Bogotá, Colombia: Universidad Nacional de Colombia, 1947.

Lowrie, John C., *A Manual of Missions or Sketches of the Foreign Missions of the Presbyterian Church*. Anson D. F. Randolph, 1854.

McCorkel, Roy J. (ed.), *Voices from the Younger Churches*. Published for the Student Volunteer Movement by Friendship Press, 1939.

Macfarland, Charles S., *Christian Unity in the Making*. Federal Council of the Churches of Christ in America, 1948.

Mackay, John A., *Christianity on the Frontier*. The Macmillan Company, 1950.

―――― *Ecumenics: The Science of the Church Universal*. Prentice-Hall, Inc., 1964.

―――― *The Presbyterian Way of Life*. Prentice-Hall, Inc., 1960.

Mackie, Robert C., and Others, *Layman Extraordinary: John R. Mott, 1865-1955*. Foreword by W. A. Visser 't Hooft. Association Press, 1965.

Macmurray, John, *The Clue to History*. Harper & Brothers, 1939.

M'Kerrow, John, *History of the Foreign Missions of the Secession and United Presbyterian Church*. Edinburgh: Andrew Elliot, 1867.

Miller, Samuel, in *Presbyterian Reunion Memorial Volume 1837–1871*. New York: De-Witt C. Lent & Co., 1871.

Minear, Paul S. (ed.), *The Nature of the Unity We Seek*. Sermon by Bishop Johannes Lilje on "The Significance of the Ecumenical Movement." The Bethany Press, 1958.

Morrill, Guy L., *Your Presbyterian Church*. Introduction by Wm. Hiram Foulkes. Privately printed, 1926.

Morrison, Charles Clayton, *The Unfinished Reformation*. Harper & Brothers, 1953.

Mott, John R., *Cooperation and the World Mission*. International Missionary Council, 1935.

—— *Five Decades and a Forward View*. Harper & Brothers, 1939.

Newbigin, J. E. Lesslie, *A Faith for This One World?* Harper & Row, Publishers, Inc., 1962.

Nichols, Robert Hastings, *Presbyterianism in New York State: A History of the Synod and Its Predecessors*, edited and completed by James Hastings Nichols. The Westminster Press, 1963.

Niebuhr, Reinhold, *Faith and History: A Comparison of Christian and Modern Views of History*. Charles Scribner's Sons, 1949.

Niebuhr, R. Richard, *The Social Sources of Denominationalism*. Henry Holt and Company, 1929.

Niles, D. T., *Upon the Earth: The Mission of God and the Missionary Enterprise of the Churches*. McGraw-Hill Book Co., Inc., 1962.

Pradervand, Marcel (ed.), *São Paulo Story*. Geneva: The World Presbyterian Alliance Offices, 1960.

Presbyterian Reunion Memorial Volume, 1837–1871. De-Witt C. Lent & Co., 1871.

Ranson, C. W. (ed.), *Renewal and Advance: Christian Witness in a Revolutionary World*. London: Edinburgh House Press, 1948.

Roberts, William Henry, *A Concise History of the Presbyterian Church in the United States of America*. The Board of Publication and Sabbath School Work, 1917.

Romig, Theodore F., and Crouch, Archie R., *The Missionary*. World Horizons, Inc., 1965.

Sanderson, Ross W., *Church Cooperation in the United States*. Hartford, Conn.: Finlay Brothers Press, 1960.

Sanford, Elias B. (ed.), *Church Federation: Interchurch Conference on Federation*, New York, November 15-21, 1905. Fleming H. Revell Company, 1906.

Sanford, Elias B., *Origin and History of the Federal Council of the Churches of Christ in America*. Hartford, Conn.: The S. S. Scranton Company, 1916.

Scovel, Myra, *My Neighbor, the Wounded: The Widening Scope of the Medical Mission of the Church*. Commission on Ecumenical Mission and Relations of The United Presbyterian Church in the U.S.A., 1966.

Slosser, Gaius Jackson, *Christian Unity*. E. P. Dutton & Co., Inc., 1929.

—— (ed.), *They Seek A Country: The American Presbyterians*. The Macmillan Company, 1955.

Sly, Virgil A., Address, "From Missions to Mission" in *The Christian Mission for Today*, five addresses presented to the Ninth Annual Assembly of the Division of Foreign Missions, National Council of Churches,

December 7-10, 1958. Division of Foreign Missions of the National Council of the Churches of Christ in the U.S.A.

Smith, Elwyn A., *The Presbyterian Ministry in American Culture: A Study in Changing Concepts, 1700–1900.* The Westminster Press, 1962.

Smith, John Coventry, in *The Christian Mission for Today.* Division of Foreign Missions of the National Council of the Churches of Christ in the U.S.A., 1958.

Sobrepeña, Enrique C., *That They May Be One,* 2d ed. Manila: United Church of Christ in the Philippines, 1964.

Speer, Robert E., *Presbyterian Foreign Missions.* The Board of Publication and Sabbath School Work, 1901.

Sweet, William Warren, *The Story of Religion in America.* Harper & Brothers, 1939.

Swift, Rev. Elliott E., "Missionary History," in *Centenary Memorial of the Planting and Growth of Presbyterianism in Western Pennsylvania and Parts Adjacent.* Pittsburgh: Benjamin Singerly, 1876.

Taylor, Theophilus M., "The Contribution of the Reformed Churches to Christian Unity." February, 1952. Unpublished manuscript.

Than, U Kyaw, Chapter, "East of New Delhi: Regionalism or Centralism?" in Keith R. Bridston and Walter D. Wagoner, eds., *Unity in Mid-Career.* The Macmillan Company, 1963.

Thomas, Winburn T., *Protestant Beginnings in Japan: The First Three Decades, 1859–1889.* Charles E. Tuttle Company, 1959.

Thompson, Charles Lemuel, *The Presbyterians.* New York: The Baker & Taylor Company, 1903.

Thompson, Robert Ellis, *History of the Presbyterian Churches in the United States* (American Church History Series, Vol. VI). Charles Scribner's Sons, 1895.

Tillich, Paul, *The Eternal Now.* Charles Scribner's Sons, 1963.

Trinterud, Leonard J., *The Forming of an American Tradition: A Re-examination of Colonial Presbyterianism.* The Westminster Press, 1949.

The Universal Church in God's Design: An Ecumenical Study Prepared Under the Auspices of the World Council of Churches. Harper & Brothers, 1948.

van de Pol, William Hendrik, *World Protestantism,* tr. by T. Zuydwijk, Foreword by Bernard J. Leeming, S.J. Herder & Herder, Inc., 1964.

Van Dusen, Henry P., Chapter, "Time of Testing for the National Council," in Keith R. Bridston, and Walter D. Wagoner, eds., *Unity in Mid-Career.* The Macmillan Company, 1963.

van Leeuwen, Arend Th., *Christianity in World History: The Meeting of the Faiths of East and West,* tr. by H. H. Hoskins, Foreword by Dr. Hendrick Kraemer. London: Edinburgh House Press, 1964.

Visser 't Hooft, W. A. *The Meaning of the Ecumenical.* London: SCM Press, Ltd., 1953.

—— "The Gathering of the Scattered Children of God," in Edward J. Jurji, ed., *The Ecumenical Era in Church and Society.* The Macmillan Company, 1959.

Wells, Kenneth E., *History of Protestant Work in Thailand 1828–1958.* Bangkok: Church of Christ in Thailand, 1958.

West, Charles C., *Outside the Camp: The Christian and the World.* Doubleday & Company, Inc., 1959.

II. PERIODICALS

America, a national Catholic weekly review, Vol. 112, No. 22 (May 29, 1965). Editorial: "Ecumenism and 'Converts.'"

The Christian Century, August 2, 1961. Richard H. Drummond, "Kyodan After 20 Years."

—— December 13, 1950. "What Is the National Council?"

ChristuspYediking in de Wereld. (Reprint.) R. Pierce Beaver, "Rufus Anderson's Missionary Principles," translated from original.

Church History, Part 1, Vol. XIV, No. 2 (June, 1945). "The American Society of Church History."

The Churchman Overseas, informal newsletter of the Committee on American Laymen Overseas, National Council of the Churches of Christ in the U.S.A., February, 1965. "Report on Overseas Laymen's Institutes."

The Ecumenical Review, Vol. VI, No. 4 (July, 1954). Charles T. Leber, "Evanston and the Ecumenical Mission."

—— Vol. XVI, No. 3 (April, 1964). J. E. Fenn, "The Mexico City Meeting—An Impression."

—— Vol. XVI, No. 5 (October, 1964). J. K. S. Reid, "The Holy Spirit and the Ecumenical Movement."

The Evangelical Repository and United Presbyterian Review, Old Series, Vol. XLVI; New Series, Vol. VIII, 1869. Joseph T. Cooper and W. W. Barr (eds.).

The International Review of Missions, October, 1961. Donald P. Smith, "A New Approach to Missionary Orientation" (reprint).

—— Vol. LIV, No. 216 (October, 1965). Gunter Linnenbrink, "Witness and Service in the Mission of the Church."

Japan Christian Quarterly, January, 1959. Malcolm R. Carrick, "The Movement Toward Church Union in Japan."

The Missionary Review of the World, Vol. 53 (February, 1930). Otis Cary, "Some 'Very Respectable Missionary Societies.'"

Occasional Bulletin, Missionary Research Library Vol. IV, No. 12 (September 30, 1953). R. Pierce Beaver, "Pioneer Single Women Missionaries."

—— Vol. XIII, No. 1 (January, 1962). "Missionaries from the Younger Churches."

The Reformed and Presbyterian World, Vol. XXIV, No. 2 (June, 1956). Charles A. Anderson, "American Presbyterians Celebrate 250 Years."
———— Vol. XXV, No. 8 (December, 1959). W. Nijenhuis, "Calvin and Ecumenism."
———— Vol. XXVI, No. 6 (June, 1961). Douglas Horton, "The Plan of Union of 1801 in the United States."
———— Vol. XXVII, No. 8 (December, 1963). Hendrik Berkhof, "The Reformed 'Confession' and the Oekumene."
Student World, No. 4, July, 1964. "The Christian Community in the Academic World," Statement Approved by the General Committee of the World Student Christian Federation.
———— No. 2, 1965. Valdo Galland, "New Perspectives in the Ecumenical Implications of the Gospel."
Theology Today, Vol. IX, No. 1 (April, 1952). Editorial: "Ecumenical: The Word and the Concept."
Youth, November, 1964. J. G. Davies, "The Church and the Society It Serves."

III. REPORTS

Advisory Study, An. Commission on Ecumenical Mission and Relations, The United Presbyterian Church in the U.S.A., 1961.
Common Evangelistic Task of the Churches in Asia, The. Papers and Minutes of the East Asia Christian Conference, Prapat, Indonesia, March 17-26, 1957. East Asia Christian Conference.
Cyclopedic Manual of the United Presbyterian Church of North America. United Presbyterian Board of Publication, 1903.
Decisive Hour for the Christian Mission, A. East Asia Christian Conference, 1959, and the John R. Mott Memorial Lectures. Norman Goodall, J. E. Lesslie Newbigin, W. A. Visser 't Hooft, D. T. Niles. London: SCM Press, Ltd., 1960.
Drumbeats from Kampala. Report of the First Assembly of the All Africa Conference of Churches, Kampala, Africa, April 20-30, 1963. London: Lutterworth Press, 1963.
Historical Sections of the Digest. United Presbyterian Church of North America and Presbyterian Church in the U.S.A., to May 27, 1958. Philadelphia: The Office of the General Assembly by the Board of Christian Education of The United Presbyterian Church in the U.S.A.
Interdenominational Conference of Foreign Missionary Boards and Societies in the United States and Canada. New York: E. O. Jenkins' Sons' Printing House, 1893.
Missionary Obligation of the Church, The. Report of Conference at Willingen, Germany, July 5-17, 1952. London: Edinburgh House Press, 1953.

New Day Outlook. Report on the Consultation at Mohonk, May, 1956. Board of Foreign Missions of the Presbyterian Church in the U.S.A.

New Delhi Report, The. The Third Assembly of the World Council of Churches, 1961. Association Press, 1962.

Report of Proceedings of the First General Presbyterian Council, Convened at Edinburgh, July, 1877 (with related documents bearing on the affairs of the Council, and the state of the Presbyterian Churches throughout the world), ed. by Rev. J. Thomson. Edinburgh: Thomas and Archibald Constable, 1877.

Reports of Situation Conferences, Convened by the East Asia Christian Conference, February–March, 1963. East Asia Christian Conference, 1963.

Witnesses in Six Continents (Ronald K. Orchard, ed.). Records of the meetings of the Commission on World Mission and Evangelism of the World Council of Churches, held in Mexico City, December 8-9, 1963. London: Edinburgh House Press, 1964.

Witnesses Together (U Kyaw Than, ed.). Report of the Inaugural Assembly of the East Asia Christian Conference, Kuala Lumpur, Malaya, May 14-24, 1959. East Asia Christian Conference.

Work Book for the Constituting Convention, Cleveland, Ohio, November 28 to December 1, 1950. Planning Committee for the National Council of Churches, 1950.

IV. SIGNIFICANT PAPERS

(Published by the Commission on Ecumenical Mission and Relations)

The Christian World Mission in Our Time, by John Coventry Smith. 1961.

Captives in Christ's Triumphal Procession, by Donald Black. 1962.

The Cosmic Dimension of the Mission of the Church, by Arnold B. Come. 1962.

The Christian Charisma, by Arnold B. Come. 1963.

The United Presbyterian Church in Ecumenical Mission and Relations, by John Coventry Smith. 1963.

Associations Between United Presbyterians and Roman Catholics. Statement adopted by the 175th General Assembly of The United Presbyterian Church in the U.S.A., 1963.

United Presbyterian Basis for Ecumenical Relations, by Harold P. Nebelsick. 1963.

The Missionary Structure of the Local Congregation, by Hans Jochen Margull. 1963.

How the Church Addresses the World, by John Coventry Smith. 1966.

NOTES

CHAPTER I. THE ECUMENICAL WITNESS OF THE UNITED PRESBYTERIAN CHURCH

1. *Presbyterian Life,* Vol. 11, No. 12 (June 15, 1958), p. 28.
2. *Ibid.*
3. *Presbyterian Life,* Vol. 11, No. 13 (July 1, 1958), p. 28.
4. *The Constitution of The United Presbyterian Church in the United States of America* (The Office of the General Assembly of The United Presbyterian Church in the U.S.A., 1958), Preface.
5. *Ibid.,* p. 36.
6. *Ibid.,* p. 119.
7. *Ibid.*
8. Arnold B. Come, *Agents of Reconciliation* (The Westminster Press, 1960), p. 20.
9. Theodore F. Romig and Archie R. Crouch, *The Missionary* (World Horizons, Inc., 1965), p. 16.
10. Reported in *Presbyterian Life,* Vol. 10, No. 13 (June 22, 1957), p. 9.
11. R. Pierce Beaver, *From Missions to Mission* (Association Press, 1964), p. 39. Quotations from this book are used by permission of the publisher.
12. W. Richey Hogg, *One World, One Mission* (Friendship Press, 1960), p. 14.
13. A. Theodore Eastman, *Christian Responsibility in One World* (The Seabury Press, Inc., 1965), p. 11.
14. Arend T. van Leeuwen, *Christianity in World History: The Meeting of the Faiths of East and West* (London: Edinburgh House Press, 1964), p. 329.
15. *Ibid.,* p. 415.
16. J. E. Lesslie Newbigin, "The Work of the Holy Spirit in the Life of the Asian Churches" in *A Decisive Hour for the Christian Mission,* a report of the East Asia Christian Conference in 1959 and the John R. Mott Memorial Lectures (London: SCM Press, Ltd., 1960), p. 21.
17. *Ibid.*
18. *Ibid.,* p. 22.
19. *Ibid.,* p. 23.
20. J. K. S. Reid, "The Holy Spirit and the Ecumenical Movement," *The Ecumenical Review,* Vol. XVI, No. 5 (October, 1964).
21. *The Constitution of The United Presbyterian Church in the U.S.A.* (1963), p. 43.
22. *Conversations with Roman Catholics on the Nature of the Church and on Ecumenism,* Resources for Ecumenical Encounter, No. 1 (Commission on Ecumenical Mission and Relations of The United Presbyterian Church in the U.S.A., 1965).
23. John Macmurray, *The Clue to History* (Harper & Brothers, 1939), p. 93.

CHAPTER II.   COLONIAL PRESBYTERIANISM AND EARLY MISSIONARY EFFORTS

1. Gaius Jackson Slosser, ed., *They Seek a Country—The American Presbyterians* (The Macmillan Company, 1955), p. 28.

2. William Henry Roberts, *A Concise History of the Presbyterian Church in the United States of America* (The Board of Publication and Sabbath School Work, 1917), p. 32.

3. Slosser, ed., *op. cit.*, quoted by William W. McKinney in his chapter "Beginnings in the North," p. 29.

4. Roberts, *op. cit.*, p. 12.

5. Robert Hastings Nichols, *Presbyterianism in New York State: A History of the Synod and Its Predecessors*, edited and completed by James Hastings Nichols. (The Westminster Press, 1963), p. 13.

6. Roberts, *op. cit.*, p. 13.

7. Nichols, *op. cit.*, p. 12.

8. Slosser, ed., *op. cit.*, p. 30.

9. *Encyclopedia of the Presbyterian Church in the United States of America*, ed. by Alfred Nevin (Presbyterian Encyclopedia Publishing Co., 1884), p. 656.

10. William Thomson Hanzsche, *Our Presbyterian Church: Its History, Organization, and Program: A Study Unit of Thirteen Lessons* (Presbyterian Board of Christian Education, 1933), p. 14.

11. Slosser, ed., *op. cit.*, p. 33.

12. Charles Hodge, *The Constitutional History of the Presbyterian Church in the U.S.A., Part II—1741 to 1788* (Philadelphia: William S. Martien, 1840), p. 504.

13. *Ibid.*

14. Wallace N. Jamison, *The United Presbyterian Story: A Centennial Study (1858–1958)* (The Geneva Press, 1958), p. 11.

15. *Ibid.*, p. 17.

16. Figures quoted by Jamison, *op. cit.*, p. 21.

17. Jamison, *op. cit.*, p. 28.

18. Slosser, ed., *op. cit.*, Chapter, "Missionary Expansion at Home," figures quoted by Clifford M. Drury, p. 170.

19. Slosser, ed., *op. cit.*, Chapter, "Service in Founding and Preserving the Nation," by H. Gordon Harold, p. 150.

20. Alfonso López, *La Estirpe Calvinista de Nuestras Instituciones* (Bogotá: Universidad Nacional de Colombia, 1947), p. 44.

21. *Encyclopedia of the Presbyterian Church in the United States of America*, p. 658.

22. *Ibid.*

23. Alan F. Geyer, *Piety and Politics: American Protestantism in the World Arena* (John Knox Press, 1963), p. 41.

24. *Ibid.*, pp. 41-42.

25. *Ibid.*, p. 43.

26. Leonard J. Trinterud, *The Forming of an American Tradition: A Re-examination of Colonial Presbyterianism* (The Westminster Press, 1949), p. 256.

27. *Ibid.*

28. Hanzsche, *op. cit.*, p. 15.

29. Charles A. and Mary R. Beard, *A Basic History of the United States* (The New Home Library, 1944), p. 45.

30. Slosser, ed., *op. cit.*, Chapter, "Service in Founding and Preserving the Nation," by H. Gordon Harold, p. 157.

31. *Encyclopedia of the Presbyterian Church in the United States of America,* p. 657.

32. Lefferts A. Loetscher, *A Brief History of the Presbyterians* (The Westminster Press, 1958), p. 61.

33. John A. Mackay, *The Presbyterian Way of Life* (Prentice-Hall, Inc., 1960), p. 28. Quotations from this book are used by permission of the publisher.

34. Loetscher, *op. cit.,* p. 54.

35. Elwyn A. Smith, *The Presbyterian Ministry in American Culture: A Study in Changing Concepts, 1700–1900* (The Westminster Press, 1962), p. 106.

36. Oliver Wendell Elsbree, *The Rise of the Missionary Spirit in America, 1790–1815* (The Williamsport Printing and Binding Company, 1928), p. 123.

37. *Ibid.,* p. 131.

38. *Ibid.,* p. 142.

39. Otis Cary, "Some 'Very Respectable Missionary Societies,'" Article in *The Missionary Review of the World,* Vol. 53 (February, 1930), p. 112.

40. Arthur Judson Brown, *One Hundred Years* (Fleming H. Revell Company, 1936), pp. 14-15.

41. Elsbree, *op. cit.,* p. 51.

42. *Ibid.,* pp. 47-48.

43. *Ibid.,* p. 145.

44. Cary, *loc. cit.*

45. Ashbel Green, *Presbyterian Missions, A Historical Sketch or Compendious View of Domestic and Foreign Missions in the Presbyterian Church in the United States of America* (Philadelphia: William S. Martien, 1838), p. 56.

46. Brown, *op. cit.,* p. 19.

47. *Ibid.*

48. *The Christian Advocate* (conducted by Ashbel Green) for the year 1833. Vol. XI, April, 1833, section "Religious Intelligence" (Philadelphia: A. Finley), p. 187.

49. Rev. Elliott E. Swift, "Missionary History," in *Centenary Memorial of the Planting and Growth of Presbyterianism in Western Pennsylvania and Parts Adjacent* (Pittsburgh: Benjamin Singerly, 1876), p. 174.

50. Green, *op. cit.,* p. 108.

51. William D. Howard, Missionary address in *History of the Origin of the Board of Foreign Missions* (New York: Mission House, 1872), pp. 8-9.

52. Swift, *op. cit.,* p. 175.

53. In 1837 the Rev. Samuel Miller was elected the first president of the Board of Foreign Missions. (See Brown, *op. cit.,* p. 40.)

54. Green, *op. cit.,* p. 173.

55. Brown, *op. cit.,* p. 33.

56. In 1837 The Western Foreign Missionary Society was transferred to New York, and renamed The Presbyterian Foreign Missionary Society. The main reason for the change of location of the Society is given in the *Centenary Memorial* as follows: "A growing conviction prevailed in the minds of many of its warmest friends in Pittsburgh and elsewhere that its efficiency would be greatly promoted by its removal to one of the principal Eastern cities." *Centenary Memorial,* p. 180.

57. Minutes of the Board of Foreign Missions of the Presbyterian Church, Baltimore, October 31, 1837, published in *Reports of the Board of Foreign Missions of the Presbyterian Church in the U.S.A.* (*1833–1846*), p. 12.

58. Green, *op. cit.,* pp. 37-38.

59. Robert E. Speer, *Presbyterian Foreign Missions* (The Board of Publication and Sabbath School Work, 1901), pp. 9-10.

60. Ashbel Green, *Presbyterian Missions,* Appendices by J. C. Lowrie (Anson

D. F. Randolph & Company, Inc., 1893), pp. 243-245. (In this revised edition, Dr. Lowrie used the shorter title for this book.)

61. *Ibid.*, p. 73.
62. *Ibid.*, p. 1.
63. Brown, *op. cit.*, p. 14.
64. *Ibid.*
65. Smith, *op. cit.*, p. 173.
66. *Minutes of the General Assembly of the Presbyterian Church in the U.S.A., 1801*, p. 224.
67. For a full discussion of the difficulties raised concerning the Plan in 1831, see *Minutes of the General Assembly of the Presbyterian Church in the U.S.A., 1831.*
68. Douglas Horton, "The Plan of Union of 1801 in the United States," Article in *The Reformed and Presbyterian World*, Vol. XXVI, No. 6 (June, 1961) (published by the World Alliance of Reformed Churches, Geneva, Switzerland), p. 249.
69. *Ibid.*, p. 250.
70. *Ibid.*
71. *Ibid.*, p. 251.
72. Charles A. Anderson, "American Presbyterians Celebrate 250 Years," Article, in *The Reformed and Presbyterian World*, Vol. XXIV, No. 2 (June, 1956), p. 65.

CHAPTER III. PRESBYTERIAN FOREIGN MISSION AGENCIES

1. *Minutes of the General Assembly of the Presbyterian Church in the U.S.A., 1837*. Report on Overture No. 7 from the Presbytery of Salem, on the subject of foreign missions, June 7, 1837, p. 452. For fuller details of the process of the formation of the Board of Foreign Missions prior to 1837, see Appendix A, "Documents."
2. *Centenary Memorial of the Planting and Growth of Presbyterianism in Western Pennsylvania and Parts Adjacent* (Pittsburgh: Benjamin Singerly, 1876), p. 181. (See also *Minutes of Board of Foreign Missions of the Presbyterian Church in the U.S.A.*, October 31, 1837, pp. 9-10.)
3. *Minutes of the General Assembly of the Presbyterian Church in the U.S.A., 1836*, p. 258.
4. Samuel Miller, "Historical Review of the Church (Old School Branch)," in *Presbyterian Reunion Memorial Volume 1837–1871* (New York: De-Witt C. Lent & Co., 1871), p. 5.
5. E. H. Gillett, *History of the Presbyterian Church in the United States of America*, Part II (revised ed., The Board of Publication and Sabbath School Work, 1864), p. 513.
6. *Presbyterian Reunion Memorial Volume*, p. 12.
7. *Ibid.*, p. 11.
8. Green, *Presbyterian Missions* (1838 ed.), p. 95 (footnote).
9. *Ibid.*, pp. 95-96.
10. Gillett, *op. cit.*, p. 453.
11. *Ibid.*
12. Brown, *op. cit.*, p. 21.
13. *Ibid.*, p. 22.
14. Earl R. MacCormac, "Missions and the Presbyterian Schism of 1837" in *Church History*, Vol. XXXII, 1963 (ed. by Robert M. Grant, Martin E. Marty, and Jerald C. Brauer) (Published by the American Society of Church History), p. 34.

15. Reference is made here to the boards of foreign missions of the Presbyterian Church in the U.S.A. and of the United Presbyterian Church of North America, the two churches which merged in 1958 to form The United Presbyterian Church in the U.S.A.

16. Gillett, *op. cit.*, p. 443.

17. *Ibid.*, p. 444.

18. Sixteenth Annual Report of the Board of Foreign Missions of the Presbyterian Church in the U.S.A., presented to the General Assembly in May, 1853 (Published for the Board at the Mission House, 23 Centre St., New York, 1853), p. 60. (In bound volume, *Reports of the Board of Foreign Missions of the Presbyterian Church in the U.S.A.*)

19. Charles Lemuel Thompson, *The Presbyterians* (New York: The Baker & Taylor Company, 1903), p. 141.

20. *Ibid.*, p. 190.

21. Miller, *loc. cit.*, p. 23.

22. Thompson, *op. cit.*, p. 200.

23. Jamison, *op. cit.*, pp. 53-54.

24. See *Minutes of the General Assembly of the United Presbyterian Church of North America, 1877*, p. 444.

25. See *Minutes of the General Assembly of the United Presbyterian Church of North America, 1878*, p. 598.

26. Earl E. Elder, *Vindicating a Vision* (Board of Foreign Missions of the United Presbyterian Church of North America, 1958), p. 10.

27. Andrew Gordon, *Our India Mission* (Published by the author, 1886), p. 20.

28. *Minutes of the First General Assembly of the United Presbyterian Church of North America*, printed in *The Evangelical Repository*, Vol. XVIII, No. 2 (July, 1859), p. 89.

29. *Ibid.*, p. 90.

30. *Minutes of the Second General Assembly of the United Presbyterian Church of North America, May, 1860*, pp. 12-13.

31. *The Evangelical Repository, Minutes of the General Assembly of the United Presbyterian Church of North America, 1860*, p. 15.

32. *Minutes of the General Assembly of the United Presbyterian Church of North America, 1860*, p. 14.

33. *Minutes of the General Assembly of the United Presbyterian Church of North America, 1878* p. 598.

34. Brown, *op. cit.*, p. 155.

35. Speer, *op. cit.*, p. 16.

36. Mrs. D. L. Child, *The History of the Condition of Women in Various Ages and Nations* (Boston: John Allen Co., 1835), Vol. II, p. 265.

37. Henry J. Carman and Harold C. Syrett, *A History of the American People,* Vol. I to 1865 (Alfred A. Knopf, Inc., 1952), p. 495.

38. *Ibid.*

39. Brown, *op. cit.*, p. 114.

40. "Christian Women in America," *Woman's Work for Woman*, Vol. I, No. 1 (April, 1871), pp. 24-25.

41. *Ibid.*

42. Child, *op. cit.*, p. 271.

43. "The Assembly's Sanction," *Woman's Work for Woman*, Vol. I, No. 2 (July, 1871), pp. 70-71.

44. *Ibid.*, p. 81.

45. *The Encyclopedia of Missions*, 2d edition, edited under the auspices of the

Bureau of Missions by the Rev. Henry Otis Dwight, the Rev. H. Allen Tupper, Jr., and the Rev. Edwin Munsell Bliss (Funk & Wagnalls Company, 1904), p. 791.

46. *Ibid.*

47. See "Pioneer Single Women Missionaries," by R. Pierce Beaver, in *Occasional Bulletin,* Missionary Research Library, Vol. IV, No. 12 (September 30, 1953).

48. *Minutes of the General Assembly of the Presbyterian Church in the U.S.A., 1789–1820* (Presbyterian Board of Publication, 1847), p. 483.

49. Beaver, "Pioneer Single Women Missionaries," *loc. cit.,* p. 2.

50. *The Encyclopedia of Missions* (2d ed.), p. 788.

51. *Ibid.*

52. Isabel Hart, ed., *Historical Sketches of Women's Missionary Societies in America and England* (Published privately by Mrs. L. H. Daggett, Boston: 1879), Frontispiece.

53. *Ibid.,* p. 140.

54. *Ibid.,* p. 123.

55. The New York Board used the word "women's." All the other boards used "woman's."

56. Brown, *op. cit.,* p. 135.

57. *Ibid.,* p. 141.

58. *Seventy-fifth Anniversary of the United Presbyterian Church of North America* (Pittsburgh, Pennsylvania, 1933), p. 74.

59. Jamison, *op. cit.,* p. 163.

60. *Ibid.,* p. 164.

61. *Ibid.*

62. Evlyn Wehling Fulton, *A History of the Women's General Missionary Society of the United Presbyterian Church of North America,* p. 7. A thesis submitted to the Faculty of the Pittsburgh-Xenia Theological Seminary in Partial Fulfillment of the Requirements for the Degree of Master of Religious Education, Pittsburgh, Pennsylvania, May, 1949.

63. *Historical Sections of the Digest,* United Presbyterian Church of North America and Presbyterian Church in the U.S.A. to May 27, 1958 (Philadelphia: The Office of the General Assembly by the Board of Christian Education of The United Presbyterian Church in the U.S.A.), pp. 595-596.

64. *Women's Missionary Magazine* of the United Presbyterian Church, Vol. I, No. 9 (April, 1888), p. 244.

65. Jamison, *op. cit.,* p. 167.

66. *Minutes of the General Assembly of the United Presbyterian Church of North America, 1956,* Vol. XXIV, No. 1, p. 88.

67. Beaver, *From Missions to Mission,* p. 15.

68. Brown, *op. cit.,* p. 1047.

69. Beaver, *From Missions to Mission,* p. 11.

CHAPTER IV.   UNITED PRESBYTERIAN INVOLVEMENT IN ECUMENICAL BODIES

1. Theophilus M. Taylor, "The Contribution of the Reformed Churches to Christian Unity," p. 7. Unpublished manuscript, February, 1952.

2. *Ibid.,* p. 6.

3. *Ibid.,* p. 1.

4. John A. Mackay, *Ecumenics: The Science of the Church Universal* (Prentice-Hall, Inc., 1964), p. 210. Quotations from this book are used by permission of the publisher.

5. Quoted by John A. Mackay in *Ecumenics*, p. 213.

6. *Report of Proceedings of the First General Presbyterian Council Convened at Edinburgh, July, 1877*, ed. by Rev. J. Thomson (Edinburgh: Thomas and Archibald Constable, 1877), p. 1.

7. *Ibid.*, p. 1.

8. *Ibid.*

9. *Ibid.*, p. 2.

10. *Ibid.*

11. *Ibid.*, p. 378.

12. For full text of the statements, see *ibid.*, pp. 4-5.

13. *Ibid.*, p. 9.

14. *Ibid.*, p. 173.

15. Hendrik Berkhof, article, "The Reformed 'Confession' and the Oekumene," in *The Reformed and Presbyterian World*, Vol. XXVII, No. 8 (December, 1963), p. 350.

16. *Ibid.*, p. 355.

17. Charles Clayton Morrison, *The Unfinished Reformation* (Harper & Brothers, 1953), p. 24. Quotations from this book are used by permission of Harper & Row, Publishers, Inc.

18. *Ibid.*, p. 24.

19. *Ibid.*, p. 3.

20. *Ibid.*, p. 23.

21. *Ibid.*

22. *Ibid.*, p. 13.

23. *Ibid.*, p. 140.

24. *Proceedings of the Union Missionary Convention held in New York May 4 and 5, 1854.* (New York: Taylor & Hogg, 1854), p. 9.

25. *Ibid.*, p. 60.

26. *Ibid.*, p. 9.

27. *Interdenominational Conference of Foreign Missionary Boards and Societies in the United States and Canada* (New York: E. O. Jenkins' Sons' Printing House, 1893), Prefatory Note.

28. *Ibid.*

29. W. Richey Hogg, *Ecumenical Foundations: A History of the International Missionary Council and Its Nineteenth-Century Background* (Harper & Brothers, 1952), p. 74.

30. *Report of the Second Conference of the Officers and Representatives of the Foreign Mission Boards and Societies in the United States and Canada, 1894*, pp. 14, 32, 41, 56.

31. *Report of the Fifth Conference of the Officers and Representatives of the Foreign Mission Boards and Societies in the United States and Canada* (Foreign Missions Library, New York, 1897), p. 100.

32. Hogg, *Ecumenical Foundations*, p. 46.

33. Quoted by Charles S. Macfarland in *Christian Unity in the Making* (Federal Council of the Churches of Christ in America, 1948), p. 352.

34. *Ibid.*, p. 19.

35. *Ibid.*

36. Elias B. Sanford, *Origin and History of the Federal Council of the Churches of Christ in America* (Hartford, Conn.: The S. S. Scranton Company, 1916), p. 34.

37. *Ibid.*, p. 35.

38. *Ibid.*, pp. 38-39.

39. Macfarland, *op. cit.*, p. 27.

40. Sanford, *Origin and History of the Federal Council of the Churches of Christ in America,* pp. 176-177.

41. See Sanford, *Origin and History,* p. 382.

42. Macfarland, *op. cit.,* p. 36.

43. Elias B. Sanford, ed., *Church Federation: Interchurch Conference on Federation* (New York, November 15-21, 1905) (Fleming H. Revell Company, 1906), p. 226.

44. Macfarland, *op. cit.,* p. 42.

45. *Ibid.,* pp. 42-43.

46. *Ibid.,* p. 330.

47. *Ibid.,* p. 261.

48. Ross W. Sanderson, *Church Cooperation in the United States* (Hartford, Conn.: Finlay Brothers Press, 1960), p. 190.

49. Sanford, ed., *Church Federation: Interchurch Conference on Federation* (New York, November 15-21, 1905).

50. National Council of the Churches of Christ in the U.S.A., *Work Book for the Constituting Convention,* Cleveland, Ohio (Planning Committee for the National Council of Churches, 1950), p. 2.

51. "What Is the National Council?" in *The Christian Century,* December 13, 1950, p. 1486.

52. Henry P. Van Dusen, Chapter, "Time of Testing for the National Council," in *Unity in Mid-Career,* ed. by Keith R. Bridston and Walter D. Wagoner (The Macmillan Company, 1963), p. 122.

53. *Ibid.,* p. 123.

54. Mackay, *Ecumenics,* p. 195.

55. W. A. Visser 't Hooft, Chapter, "The Gathering of the Scattered Children of God," in *The Ecumenical Era in Church and Society,* ed. by E. J. Jurji (The Macmillan Company, 1959), p. 33.

56. *Minutes of the General Assembly of the Presbyterian Church in the U.S.A., 1938,* Part I, p. 224.

57. *The Universal Church in God's Design: An Ecumenical Study Prepared Under the Auspices of the World Council of Churches* (Harper & Brothers, 1948), p. 207.

58. *Minutes of the General Assembly of the United Presbyterian Church of North America, 1949.* Report of the American Committee of the World Council of Churches, p. 415.

59. Visser 't Hooft, *loc. cit.,* pp. 33-34.

60. U Kyaw Than, Chapter, "East of New Delhi: Regionalism or Centralism?" in *Unity in Mid-Career,* ed. by Keith R. Bridston and Walter D. Wagoner, p. 60.

61. *Ibid.,* p. 62.

62. *Ibid.,* p. 57.

63. *The Common Evangelistic Task of the Churches in East Asia* (Papers and Minutes of the East Asia Christian Conference. Prapat, Indonesia, March 17-26, 1957), p. ii.

64. Mackay, *Ecumenics,* p. 217.

65. *Ibid.,* p. 217.

66. *Minutes of East Asia Consultation on Ecumenical Mission* (Kowloon, Hong Kong, July 23-25, 1954).

67. Than, Chapter, "East of New Delhi: Regionalism or Centralism?" in *Unity in Mid-Career,* Bridston and Wagoner, eds., p. 61.

68. U Kyaw Than, ed., *Witnesses Together,* The Official Report of the Inaugural Assembly of the East Asia Christian Conference, Kuala Lumpur, Malaya, 1959 (Burma, 1959), p. 145.

69. *Drumbeats from Kampala,* Report of the First Assembly of the All Africa Conference of Churches, Kampala, 1963 (London: Lutterworth Press, 1963), p. 35.

70. Glen Garfield Williams, *The Conference of European Churches.* Unpublished report to the World Council of Churches, November 10-13, 1964.

71. Hogg, *Ecumenical Foundations,* p. 81.

72. *Ibid.,* pp. 81-82.

73. Quoted by Galen M. Fisher in *John R. Mott: Architect of Co-operation and Unity* (Association Press, 1953), p. 23.

74. *Ibid.,* p. 24.

75. *Ibid.*

76. Dr. Speer was appointed as Secretary of the Board of Foreign Missions of the Presbyterian Church in the U.S.A. in 1891.

77. Fisher, *op. cit.,* p. 11.

78. Basil Mathews, *John R. Mott: World Citizen* (London: SCM Press, Ltd., 1934).

79. *Progress in Mass Communication,* A mimeographed report of the Committee of Radio, Visual Education and Mass Communication, Bulletin #2, August, 1950, p. 8.

80. Donald P. Smith, "A New Approach to Missionary Orientation," *The International Review of Missions,* October, 1961, p. 3.

CHAPTER V.   THE PRESBYTERIAN SEARCH FOR WHOLENESS

1. Eph. 4:13.

2. Mackay, *Ecumenics,* p. 187.

3. John Coventry Smith, "The Christian Mission from the Standpoint of United Churches," in *The Christian Mission for Today* (Division of Foreign Missions of the National Council of the Churches of Christ in the U.S.A., 1958), p. 16.

4. *Webster's New Collegiate Dictionary* (G. & C. Merriam Co., 1959), p. 930.

5. Paul S. Minear, ed., *The Nature of the Unity We Seek* (The Bethany Press, 1958), p. 120.

6. *Ibid.,* p. 242.

7. *Ibid.*

8. *Ibid.,* p. 38.

9. *Ibid.,* p. 39.

10. John 17:21-22.

11. Eph. 4:4-6.

12. Minear, *op. cit.,* p. 125.

13. Quoted in *The General Assembly Daily News* (of the United Presbyterian Church), May 30, 1958.

14. Minear, *op. cit.,* pp. 32-33.

15. Mackay, *Ecumenics,* p. 194.

16. W. Nijenhuis, article on "Calvin and Ecumenism," in *The Reformed and Presbyterian World,* Vol. XXV, No. 8 (December, 1958), p. 345.

17. Quoted by Nijenhuis, *loc. cit.,* p. 345.

18. *Ibid.,* p. 346.

19. *Ibid.*

20. Wayne H. Christy, *The United Presbyterian Church and Church Union,* p. 255. Doctoral thesis presented to the University of Pittsburgh, 1947.

21. Mackay, *The Presbyterian Way of Life,* p. 215.

22. Minear, *op. cit.,* p. 130.

23. Hogg, *Ecumenical Foundations,* p. 19.

24. *Ibid.,* p. 20.

25. *Ibid.,* p. 26.

26. Jamison, *op. cit.,* p. 219.

27. Christy, *op. cit.,* p. 159.

28. *Ibid.,* p. 115. (NOTE: At that time the United Presbyterian Church used metrical psalms rather than hymns in their worship services. This in practice proved a stumbling block to union in many negotiations.)

29. *The Evangelical Repository and United Presbyterian Review.* Old Series, Vol. XLVI; New Series, Vol. VIII, No. 7, p. 462. December, 1869. Joseph T. Cooper and W. W. Barr, eds. (Philadelphia: William S. Young, 1869).

30. Christy, *op. cit.,* p. 118.

31. *Ibid.,* p. 143.

32. Clifford Merrill Drury, *Presbyterian Panorama* (Board of Christian Education, Presbyterian Church in the U.S.A., 1952), p. 70.

33. *Ibid.,* p. 71.

34. *Ibid.,* p. 70.

35. *Ibid.*

36. H. Paul Douglass, *Church Unity Movements in the United States* (Institute of Social and Religious Research, 1934), p. 52.

37. Drury, *op. cit.,* p. 221.

38. Quoted by Christy, *op. cit.,* p. 151.

39. Jamison, *op. cit.,* p. 214.

40. Christy, *op. cit.,* pp. 166-167.

41. *Historical Sections of the Digest,* United Presbyterian Church of North America and Presbyterian Church in the U.S.A. to May 27, 1958 (Philadelphia: The Office of the General Assembly by the Board of Christian Education of The United Presbyterian Church in the U.S.A.), pp. 530-531.

42. Cited by Christy, *op. cit.,* p. 201. (See footnote.)

43. Quoted by Christy, *op. cit.,* p. 229.

44. *Minutes of the General Assembly of the United Presbyterian Church of North America, 1950,* Vol. XXII, No. 3, p. 796.

45. *Ibid.,* Vol. XXII, No. 4, p. 1204.

46. Arthur Judson Brown, *Unity and Missions* (Fleming H. Revell Company, 1915), p. 177.

47. *Minutes of the General Assembly of the Presbyterian Church U.S.A., 1955,* p. 43; *Minutes of the General Assembly of the Presbyterian Church U.S., 1955,* p. 69; *Minutes of the General Assembly of the United Presbyterian Church of North America, 1955,* p. 1343. The reader should note that there were two documents dealing with union, one in 1954, sometimes called the "three-way Plan" (Presbyterian U.S.A., Presbyterian U.S., and United Presbyterian), the other issued in 1956, and sometimes referred to as the "two-way Plan" (Presbyterian U.S.A. and United Presbyterian). They were printed in quantities sufficient for distribution among the churches concerned in each case. For a discussion of these Plans, see: *Minutes of the General Assembly of the Presbyterian Church in the U.S.A.* for 1953, Part I, Journal, pp. 211 ff.; 1955, Part I, Journal, pp. 237 ff.; 1956, Part I, Journal, pp. 237 ff.

48. *Minutes of the General Assembly of the Presbyterian Church U.S.A., 1955,* Part I, Journal, p. 240.

49. *Ibid.,* p. 238.

50. Mackay, *Ecumenics,* p. 202.

51. *Ibid.,* p. 203.

52. *News, Presbyterian Office of Information* (New York: The United Presbyterian Church in the U.S.A.), January 24, 1965, p. 1.

53. *Ibid.*, p. 2.
54. *Ibid.*
55. *Ibid.*
56. From unpublished report of sermon preached by Dr. Eugene Carson Blake on January 24, 1965.
57. Mackay, *Ecumenics*, p. 189.

CHAPTER VI. THE FORMATION OF THE COMMISSION ON ECUMENICAL
MISSION AND RELATIONS

1. J. Merle Davis, *New Buildings on Old Foundations* (International Missionary Council, 1945), p. 75.
2. R. Pierce Beaver, "Rufus Anderson's Missionary Principles," p. 43, translated and reprinted from *Christusprediking in de Wereld.*
3. *Ibid.*, p. 56.
4. *The Jerusalem Meeting of the International Missionary Council, March 24–April 8, 1928*, Vol. III, "The Relation Between the Younger and the Older Churches" (International Missionary Council, 1928), p. 25.
5. Hogg, *Ecumenical Foundations*, pp. 32-33.
6. *The Jerusalem Meeting of the International Missionary Council*, Vol. III, p. 113.
7. *Ibid.*
8. Hogg, *Ecumenical Foundations*, p. 124.
9. *The Jerusalem Meeting of the International Missionary Council*, Vol. III, p. 3.
10. *Ibid.*, Vol. III.
11. *Ibid.*, Vol. III, p. 115.
12. Hogg, *Ecumenical Foundations*, p. 254.
13. *Report of the World Consultation of The Board of Foreign Missions of the Presbyterian Church in the U.S.A.*, held at Mountain House, Lake Mohonk, New York, April 22 to May 1, 1956 (mimeographed document), p. 1.
14. *Ibid.*, pp. 1-2.
15. *Ibid.*, p. 5.
16. *Ibid.*, p. 65.
17. *Ibid.*
18. W. Richey Hogg, *New Day Dawning* (World Horizons, Inc., 1957), p. 4. (The author is indebted to Dr. Hogg for many of the facts about Dr. Han's life included in this chapter.)
19. *Manual* of The Board of Foreign Missions of the Presbyterian Church in the U.S.A. (Revised 1952), p. 48.
20. The Presbyterian Church in the Cameroun had not yet achieved the independent status it now has, with its own General Assembly. The Cameroun Synod was related to the General Assembly of the Presbyterian Church U.S.A.
21. *New Day Outlook*, Report on the Consultation at Mohonk, Special Issue, May, 1956 (Board of Foreign Missions of the Presbyterian Church in the U.S.A.), p. 8.
22. Hogg, *New Day Dawning*, p. 100.
23. *Minutes of the General Assembly of the Presbyterian Church in the U.S.A., 1949*, Part I, p. 51.
24. *Minutes of the General Assembly of the Presbyterian Church in the U.S.A., 1954*, Part I, p. 162.
25. *Minutes of the General Assembly of the Presbyterian Church in the U.S.A., 1956*, Part I, p. 176.

26. *Minutes of The Board of Foreign Missions of the Presbyterian Church in the U.S.A.*, April 21-22, 1958 (action 58-347).

27. For full text of General Assembly action, see Appendixes.

28. *Minutes of the General Assembly of The United Presbyterian Church in the U.S.A., 1958*, Part I, p. 155.

29. Mackay, *Ecumenics*, p. 9.

30. Charles T. Leber, *The Church Must Win!* (Fleming H. Revell Company, 1944), p. 114.

31. *Ibid.*, p. 115.

32. Charles T. Leber, "Evanston and the Ecumenical Mission," in *The Ecumenical Review*, Vol. VI, No. 4 (July, 1954), p. 371.

33. Charles T. Leber, from an address delivered in Louisville, Kentucky, 1959.

34. Charles T. Leber, from an unpublished letter to the staff.

35. For the concepts underlying Dr. Blake's role in the formation of the Commission, the author is indebted to Dr. Glenn W. Moore, who was one of several who paid a tribute to Dr. Eugene Carson Blake at a dinner given in his honor by the Commission on Ecumenical Mission and Relations in New York on March 21, 1966, following Dr. Blake's election as General Secretary of the World Council of Churches, in February, 1966, to succeed Dr. W. A. Visser 't Hooft.

36. *Minutes of the General Assembly of the Presbyterian Church in the U.S.A.*, New Series, Vol. III, No. 2, 1903, p. 91.

37. *Minutes of the General Assembly of the United Presbyterian Church of North America, 1910*, p. 649.

38. *Ibid.*

39. *Minutes of the General Assembly of the United Presbyterian Church of North America, 1944*, p. 55.

40. *Minutes of the General Assembly of the United Presbyterian Church of North America, 1951*, p. 1240.

41. John A. Mackay, *An Interpretation: The Commission on Ecumenical Mission and Relations, The United Presbyterian Church in the United States of America* (New York, 1958), p. 2.

42. Mimeographed paper: "Re: A New Name for The Foreign Board issued by the Board of Foreign Missions of the Presbyterian Church in the U.S.A.," January 31, 1955, p. 5.

43. Minear, *op. cit.*, p. 127. Sermon by Bishop Johannes Lilje, on "The Significance of the Ecumenical Movement."

44. W. A. Visser 't Hooft, *The Meaning of Ecumenical* (London: SCM Press, Ltd., 1953), p. 5.

45. *Ibid.*, p. 7.

46. Albert H. van den Heuvel, Article, "Toward a Secular Understanding of the Ecumenical?" in *Youth*, No. 10 (November, 1964), Youth Department, World Council of Churches, p. 7.

47. From "The Calling of the Church to Mission and to Unity," a statement received by the Central Committee of the World Council of Churches at Rolle, Switzerland, 1951.

48. *Manual* of The Board of Foreign Missions of the Presbyterian Church in the U.S.A. (Revised 1952), p. 23.

49. Beaver, *From Missions to Mission*, pp. 6-7.

50. *Introductory Information on the Commission on Ecumenical Mission and Relations* (Pamphlet published by the Commission, 1958), p. 30.

51. Mackay, *An Interpretation: The Commission on Ecumenical Mission and Relations.*

52. John Coventry Smith, *The United Presbyterian Church in Ecumenical Mission and Relations*, Significant Papers No. 5 (Commission on Ecumenical Mission and Relations, 1963), p. 3.

53. Col. 1:17-20 (Phillips translation).

CHAPTER VII. THE FIRST SEVEN YEARS OF THE COMMISSION

1. *Minutes of the General Assembly of The United Presbyterian Church in the U.S.A., 1958*, Part I, Journal, p. 251.

2. *Ecumenical Press Service*, No. 26, 32d year, July 22, 1965.

3. *Blue Book* to the General Assembly of The United Presbyterian Church in the U.S.A., May, 1966, p. 402.

4. Facts taken from the Report on Overseas Laymen's Institutes, in *The Churchman Overseas*, informal newsletter of the Committee on American Laymen Overseas, National Council of the Churches of Christ in the U.S.A., February, 1965.

5. Joseph Berton Gremillion, *The Other Dialogue* (Doubleday & Company, Inc., 1965), p. 15.

6. *Ibid.*

7. R. Pierce Beaver, *Ecumenical Beginnings in Protestant World Mission: A History of Comity* (Thomas Nelson & Sons, 1962), p. 39.

8. The Philippine Methodist Church separated from the main body of The Methodist Church in 1933.

9. Enrique C. Sobrepeña, *That They May Be One* (2d ed., Manila: United Church of Christ in the Philippines, 1964), p. 67.

10. *Ibid.*, p. 82.

11. Charles W. Iglehart, *A Century of Protestant Christianity in Japan* (Charles E. Tuttle Company, 1959), p. 55.

12. Malcolm R. Carrick, "The Movement Toward Church Union in Japan," in *Japan Christian Quarterly*, January, 1959, p. 46.

13. Richard H. Drummond, "Kyodan After 20 Years," *The Christian Century*, August 2, 1961, p. 926.

14. *Manual* of The Board of Foreign Missions of the Presbyterian Church in the U.S.A. (Revised 1952), pp. 27-28.

15. Virgil A. Sly, Address, "From Missions to Mission," in *The Christian Mission for Today*, five addresses presented to the Ninth Annual Assembly of the Division of Foreign Missions, National Council of Churches, December 7-10, 1958 (Division of Foreign Missions of the National Council of the Churches of Christ in the U.S.A.), p. 8.

16. *Ibid.*

17. Beaver, *From Missions to Mission*, p. 79.

18. I Peter 2:9.

19. Thomas J. Liggett, *The Role of the Missionary in Latin America Today* (The Committee on Cooperation in Latin America, Division of Foreign Missions, National Council of the Churches of Christ in the U.S.A., 1963), p. 2.

20. D. T. Niles, *Upon the Earth: The Mission of God and the Missionary Enterprise of the Churches* (McGraw-Hill Book Co., Inc., 1962), p. 163.

21. *Ibid.*

CHAPTER VIII. DIMENSIONS AND CHALLENGES OF THE TASK AHEAD

1. *An Advisory Study.* Report of a specially-appointed Committee, published by the Commission on Ecumenical Mission and Relations of The United Presbyterian Church in the U.S.A., 1963.

2. *Ibid.,* p. 15.

3. *Ibid.,* p. 18.

4. Donald Black, *Captives in Christ's Triumphal Procession,* An address delivered at the West Africa Consultation of the World Presbyterian Alliance, Ibadan, Nigeria (Commission on Ecumenical Mission and Relations, 1962), p. 8.

5. *An Advisory Study,* p. 13.

6. John 6:21.

7. *An Advisory Study,* p. 25.

8. *Ibid.,* p. 27.

9. *Ibid.,* p. 4.

10. From a privately circulated memorandum of the Office of Interpretation, Commission on Ecumenical Mission and Relations, January, 1962.

11. *An Advisory Study,* p. 66.

12. *Ibid.,* p. 83.

13. *Reports of Situation Conferences* convened by the East Asia Christian Conference, February–March, 1963 (published by the East Asia Christian Conference, 1963), p. 7.

14. *An Advisory Study,* p. 81.

15. *Minutes of the Commission on Ecumenical Mission and Relations of The United Presbyterian Church in the U.S.A.,* March 16-17, 1964, p. 50.

16. *Reports of Situation Conferences* convened by the East Asia Christian Conference, February–March, 1963, p. 36.

17. *Ibid.,* pp. 17-18.

18. *Minutes of Assembly of the East Asia Christian Conference* (Part I) (Bangkok, February 25 to March 5, 1964), p. 27.

19. *Ibid.,* p. 28.

20. *Minutes of the Commission on Ecumenical Mission and Relations, The United Presbyterian Church in the U.S.A.,* March 16-17, 1964.

21. *Issues in Theological Education 1964–1965. Asia—Africa—Latin America,* A report of the Theological Fund, A Service of the Commission on World Mission and Evangelism of the World Council of Churches (New York and London), p. 7.

22. *Findings of the North India–Punjab Synod Consultation* (Rajpur, November 11-14, 1963; mimeographed document), p. 11.

23. *Ibid.*

24. "Missionaries from the Younger Churches," *Occasional Bulletin,* Vol. XIII, No. 1 (January, 1962) (New York: Missionary Research Library).

25. *Minutes of the Assembly of the East Asia Conference,* Part I, Bangkok, February 25 to March 5, 1964, p. 27.

26. *Ibid.*

27. *The Missionary Obligation of the Church,* Report of the Willingen Conference, 1952, International Missionary Council (London: Edinburgh House Press, 1953), p. v.

28. *Ibid.,* p. 22.

29. *Frontier Internship in Mission,* A Program of the Commission on Ecumenical Mission and Relations of The United Presbyterian Church in the U.S.A. (New York: 1963), p. 13.

30. John A. Mackay, *Christianity on the Frontier* (The Macmillan Company, 1950), p. 67.

31. In Unity—For Mission, Statement adopted by the General Assembly of The United Presbyterian Church in the U.S.A., May 30, 1958. *Minutes of the General Assembly, 1958,* p. 159.

32. Valdo Galland, article, "New Perspectives in the Ecumenical Implications of the Gospel," in *The Student World,* No. 2, 1965, p. 136.

33. John A. Mackay, Address, "With Christ to the Frontier," in *Renewal and Advance: Christian Witness in a Revolutionary World,* ed. by C. W. Ranson (London: Edinburgh House Press, 1948), p. 205.

34. "The Christian Community in the Academic World," a statement approved by the General Committee of the World Student Christian Federation, July, 1964, in *The Student World,* No. 4, July 1964, p. 362.

35. Johannes Blauw, *The Missionary Nature of the Church* (McGraw-Hill Book Co., Inc., 1962), p. 112.

36. Harvey Cox, *The Secular City* (The Macmillan Company, 1965), p. 26.

37. J. E. Lesslie Newbigin, *A Faith for This One World?* (Harper & Row, Publishers, Inc., 1962), p. 101.

38. II Cor. 5:17.

39. Luke 4:18-19 (Revised Standard Version).

40. *The Constitution of The United Presbyterian Church in the United States of America,* Ch. III, Sec. I, p. 119, in *The Presbyterian Constitution and Digest* (Philadelphia: The Office of the General Assembly of The United Presbyterian Church in the U.S.A., 1963).

41. Acts 1:7.

42. John 17:18.

43. Blauw, *op. cit.,* p. 121.

44. Nicolas Berdyaev, "The End of Things and the New Aeon," in *Four Existentialist Theologians,* ed. by Will Herberg (Doubleday & Company, Inc., 1958), p. 151.

45. Mackay, *The Presbyterian Way of Life,* p. 109.

46. Marcel Pradervand, *São Paulo Story* (Geneva: The World Presbyterian Alliance Offices, 1960), p. 49.

47. *Ibid.*

48. *Ibid.,* p. 37.

49. Myra Scovel, *My Neighbor, the Wounded: The Widening Scope of the Medical Mission of the Church* (Commission on Ecumenical Mission and Relations of The United Presbyterian Church in the U.S.A., 1966), pp. 37-38.

50. *Minutes of the General Assembly of The United Presbyterian Church in the U.S.A., 1962,* Part I, p. 307.

INDEXES

Subjects

Advisory Study, An, 212, 230 ff.

Africa, 84, 115, 128, 138; All Africa Conference of Churches, 120 f.; Cameroun Presbyterian Church, 214, 225; changing pattern of life in, 25; Christian art in, 189; the churches and the new frontiers, 244; a dark continent, 84; fraternal delegates of Presbyterian churches to General Assembly of Presbyterian Church U.S.A., 27; maturing churches in, 222; missions in, 27, 78; new nations in, 23; selfhood of the churches in, 121; theological education in, 240 f.

Allahabad (India), 66

Allegheny City (Pa.), 67, 80 f.

Alliance of Reformed Churches Throughout the World Holding the Presbyterian Order, 86, 88, 91. See also World Presbyterian Alliance

American Bible Society, 87 ff.

American Board of Commissioners for Foreign Missions, 44, 47, 58, 60, 159

American colonies, Presbyterian Church in, 29

American Home Missionary Society, 57

Andover Theological Seminary, 44

Asia, 119 f.; changing pattern of life in, 25; the churches and the frontiers of social, economic, and political life, 244; fraternal delegates of Presbyterian churches to General Assembly of Presbyterian Church U.S.A., 27; maturing churches in, 222; missions in, 27; regional ecumenical organiza-

tions in, 115 f.; theological education in, 240 f.

Associate Presbyterian Church, 17, 36, 64

Associate Presbyterian Synod, 67

Associate Reformed Church, 44, 67, 141

Associate Reformed Presbyterian Church, 17, 64 f.

Associate Reformed Presbyterian Synod, 65 f.

Associate Reformed Synod, 37, 88, 141

Associate Synod, 69

Association of Presbyterian and Reformed Churches in Latin America, 124

Australia, 28, 119, 157, 241

Baltimore (Md.), 49

Bandung, Afro-Asian Conference of, 119

Bangkok (Thailand), 117, 119, 201, 207, 239, 245

Baptists, 32, 37, 40, 207

Barn Playhouse, Stony Point (N.Y.), 181

Basis of Union (Presbyterian U.S.A. and Protestant Episcopal Church), 147

Berkshire and Columbia Missionary Society, 43

Bible, 42

Blake Proposal, 153 ff.

Board of Domestic Missions (Presbyterian Church U.S.A.), 51

Board of Foreign Missions of the Pres-

Names